CAMBRIDGE TE
THE HISTORY OF PI

GREEK AND ROMAN
AESTHETICS

CAMBRIDGE TEXTS IN THE HISTORY OF PHILOSOPHY

Series editors

KARL AMERIKS
Professor of Philosophy, University of Notre Dame

DESMOND M. CLARKE
Emeritus Professor of Philosophy, University College Cork

The main objective of Cambridge Texts in the History of Philosophy is to expand the range, variety, and quality of texts in the history of philosophy which are available in English. The series includes texts by familiar names (such as Descartes and Kant) and also by less well-known authors. Wherever possible, texts are published in complete and unabridged form, and translations are specially commissioned for the series. Each volume contains a critical introduction together with a guide to further reading and any necessary glossaries and textual apparatus. The volumes are designed for student use at undergraduate and postgraduate level, and will be of interest not only to students of philosophy but also to a wider audience of readers in the history of science, the history of theology, and the history of ideas.

For a list of titles published in the series, please see end of book.

Greek and Roman Aesthetics

TRANSLATED AND EDITED BY

OLEG V. BYCHKOV
St Bonaventure University, New York

ANNE SHEPPARD
Royal Holloway, University of London

CAMBRIDGE UNIVERSITY PRESS
Cambridge, New York, Melbourne, Madrid, Cape Town, Singapore,
São Paulo, Delhi, Dubai, Tokyo

Cambridge University Press
The Edinburgh Building, Cambridge CB2 8RU, UK

Published in the United States of America by Cambridge University Press, New York

www.cambridge.org
Information on this title: www.cambridge.org/9780521547925

First published 2010

Printed in the United Kingdom at the University Press, Cambridge

A catalogue record for this publication is available from the British Library

Library of Congress Cataloguing in Publication Data
Greek and Roman aesthetics / [edited and translated by] Oleg V. Bychkov.
p.   cm. – (Cambridge texts in the history of philosophy)
ISBN 978-0-521-83928-0 (hardback)
1. Aesthetics, Ancient.   2. Arts–Philosophy.   3. Philosophy, Ancient.
I. Bychkov, O. V.   II. Title.   III. Series.
BH90.G74 2010
111′.850938–dc22
2010015191

ISBN 978-0-521-83928-0 Hardback
ISBN 978-0-521-54792-5 Paperback

Contents

v

Contents

Contents

Preface

Although Anne Sheppard has had primary responsibility for the Greek texts in this volume, and Oleg Bychkov for the Latin, we have commented closely on each other's material and consulted on many issues, large and small. We worked together in preparing the Introduction and other preliminary material. Transatlantic collaboration was made much easier by a British Academy Small Research Grant which enabled Oleg Bychkov to spend some time in London in the summer of 2005. A number of people have helped us with advice of various kinds. Particular thanks are due to Carol Harrison, who gave advice about Augustine at a very early stage, to Brian Stock who kindly reviewed and commented on the translation of Augustine and to Daniel Delattre who generously allowed us to see his Greek text of Philodemus, *On Music* 4 in advance of publication and checked our translation of this difficult text. We should like to thank both Desmond Clarke and Hilary Gaskin for their patience with a project which has taken rather longer, and proved to be rather more complex, than was anticipated, and for their advice and comments. We are also grateful to Linda Woodward for her careful copy-editing.

Introduction

The title of this volume is *Greek and Roman Aesthetics*. However, aesthetics as a separate branch of philosophy with a distinctive subject matter (questions about beauty, the nature of fine art, forms of aesthetic judgement, etc.) which admits of a systematic but unitary treatment, is hardly older than the eighteenth century. Its origin is generally dated to Alexander Baumgarten (1714–62), who coined the term and devoted a specific treatise to the nascent discipline, and to Immanuel Kant, who investigated the issue of aesthetic judgement and its fundamental role in philosophy in more depth in the *Critique of Judgement* in 1790. What, then, is Greek and Roman aesthetics? How do ancient discussions relate to what we now call aesthetics and on what basis have we selected the particular texts included in this volume? This introduction will begin by briefly addressing these questions, before offering an account of the Greek and Roman precursors of aesthetics which should help to place the texts in this volume within their intellectual context.

Ancient texts and modern aesthetics

One way of approaching the connection between ancient texts and modern aesthetics is to examine the ancient texts that directly influenced what is now called aesthetic thought. A number of the texts in this volume, such as the selections from Plato's *Republic*, Aristotle's *Poetics* or the work *On Sublimity* attributed to Longinus, are frequently presented as forerunners of modern aesthetic thought and rightly so, since they have clearly influenced its development from Baumgarten and Kant in the eighteenth century down to the present.[1]

Another approach is to formulate what are commonly held to be aesthetic concerns in modern thought and to see if they can already be found in ancient texts, without limiting the choice of texts to those which have demonstrably influenced modern aesthetics. Our volume also includes material, particularly from Latin sources, which is less commonly cited by historians of aesthetics but which raises what we regard as aesthetic issues. What sort of issues that would now be described as 'aesthetic' were discussed by ancient authors?

The most common description of the subject of modern aesthetics, arising out of eighteenth- and nineteenth-century theories, is that aesthetics is concerned with issues connected to natural and artistic beauty and with art, including all aspects of its appreciation and production. Interest in natural beauty, and the issue of beauty as such, faded for a while but is now reviving. If one assumes this understanding of 'aesthetics', discussions of what we would now call 'aesthetic' topics can certainly be found in antiquity, since it had its share of treatments of both beauty and art, although the meaning of both these terms was rather different in the ancient world.[2] Ancient authors do discuss in their own way a wide range of issues concerning the nature of beauty, the principles of art, and the questions of both the appreciation of art and its production by artists.

Most modern aesthetic theories focus on art – rather than, for instance, on questions about natural beauty – and in particular on the nature of art, or its common foundational principles such as imitation or expression, as well as on its formal principles. The institutional theory of art claims that works of art are simply those works which we choose to regard as such by placing them in galleries or collections while Marxist theories hold that art reflects social and economic reality in some way. Another type of theory claims that the interest we take in works of art and in natural beauty cannot be explained by particular characteristics of the objects, nor by social concerns; rather, there is a special aesthetic kind of interest, judgement or attitude. Here Kant's account of aesthetic judgement is of central importance. In Kant's view the objects of aesthetic judgement

[1] See, for example, Eva Schaper, *Prelude to Aesthetics* (London: Allen and Unwin, 1968) on Plato and Aristotle.
[2] See the discussion of some key terminology in our Note on the texts and the translations.

have 'purposiveness without purpose' and aesthetic experience can be described as revealing a reality that transcends our understanding.

The theory of art as imitation or expression has well-known ancient roots. So do some formalist theories of art. Others, such as the institutional theory of art, are absent from Greek and Roman texts. The institutional theory of art assumes modern habits of collecting and viewing art[3] and it is not surprising that we find no trace of it in antiquity. Similarly, theories which hold that art reflects social and economic reality, or promotes a particular ideology, have no counterpart in ancient thought. At the same time, the theories concerned with the nature of aesthetic judgement, and especially with its revelatory nature, do have ancient roots: this fact is not often acknowledged in the Anglo-American tradition but is commonly accepted in Continental philosophy.

Modern discussions of the arts, and modern aesthetics, tend to emphasize subjectivity and individual taste. Ancient thinkers on the other hand assumed that there are objective criteria of beauty and objective principles of art. The contrast comes out clearly if we consider theories of art as expression. Since the rise of the Romantic movement, the idea that artists express their feelings and personality through their art has not only formed the basis for some theories in philosophical aesthetics, such as the idealist theories of Croce and Collingwood, but has pervaded criticism of art, literature and music. Although Longinus, *On Sublimity*, foreshadows this modern interest in subjective expression, most ancient authors who regard art as expressive hold, either implicitly or explicitly, that what is expressed is not just individual feeling but some kind of objective reality. In consequence their ideas are best considered alongside theories of art as imitation or representation.

Although discussion of the objective principles of beauty and art has received comparatively little emphasis since the nineteenth century as a result of the subjective turn in aesthetics, it is again becoming increasingly popular as scholars and scientists alike realize how much in aesthetics is objective, i.e., dependent on human physiology, neurobiology and universal environmental and social experiences.[4] From this point of

---

[3] See especially G. Dickie, *Art and the Aesthetic: an Institutional Analysis* (Ithaca and London: Cornell University Press, 1974).

[4] See, for example, I. Rentschler, B. Herzberger and D. Epstein, eds., *Beauty and the Brain: Biological Aspects of Aesthetics* (Basle, Boston and Berlin: Birkhäuser Verlag, 1988).

view, the observations of ancient authors such as Cicero and Philodemus become increasingly topical.

Another common point of discussion in modern aesthetics is emotion. The Romantics not only claimed that art expressed the emotions of the artist but also emphasized the power of both art and beauty to evoke emotions. Many ancient texts discuss the emotional effect of art: the theme is already present in Gorgias' *Encomium of Helen*, runs through all Plato's discussions of art and poetry and makes a notoriously puzzling appearance in Aristotle's claim that tragedy produces a *katharsis* ('purification') of pity and fear. In late antiquity the 'paradox of tragedy', that we enjoy the vicarious sufferings we experience as the members of a theatre audience, is highlighted by Augustine at the beginning of *Confessions* 3. The idea that our reaction to beauty involves the emotions also goes back to antiquity: it is already present in Plato's *Symposium* and *Phaedrus* and is particularly stressed by Plotinus, in *Ennead* 1.6 and elsewhere.

Greek and Roman aesthetics developed over a long period. The earliest text included in this volume (Gorgias' *Encomium of Helen*) was written before 400 BC, the latest in the sixth century AD. By AD 600 the Mediterranean world was a very different place, politically, socially and intellectually, from what it had been in 400 BC. Nevertheless the texts presented here have many themes in common and share a broadly similar approach to beauty and the arts, assuming that beauty can be objectively defined and that art is in some way imitative or representational. Some of our texts were written by philosophers, others by intellectuals interested in the arts and knowledgeable about philosophy. Many of them have directly influenced subsequent thinking about aesthetic issues in the European tradition. All of them, we believe, are worth reading and studying by anyone interested in philosophical aesthetics.

Classical Greek aesthetics: Gorgias, Plato, Xenophon, Aristotle

Early Greek poets, such as Homer, Hesiod and Pindar, include in their work some comments on their own craft of poetry; Gorgias, one of the first teachers of rhetoric, includes an interesting discussion of the power of speech in his *Encomium of Helen*, as mentioned above; the sophist Damon is said to have held that music had ethical effects; and comments about poetry and beauty are attributed to the atomist philosopher, Democritus.[5] The comedy, *Frogs*, by the Athenian playwright Aristophanes includes a contrast between two tragic poets, Aeschylus and Euripides. The poets are presented as arguing both about the appropriate style for tragedy and about its moral significance. However, as in many other areas of philosophy, it is Plato who offers the first extended treatment of both beauty and the arts and who raises many of the questions considered by subsequent ancient thinkers. Notoriously, Plato expels the poets (or most of them) from the ideal state depicted in the *Republic* and criticizes both poets and painters as mere copyists of objects in the physical world which are themselves only copies of intelligible Forms. But Plato does not offer one unified theory in aesthetics, any more than he does in any other area of philosophy, and there is much more to his views of beauty and the arts than this. Plato discusses beauty and the arts in a variety of different contexts. Often we need to look at the context of a particular passage in order to understand the point of view expressed in it and to make sense of apparent contradictions with passages from other dialogues. Despite the variety, there are some constant themes which reappear in all Plato's discussions of aesthetic topics: he always stresses that poets, and other artists, lack knowledge, and he frequently draws attention to the emotional effects of poetry and music. For Plato poetry and music have a significant role to play in moral education because they have such a powerful effect on the emotions.

Most of Plato's dialogues depict Socrates in discussion with one or more interlocutors. It is impossible to know how far these discussions reflect the interests of the historical Socrates although it is tempting to speculate that dialogues such as the *Ion* and the *Hippias Major*, which are usually regarded as having been written early in Plato's career, do bear some relation to Socrates' own views about poetry and about 'the fine'.[6]

In the *Ion* Socrates argues that divine inspiration, not knowledge, is responsible both for the facility with which poets compose their work and for the power which those works can have over the emotions of an audience. Socrates tries to show Ion, a professional reciter and interpreter

---

[5] See, for example, Homer, *Iliad* 2.484–92, *Odyssey* 1.336–52, 8.479–98, 22.340–9; Hesiod, *Theogony* 21–34; Pindar, *Nemean* 7.11–24, fr. 137; Gorgias, *Encomium of Helen* 8–14, pp. 3–4 below; Democritus, frr. B18, B21DK. On Damon, see A. Barker, *Greek Musical Writings* I (Cambridge University Press, 1984) 168–9.

[6] There is however some dispute over whether the *Hippias Major* is by Plato at all. See Paul Woodruff, *Plato. Hippias Major* (Oxford: Blackwell, 1982) 93–105.

of Homer, that his abilities, like those of the poets, are due to inspiration and in 535b–e he describes Ion as manipulating the emotions of his audience. In the *Ion* Socrates' praise of inspiration seems somewhat ironical, since he emphasizes the poets' lack of knowledge, whereas in the *Phaedrus* (245a) he appears more genuinely favourable to inspired poetry. In the *Hippias Major* Socrates is engaged in a lengthy discussion with the sophist Hippias about how to define beauty or 'the fine'.⁷ The suggestion that the fine is the appropriate is rejected, and the fine is firmly distinguished from the useful and the beneficial. A final suggestion that 'the fine is what is pleasant through hearing and sight' (298a) is also rejected and the dialogue ends inconclusively.

In the *Symposium* and the *Phaedrus* Plato returns to discussion of beauty or 'the fine' in quite a different way. In these dialogues we find the idea that beauty in the physical world awakens in us the realization that true beauty is located in a higher, intelligible world. *Symposium* 209e–212a recounts how the soul can ascend from the physical world to the Platonic Form of Beauty, moving from admiration for physical beauty to appreciating beauty in souls, in practices and laws, and in types of knowledge and finally to a revelation of true beauty itself. *Phaedrus* 249d–251a portrays the vision of true beauty in mythical terms, describing it as 'shining brightly'. In both dialogues, love is presented as the force driving the soul towards a vision of ultimate beauty which transcends conceptual knowledge. Both dialogues are concerned with moral as well as aesthetic beauty: that is why 'beauty in practices and laws' is mentioned in the *Symposium* while in the *Phaedrus* the souls which have lost sight of true beauty are described not just as having 'forgotten holiness' but as 'turned towards injustice'. In both dialogues the ladder which the soul must climb starts in the physical world. The beauty of the physical world is recognized as essentially attractive, drawing us to the revelation of something beyond it. In the *Timaeus* we find a passage (28a–29b) praising the beauty of the world as a whole and arguing explicitly that if the world is so well arranged and beautiful it must have an intelligent creator, just as a work of art has an artist who created it.

In the *Republic* Plato's standpoint is in some ways rather different. Here, in the context of describing an ideally just state, ruled by

---

⁷ The Greek adjective *kalos* can be translated as 'fine', 'beautiful', or even 'good': see Note on the texts and the translations.

philosophers who have knowledge of the Good, he is concerned with the role of poetry and music in education and with the relationship between works of art and what they represent. Yet here too, as elsewhere, he argues that poets and other artists do not have knowledge and draws attention to the effect of art on the emotions. In *Republic* 2 and 3 Socrates criticizes Homer and Greek tragedy on moral grounds: the future guardians of the ideal state are not to be taught any poetry which will give them mistaken ideas about the gods or encourage the development of strong emotions such as grief, upsetting the harmonious balance of the virtuous soul ruled by reason. At 392d he turns to the discussion of poetic imitation, distinguishing between 'narrative, narrative expressed through imitation and a combination of the two'. By narrative he means telling a story in the third person; tragedy, which presents a story in dramatic form, is 'narrative expressed through imitation' while Homeric poetry, which combines third-person storytelling with passages of direct speech by the character, is a combination of narrative and imitation. The main problem with imitation, in *Republic* 3, is that dramatic actors expose themselves to psychological damage, both by playing the parts of many different kinds of people and by playing villains. Music is criticized on similar grounds. Musical modes which encourage either excessive grief or indulgence in luxury are not to be permitted. Only modes which encourage brave, steadfast and wise behaviour will be allowed, played on simple instruments, with rhythms appropriate to 'a self-disciplined and courageous life'.

Much of the discussion of poetry and music in *Republic* 2 and 3 is harshly critical of these arts. However, there is also a positive side to Plato's treatment of the arts in these books. At 398a–b, we are told that the versatile poet who can imitate anything would be expelled from the ideal state but a 'simpler … poet and storyteller, who can imitate the decent man's way of speaking' remains acceptable. At 400d–402a, after the discussion of music, there are some important remarks on the educational value of aesthetic experience. Here Socrates expresses the idea that the aesthetic experience of sensible beauty leads directly to the beauty of speech and thought, just as healthy air in a healthy environment leads directly to health. He goes on to argue that being exposed to aesthetic experiences, which infuse the idea of harmony as a universal principle, leads directly to improved morals. Recognizing aesthetic harmony in things leads us to think of preserving such harmony in our souls as well, even before we master conceptual arguments for moral behaviour.[8]

In *Republic* 10 Socrates returns to the topic of poetry and claims that all imitative poetry had earlier been excluded from the ideal state. This misleading claim signals clearly that the treatment of poetry in the final book of the *Republic* will be both wider ranging and harsher than the treatment in Books 2 and 3. The discussion focuses on imitation and both painters and poets are attacked on the grounds that they imitate objects in the physical world which are themselves only imitations of the Platonic Forms. At 596b–e the painter is compared to someone holding a mirror who creates things 'as they appear to be' but not 'as they truly are'. Art here is seen as pandering to illusion, giving its audience a false view of reality. These arguments about imitation are the prelude to a renewed attack on the poets as lacking in knowledge and as producing work which appeals only to the emotions, not to the rational part of the soul.[9] Once again most poets are expelled from the ideal state. This time the only poetry allowed in is 'hymns to the gods and verses in praise of good men' (607a). The view of imitation found in *Republic* 10 reappears in the *Sophist* where at 235c–236c the Eleatic Stranger argues that most sculptors and painters who practise the imitative art are concerned only with appearances.

Plato's discussions of the arts focus mainly on poetry, occasionally including music and the visual arts. There are striking parallels between his attitude to poetry and his attitude to rhetoric, that is, the techniques of persuasion and the skills required to compose speeches in prose. In the *Gorgias* Plato is harshly critical of rhetoric, contrasting its persuasive power, which aims only at pleasing the audience, with philosophy which aims for knowledge of the truth. In the *Phaedrus*, although Socrates criticizes severely a speech said to be by the orator Lysias, he also raises the possibility that there could be an ideal kind of rhetoric, based on knowledge. Our selection contains a passage from the *Phaedrus*, 264c, expressing the requirement that a speech should have organic unity, which influenced later views about the organic unity of works of literature.

---

[8] The role of the arts in education is also discussed in *Laws* 2 (653c–660d, 667b–670e), 3 (700a–701b) and 7 (798d–802e, 810b–817e), passages not included in this volume.

[9] The mixture of emotions experienced by the audience for both tragedy and comedy is further discussed in *Philebus* 48a–50d, a passage not included in this volume.

Xenophon's *Memoirs of Socrates*, like Plato's dialogues, offer us fictional conversations which attempt to recreate what talking to Socrates was like. A passage from these *Memoirs*, included in our selection, presents Socrates discussing painting and sculpture with practitioners of those arts. Xenophon presents both Socrates and his interlocutors as assuming that painting is concerned 'to produce a likeness' and that sculptors aim to make their work 'look like the figures of living people'. The discussion focuses on whether it is possible to imitate moral character and emotion as well as physical appearance.

A reader turning from the dialogues of Plato or Xenophon to the work of Aristotle will immediately be struck by the very different way in which Aristotle's philosophy is presented. The surviving works of Aristotle probably derive from lectures delivered in his philosophical school, the Lyceum, and can seem both dense and elliptical to a modern reader. Aristotle's *Poetics*, as we have it, focuses on the nature of tragic drama (a lost second book dealt with comedy) but opens with reflections on poetry in general and includes some discussion of epic. Like Plato and Xenophon Aristotle assumes that both painters and poets are engaged in imitation and defines tragedy as 'an imitation of an action' in *Poetics* 6.1449b. However unlike Plato in *Republic* 10 he does not regard the art of the dramatist as simply copying: in *Poetics* 9.1451a–b he argues that the poet, unlike the historian, imitates 'not what happened but the sort of thing that would happen' and so 'tends to make universal statements'. This suggests that art can convey truth and can be, in its own way, a source of knowledge.

Aristotle recognizes that a good tragedy will contain a number of different components, such as striking characterization, attractive diction, and spectacle, all of which will contribute to its overall effect (1449b ff.). However in his view plot is by far the most important component: the best tragedy is one which is well constructed and he devotes considerable space to setting out what makes for a good plot. However he is not concerned only with the formal characteristics of tragic drama, or of epic. His moral concerns become clear when he discusses what kinds of character should be portrayed in tragedy in *Poetics* 13.1452b–1453a and again in 15.1454a–b: tragedy should present characters who, while 'better than we are', are not perfect and who fall into misfortune through some kind of error or failing. Exactly what kind of error or failing this is has been a continuing topic of discussion in later aesthetics, and no consensus has ever been reached. In his discussion of tragic error, Aristotle is not simply concerned with what kinds of characters make for a successful tragic plot; he is assuming that tragedy has a role to play in moral education.

Aristotle's view of the effect of art on the emotions is more complex than Plato's but is expressed with tantalizing brevity. In *Poetics* 4.1448b he recognizes that human beings naturally take pleasure in viewing imitations while in 6.1449b he makes the puzzling claim that tragedy somehow purifies our emotions of pity and fear. Exactly what Aristotle means by his claim that a good tragedy will effect a 'purification' (*katharsis*) of emotions is another issue of recurring debate in later philosophy, and one on which no general agreement has ever been reached. Talk of purification or *katharsis*, however, appears again in Aristotle's discussion of music in *Politics* 8 where, like Plato, he takes it for granted that music arouses emotion and discusses its use in education.

Parts of the *Poetics* discuss matters such as language (19.1456a–b) and the use of metaphor (21.1457b). At 19.1456a Aristotle refers the reader to the *Rhetoric* for discussion of 'the effects to be produced by speech'. The *Rhetoric* deals with a range of philosophical issues raised by rhetorical practice: rhetorical reasoning, prose style and the emotions which an orator will need to understand in order to persuade his audience effectively. We have not included any Aristotelian material on rhetoric, partly because there simply is not room in one volume for all the texts that might be included. Nevertheless, his views on rhetoric, like Plato's, deserve mention in any discussion of the development of Greek and Roman aesthetics since rhetoric, including both rhetorical theory and the literary criticism of prose style, played an important role in Greek and Roman education and influenced the way in which both poets and prose authors wrote as well as the way in which ancient readers responded to their work. Many of the later thinkers included in our selection will have learned rhetoric before they learned philosophy, and rhetorical theory and criticism affect both their views on aesthetics and the way in which they present those views.

The influence of Plato and Aristotle can be found almost everywhere in later Greek and Roman aesthetics. As in other areas of philosophy, they raised fundamental questions and set the terms of subsequent debate.

Aesthetics in Republican Rome: Philodemus, Cicero

A glance at the Chronology at the end of this Introduction will immediately reveal that our selection jumps some 300 years from Plato, Xenophon and Aristotle to Philodemus and Cicero. Why is this, and what happened to Greek philosophy, and to aesthetics in those 300 years? A great deal happened in Greek philosophy: while the intellectual heirs of Plato and Aristotle continued to discuss problems and develop ideas along the lines laid down in Plato's Academy and in the Lyceum, new schools of philosophy developed in the Hellenistic period, especially Stoicism and Epicureanism. Whereas Stoics put great emphasis on the rational nature of the universe as a whole and on the need for humans to cultivate a form of 'virtue' which was associated with insight into that rationality, Epicureans claimed that the goal or end of human life was pleasure, by which they meant not so much sensual pleasure as tranquillity and freedom from pain. Vigorous debates took place within these schools and between philosophers of different schools. Within the Academy, debate over what was most important in the tradition inherited from Socrates and Plato contributed to the development of Scepticism. Sadly, most of the philosophical texts written during this period do not survive in their entirety. In reconstructing the history of philosophy in the Hellenistic period we have to rely largely on quotations and paraphrases by later authors and on fragmentary papyri.

However, once we reach the first century BC, there is much more evidence available. By this time Rome was the dominant power in the Mediterranean world, although Greek continued to be the language of philosophical culture and education. Philodemus and Cicero, the two authors of the first century BC included in our selection, offer two different perspectives on Hellenistic aesthetics.

Philodemus was both a teacher of Epicurean philosophy and a poet. Born in Gadara in Syria, he studied philosophy in Athens before arriving in Rome in the mid-70s BC. He enjoyed the patronage of powerful Roman aristocrats and taught philosophy at Naples and at Herculaneum, on the Bay of Naples, to a group of students which included the poet Virgil. His works were preserved on papyrus rolls in a philosophical library at Herculaneum which was buried in the eruption of Vesuvius in AD 79 that destroyed Pompeii and was only rediscovered in the eighteenth century. In recent years new techniques have made it possible to read the papyri of Philodemus much more fully and accurately than before and his work on aesthetics has aroused great interest, both because it opens a window on the lost world of aesthetic theory between the time of Aristotle and the first century BC and because it informs us about Philodemus' own distinctive aesthetic views.

Philodemus writes as a philosopher working within a school tradition of controversy and debate. He proceeds by first expounding the views of earlier thinkers and then criticizing those views. His own positive theories emerge only through his criticism of others but he does put forward some radical views which differ sharply from the mainstream of Greek and Roman aesthetics. As an Epicurean, his prime targets for attack are philosophers from the rival school of Stoicism. In *On Poems* 5 he attacks not only Stoic views of what makes poetry good but also the views of Heraclides Ponticus, who studied with both Plato and Aristotle, and of Neoptolemus of Parium, who belonged to the Aristotelian school. (The discussion of Neoptolemus has aroused particular interest among scholars because Neoptolemus is probably the main source for the views on poetry found in Horace's *Art of Poetry*.[10]) *On Music* 4 is largely devoted to criticizing the views of Diogenes of Babylon, a Stoic. Epicurus himself expressed considerable hostility to poetry and opposed its use in education; nevertheless he was prepared to accept poetry as a means to pleasure. It is in keeping with this that Philodemus objects to any view which values poetry simply because its content is morally improving. Philodemus insists that form and content in poetry are not separable and in other parts of *On Poems*, particularly the rather technical Book 1, he criticizes theorists, such as the Stoic Crates of Mallos, who studied the sound of poetry in detail and attached great importance to euphony. In *On Poems* 5.XVI.28–XVII.31 Philodemus argues that poems whose content conforms to the lofty Stoic ideals of virtue have never been written, and never will be written. As an Epicurean, he believes that both poetry and music are simply sources of pleasure. The pleasure we take in hearing certain types of music, for instance, is an automatic reaction, produced by the impression of atoms on our sense-organ. In *On Music* 4, cols.115.44–117.35 he describes such impressions as 'not subject to reason' and firmly distinguishes between our initial reactions of pleasure and our subsequent rationalization of those reactions. The moral qualities which Stoics like Diogenes of Babylon attribute to music are the result of subjective interpretation, with no basis in the atomic structure of reality.

---

[10] See C. O. Brink, *Horace on Poetry, I. Prolegomena to the Literary Epistles* (Cambridge University Press, 1963).

That is why he attacks Diogenes for talking of the parts of the soul as 'in proportion with each other' (col. *78*.3–45) and for claiming that music imitates the emotions in a way which brings moral benefit (cols. *91*.3–*92*.5) and that music displays moral qualities (col. 117.28–35).

Cicero was not a professional philosopher but a lawyer and a politician. However, he too, like Philodemus, studied philosophy in Athens. As a young man he wrote the theoretical work *On Rhetorical Invention*, and made some translations from Greek writers such as Xenophon. At two later times in his life, in 55–51 BC and again in 45–44 BC, he turned from the frustration of politics in the final years of the Roman Republic to the composition of philosophical works. His aim in these works was to present Greek philosophy in Latin, for Roman readers. What he presented was Greek philosophy as it looked in the first century BC: some Platonism, a little Aristotle, a good deal of Stoicism and Epicureanism, and various viewpoints deriving from the philosophical battles taking place within the Academy. By the first century BC the philosophers in the Academy were Sceptics rather than Platonists. Their views came under attack from Antiochus of Ascalon who claimed to be returning to the views of Plato – but to us Antiochus' philosophy appears to be a combination of Platonism, Stoicism and some Aristotelian views. In works such as *On the Nature of the Gods* and *On Moral Ends* Cicero pits the views of the different philosophical schools of his own time against one another. In the *Tusculan Disputations* he discusses death, pain, the passions and the happy life from a largely Stoic point of view while *On Duties* draws heavily on the ideas of the second-century BC Stoic Panaetius. His mature philosophical output included further theoretical works on oratory such as *On the Ideal Orator* and *Orator*; in these as in *On Rhetorical Invention* he draws on earlier philosophical discussions of rhetoric, on contemporary theorizing and on his own experience as a highly successful advocate in the Roman lawcourts.

Passages such as the ones we have selected from *On Moral Ends* and *On Duties* make it clear that, following Stoic usage, Cicero understands the notions of 'excellence' and 'the fitting' in aesthetic, as well as moral, terms – or rather, that he makes no distinction between the moral and the aesthetic. So, for example, in *Tusculan Disputations* 4.13.30–1 and *On Duties* 1.27.93–9 he uses a Stoic comparison between the harmonious arrangement of powers in the soul and the analogous arrangement of elements in the body, which results in health and beauty. Similarly he reflects Stoic views when he claims in *On Duties* 1.4.14 and *On Moral Ends* 2.14.47 that beauty serves as a sure guide in moral life, indicating clearly what must be preferred in morals by analogy with what is preferred among visual forms on the basis of their beauty and noble appearance.

The admiration for the ordered beauty of the world expressed in Plato's *Timaeus* 28a–29b influenced much later thought. Many ancient authors believed that a universal law of patterns and proportions underlies all reality, governing both physical things and human souls and minds. In several of our Cicero texts (*On the Ideal Orator* 3.25.96–26.101; 3.45.178; 3.50.195–51; *Orator* 51.173; 53.177–8) we find the observation that humans have an innate capacity to perceive metrical patterns in speech, rhythms and harmonies in music, and proportions in the visual arts, such as painting and architecture, as well as in natural bodies. In *Orator* 55.183–4 Cicero notes that such patterns cannot be explained unless one assumes that they depend on the innate qualities of our sensory powers alone.

These observations about the human perception of order are probably of Stoic origin but the story Cicero tells in *On Rhetorical Invention* 2.1.1–3, according to which Zeuxis drew on a number of different models in order to paint a picture of Helen of Troy, is a traditional one, probably first told by the fourth-century BC historian Duris of Samos[11] while the suggestion in *Orator* 2.8–9 that the sculptor Phidias imitated 'some exquisite form of beauty present in his own mind' introduces an element of Platonism, perhaps due to Antiochus of Ascalon. The shift from the idea which we find in Plato's *Republic*, that the artist 'imitates' some particular object in the sensory world, to the suggestion that art is an 'imitation' of something ideal present in the artist's mind, is a historically momentous one.

Aesthetics under the Roman Empire: Seneca, Longinus, Philostratus, Philostratus the Younger, Aristides Quintilianus

The student of philosophy between the time of Cicero and the time of Plotinus encounters similar problems to the student of Hellenistic

---

[11] For the origins of this story and its popularity in the Renaissance, see K. Jex-Blake and E. Sellers, *The Elder Pliny's Chapters on the History of Art* (London: Macmillan, 1896, revised edition by R. V. Schoder, Chicago: Argonaut, 1968) lxi–lxii, and E. Panofsky, *Idea. A Concept in Art Theory* (trans. J. J. S. Peake, Columbia: University of South Carolina Press, 1968) 15, 49, 58, 157.

philosophy. Although philosophical teaching flourished during this period, very few works survive by authors whom we would now regard as 'professional philosophers'. Instead there is a wealth of material by philosophically educated writers such as Philo of Alexandria or Plutarch who used philosophical ideas in other kinds of writing, assuming a high level of philosophical culture and understanding in their readers. The material in our selection that dates from this period all comes from writers of this kind. Seneca, tutor and adviser to the Emperor Nero, writes about philosophy primarily from a Stoic viewpoint but the account of five kinds of cause in *Letter* 65.2–10 explicitly draws on Plato and Aristotle as well as on 'our own Stoics'. The suggestion that rather than merely imitating objects in the physical world the artist looks to ideas in his own mind which are themselves reflections of the Platonic Forms, already made in Cicero, *Orator* 2.8–9, reappears here. Meanwhile, in the passages we have selected from *On the Award and Reception of Favours*, Seneca follows Stoic thought in describing 'the noble' as beautiful and in expressing admiration for the beauty and order of the world.

The work *On Sublimity* attributed to Longinus was probably written at around the same time, in the first century AD, though we know nothing of its author. Written in response to a lost work by Caecilius of Caleacte, with the expressed intention of teaching budding orators how to achieve sublimity in their writing, this text combines ideas drawn from the rhetorical tradition of literary criticism with ideas drawn from philosophy, particularly from Platonism.

Longinus tries to define and illustrate the peculiar quality which makes certain literary works great, a quality which he calls 'the sublime'. 'Sublime' seems originally to have referred to a type of style: the 'high' or elevated style as opposed to a more colloquial mode of expression. It then comes to be used as a moral and psychological property, and finally as what we would call an 'aesthetic' category, which is a potential alternative to 'beauty'. Thus Longinus (in 9.2) illustrates the point that ideas can be grand, or sublime, in themselves 'without verbal expression' by referring to Homer's account of the silence of Ajax in the Underworld (in *Odyssey* 11.541–67). Ajax had been defeated by Odysseus in a contest for a prize of honour – the armour of the dead Achilles – and had thereupon killed himself. When Odysseus sees him in the Underworld and tries to make peace with him, Ajax does not respond, but simply goes off in silence.

When Longinus defines what he means by the sublime in literature, he appeals to the test of time, claiming in 7.4 that we should 'reckon those things which please everybody all the time as genuinely and finely sublime'. In 8.1 he lists five sources of sublimity, including strong emotion. In fact emotion does not receive separate discussion but it is clear throughout the work that Longinus regards the successful expression of emotion as a very important mark of sublimity and also assumes that sublime works have a powerful effect on the emotions of their audience. He admires the genius of great writers, going so far as to describe this genius as divine in passages such as 33.5 and 34.4. Longinus' main way of arguing for his views is to discuss particular passages of poetry and prose in some detail, drawing attention to their good and bad qualities. He presents these passages as models to be followed by those who aim at sublimity in their own writing. Some parts of his text, omitted from our selection, discuss matters such as figures of speech and word-order which were regularly studied in the rhetorical schools.

Longinus focuses on literature, both poetry and prose, but we can see from the probably somewhat later works by the two Philostrati and by Aristides Quintilianus that the aesthetic interests of intellectuals in this period included painting, sculpture and music. The *Life of Apollonius of Tyana* is a long work in eight books commissioned from the elder Philostratus, the Athenian, by the wife of the Emperor Septimius Severus. Apollonius is represented as a holy man with philosophical interests and the work includes reports of many conversations which Apollonius is alleged to have held with a variety of people. Our selection includes two passages in which he is presented as discussing the visual arts. In 2.22 he is discussing painting with Damis, his disciple and companion, while in 6.19, in conversation with Thespesion, an Egyptian, he is contrasting the animal images used to represent the Egyptian gods with the ways in which Greek sculptors portrayed the divine. Here he makes the striking claim that it was imagination, rather than imitation, which made sculptors like Phidias able to reproduce the appearance of the gods.

Two works entitled *Pictures* which contain literary descriptions of pictures and whose prefaces include interesting general comments about painting are attributed to authors called Philostratus. It is probable that one of them was written by the author of the *Life of Apollonius of Tyana* and the other by his younger relative, Philostratus the Lemnian. In the first we find praise of the painter as a more skilful imitator than the sculptor. The second develops the point already found in Xenophon that the painter can portray character and emotion, not just physical appearance.

The work *On Music* by Aristides Quintilianus probably dates from the third century AD. Book 1 deals with technical aspects of music – harmonics, rhythmics and metrics – while Book 2 deals with music's use in education and as therapy. Book 3 uses numerology, mathematics and natural science to connect the phenomena of music with the structure of reality overall. Although Aristides draws on a variety of earlier writings about music, his philosophical viewpoint is that of a Platonist. We have included in our selection the opening chapters of Book 1, which introduce the work as a whole, and material from Book 2 on the role of music in education. Aristides sees music as playing an important role in moral education through its effect on the emotions. He refers explicitly to Plato and develops the positive side of Plato's discussion of music.

Aesthetics in late antiquity: Plotinus, Augustine, Proclus, Anonymous Prolegomena

The latest texts in our selection bear witness to the two most significant intellectual currents in late antiquity: pagan Neoplatonism and Christian thought. The *Enneads* of Plotinus reflect teaching and discussion in his philosophical school in Rome. By the time of Plotinus Platonism had become the dominant philosophy, absorbing and transposing many Aristotelian and Stoic ideas. The teaching of philosophy consisted of the study and exposition of the texts of both Aristotle and Plato, interpreting these authorities with the aim of showing that, rightly understood, they offered a unified doctrine. Plotinus' approach to beauty clearly owes a good deal to Plato's *Symposium*, *Phaedrus* and *Timaeus* but he develops Plato's suggestions into something more systematic. He emphasizes not only that the Platonic Forms are the source of all beauty in this world but also that ultimately intelligible beauty derives from the Good, or the One, the highest entity in his metaphysical system. The suggestion found in Cicero and Seneca that the artist has access to the Platonic Forms now becomes a claim that the best art is not representational at all but rather symbolic of higher realities. In *Ennead* 5.8.1 Plotinus claims that 'Phidias ... made his statue of Zeus not from any perceptible model but grasping what Zeus would look like if he chose to appear before our eyes.'

As Christianity spread and developed, Christian intellectuals adopted and transformed many aspects of pagan Greek philosophy. Augustine, the only Christian writer included in our selection, offers a particularly interesting and influential synthesis of Platonist philosophy with Christian theology and spirituality. His extensive output includes considerable discussion of aesthetic issues. In his earlier works Augustine was trying to provide a stable foundation for the Christian faith through means that would appeal to the general public, not only to the circle of believers, i.e., through philosophy and common experience. Accordingly, in works such as *On Order*, *On Music* and *On Free Choice of the Will*, based on the model of Platonic dialogues, as well as in *On True Religion* Augustine makes the 'transcendental' nature of aesthetic experience the key point in his demonstration of the existence of the divine. Such experience seems to point beyond the limitations of the human mind and beyond immediately experienced reality. In *On True Religion* 40.76 Augustine makes a distinction between judgements of truth and judgements of beauty. In this passage he argues that in judging whether something is beautiful we should consider it not in isolation but as part of an ordered whole whereas 'the truth of our judgement does not depend on whether it is about the whole or a part'.

In some passages of Augustine, such as *Confessions* 7.17.23 and *On the Trinity* 9.6.11, we find a Platonist account of the love of beauty very similar to what we find in Plotinus. In other passages, such as *On True Religion* 30.56–32.60 and 39.72 or *On Free Choice of the Will* 2.12.34 and 16.41–3, Augustine combines this with a version of the argument from design found in Stoic aesthetics. In passages such as *On Free Choice of the Will* 2.16.42, *On Order* 2.11.32–4 and *On Music* 6.4.5 he follows the Stoics in appealing, like Cicero before him, to a universal law of patterns and proportions underlying all reality. In *On Music* he regards art as a combination of natural principles, that can always be 'consulted' in our minds and restored, with purely learned rules, such as the length of syllables, that must be retained by memory.

In *Confessions* 3.2.2 Augustine deplores the effect of drama on the emotions in a manner which is strongly reminiscent of Plato. At the same time he follows both Plato and the Stoics in making a close connection between aesthetic and moral harmony. In *On Order* 2.19.50–1 he asks how, when we perceive a harmoniously sounding cithara, we can tolerate 'discordant sounds' in our soul.

Despite the spread of Christianity, pagan philosophy in the Platonic tradition continued well into the sixth century AD. In the fifth century Proclus wrote commentaries on Plato based on the lectures he gave at the revived Platonic Academy in Athens.[12] Proclus believed that the poetic and religious texts of the Greek tradition contained the same essential truths as the philosophy of Plato. In his *Commentary on the Timaeus* 1.265.18–26 he makes a similar point about Phidias' statue of Zeus to that made by Plotinus in *Ennead* 5.8.1 but claims that Phidias represented the Homeric Zeus rather than 'the intellectual god himself'. In his *Commentary on the Republic* he develops Plotinus' claim that the best art is symbolic of higher realities with reference to poetry rather than sculpture, trying to show that Plato's criticisms of poetry do not apply to most of Homer's work. In 1.177.7–179.32 he offers an account of three types of poetry, contrasting the highest, inspired type with the lowest, 'simply imitative' type. It is clear from the wider context of Proclus' account that inspired poetry is symbolic and that when Proclus claims most of Homer is inspired what he means is that it must be interpreted allegorically. A similar approach to mythical stories as symbolic can be found in *Commentary on the Republic* 2.107.14–108.16, in a context where Proclus is about to comment on the myth of Er told by Plato at the very end of the *Republic*. In Proclus' account of the three types of poetry there is also a middle type, 'full of admonition and excellent advice', between the highest, inspired poetry and the lowest, imitative type. This type of poetry affects morals in a straightforward way and would have been quite acceptable in Plato's ideal state.

The *Anonymous Prolegomena to the Philosophy of Plato* was probably written at Alexandria, the other great centre of philosophy in late antiquity, some time in the sixth century. This work reflects many of the ideas about literature found in Proclus and his contemporaries and successors.[13] Its author returns to the effect of literature on morals and defends Plato's own use of the dialogue form by claiming that Plato shows us bad characters 'being changed by the good and instructed and purified' and that he uses the characters in his dialogues to exemplify moral qualities such as friendship and ambition.

---

[12] Plato's original foundation disintegrated in the first century BC. The institution at which Proclus taught was a re-foundation, probably dating only from the fourth century AD.

[13] Cf., for example, the opening pages of Olympiodorus, *Commentary on Plato's Gorgias*, trans. R. Jackson, K. Lycos and H. Tarrant (Leiden: Brill, 1998).

Medieval aesthetics, both in the Byzantine world and in the Latin West, was heavily influenced by the Platonism of late antiquity, both pagan and Christian. In every subsequent period, from the Renaissance onwards, some ancient writers on aesthetics have been 'rediscovered' and regarded as of central importance: for example, Aristotle's *Poetics* was enormously influential on the theory and practice of Renaissance drama while Longinus strongly influenced the development of aesthetic thought in the Romantic period.[14] We have tried in our selection to reflect the range and variety of Greek and Roman aesthetic thought over its long period of development.

[14] On Longinus, see M. H. Abrams, *The Mirror and the Lamp* (New York: Oxford University Press, 1953) esp. ch. 4.

Chronology

Note that some dates are approximate.

Dates	Authors	Historical events
c. 484–*c.* 380 BC	Gorgias	
427 BC		Gorgias visits Athens as an ambassador from Leontini and displays his rhetorical skill
c. 429–347 BC	Plato	
c. 428–*c.* 354 BC	Xenophon	
404 BC		End of the Peloponnesian War
399 BC		Death of Socrates
384–322 BC	Aristotle	
323 BC		Death of Alexander the Great
146 BC		Roman defeat of the Achaean Confederacy – Greece becomes a Roman province
c. 110–*c.* 40/35 BC	Philodemus	

106–43 BC	Cicero	
86 BC		Sack of Athens by the Roman general, Sulla
44 BC		Murder of Julius Caesar
31 BC		Battle of Actium
AD 14		Death of Augustus
c. AD 1–65	Seneca	
AD 54–68		Reign of Nero
?1st century AD	Longinus	
AD 161–80		Reign of Marcus Aurelius
c. AD 172–244/9	Philostratus	
AD 193–211		Reign of Septimius Severus
3rd century AD	Philostratus the Younger	
?3rd century AD	Aristides Quintilianus	
AD 205–269/70	Plotinus	
AD 242–3		Expedition against Persia by Gordian III, accompanied by Plotinus
AD 253–68		Reign of Gallienus, Plotinus' patron
AD 312–337		Reign of Constantine
AD 354–430	Augustine	
AD 378–95		Reign of Theodosius. Christianity becomes the official religion of the Roman Empire.
AD 395		The Roman Empire is divided into eastern and western parts on the death of Theodosius.

4th century AD		Probable re-founding of Plato's Academy at Athens
AD 410		Sack of Rome by the Goths
AD 410/12–85	Proclus	
AD 415		Lynching of the philosopher Hypatia at Alexandria
AD 529		Justinian forbids pagans to teach philosophy or law. The Neoplatonist philosophers leave Athens.
?6th century AD	*Anonymous Prolegomena to the Philosophy of Plato*	
AD 641		Capture of Alexandria by the Arabs

Further reading

There are complete English editions of some of the works from which we have extracted selections specifically concerned with aesthetics. A complete text and translation of Gorgias' *Encomium of Helen* can be found in D. M. MacDowell, ed., *Gorgias. Encomium of Helen* (Bristol Classical Press, 1982). Two useful collections of translations of all Plato's dialogues are: E. Hamilton and H. Cairns, eds., *Plato: The Collected Dialogues* (Princeton University Press, 1961) and J. Cooper and D. S. Hutchinson, eds., *Plato: Complete Works* (Indianapolis, IN: Hackett, 1997). A complete translation of the *Memoirs of Socrates* is available in Xenophon, *Conversations of Socrates*, trans. H. Tredennick and R. Waterfield, ed. R. Waterfield (London and New York: Penguin, 1990). Among the many other translations of Aristotle's *Poetics*, we would particularly recommend the translation by M. E. Hubbard in D. A. Russell and M. Winterbottom, eds., *Ancient Literary Criticism. The Principal Texts in New Translations* (Oxford: Clarendon Press, 1972), and the translation by Malcolm Heath, *Aristotle. Poetics* (London: Penguin, 1996). The most readily available translation of Aristotle's *Politics* is probably that of T. J. Sinclair, revised by T. J. Saunders (Harmondsworth: Penguin, 1981). A translation of Philodemus, *On Poems* Book 5, by David Armstrong can be found as Appendix 1 to D. Obbink ed., *Philodemus and Poetry: Poetic Theory and Practice in Lucretius, Philodemus, and Horace* (Oxford University Press, 1995).

Translations of the Cicero works from which our selections are drawn include: *Cicero. On the Ideal Orator (De oratore)*, trans. J. M. May and

J. Wisse (Oxford University Press, 2001); *Cicero. On Moral Ends*, ed. J. Annas, trans. R. Woolf (Cambridge University Press, 2001); *Cicero. The Nature of the Gods*, trans. P. G. Walsh (Oxford: Clarendon Press, 2007); *Cicero on the Emotions. Tusculan Disputations 3 and 4*, trans. M. Graver (Chicago University Press, 2002); *Cicero. On Duties*, ed. E. M. Atkins, ed. and trans. M. T. Griffin (Cambridge University Press, 1991); and *Cicero. On Obligations*, trans. P. G. Walsh (Oxford University Press, 2000). A useful translation of Seneca's *Letters* is *Seneca. Letters from a Stoic. Epistulae morales ad Lucilium*, trans. R. Campbell (Harmondsworth: Penguin, 1969). A translation of *On the Award and Reception of Favours* can be found in *Seneca. Moral and Political Writings*, trans. J. M. Cooper and J. F. Procopé (Cambridge University Press, 1995). The Loeb edition of Philostratus and Philostratus the Younger, *Imagines* (ed. A. Fairbanks, The Loeb Classical Library, Harvard University Press, 1931), includes an English translation, as does the Loeb edition of the *Life of Apollonius of Tyana* (ed. C. P. Jones, 2005).

The most reliable English translation of Plotinus is that of A. H. Armstrong in his Loeb edition (1966–88). Some of the Augustine selections included here are also translated in the following English editions: *Augustine. On Free Choice of the Will*, trans. T. Williams (Indianapolis, IN: Hackett, 1993); *St. Augustine. Confessions*, trans. H. Chadwick (Oxford University Press, 1991); and *Augustine. On the Trinity*, ed. G. B. Matthews, trans. S. McKenna (Cambridge University Press, 2002). An English translation of Proclus, *Commentary on the Timaeus*, in four volumes, is in course of publication. The passage used in this volume can be found in volume I of that translation, by H. Tarrant (Cambridge University Press, 2007). The first of our passages from the *Commentary on the Republic* is also translated by D. A. Russell in the Appendix to *Criticism in Antiquity* (London: Duckworth, 1981). There is a complete French translation of the *Commentary on the Republic* by A. J. Festugière (Paris: J. Vrin, 1970).

For a recent general study of ancient aesthetics, with special emphasis on Plato, Aristotle and Plotinus, see S. Büttner, *Antike Ästhetik. Eine Einführung in die Prinzipien des Schönen* (Munich: C. H. Beck, 2006). For a detailed study of ancient and medieval aesthetic texts, including authors from Plato to Augustine, as well as of theoretical approaches to the study of ancient aesthetics and philosophical and theological issues in ancient aesthetics, see O. Bychkov, *Aesthetic Revelation: Reading*

Ancient and Medieval Texts after Hans Urs von Balthasar (Washington, DC: Catholic University of America Press, 2010). The aesthetics of Plato, Plotinus and their ancient and more recent followers is covered in V. Olejniczak Lobsien and C. Olk, eds., *Neuplatonismus und Ästhetik* (Berlin and New York: Walter de Gruyter, 2007). Comprehensive coverage of the history of ancient literary criticism, up to the early Christian authors, can be found in G. A. Kennedy, ed., *Classical Criticism*, vol. I of *The Cambridge History of Literary Criticism* (Cambridge University Press, 1989). Two similarly broad studies that include aesthetic topics other than literature are D. T. Benediktson, *Literature and the Visual Arts in Ancient Greece and Rome* (Norman, OK: University of Oklahoma Press, 2000) and K. Boudouris, ed., *Greek Philosophy and the Fine Arts*, 2 vols. (Athens: International Center for Greek Philosophy and Culture, 2000). For a general study on the specific notion of mimesis in aesthetics see S. Halliwell, *The Aesthetics of Mimesis* (Princeton University Press, 2002).

There are a number of studies of aesthetic issues in particular ancient authors. Plato's aesthetics is very well covered in: C. Janaway, *Images of Excellence: Plato's Critique of the Arts* (Oxford: Clarendon Press, 1998); and J. M. E. Moravcsik and P. Temko, eds., *Plato on Beauty, Wisdom and the Arts* (Totowa, NJ: Rowman and Littlefield, 1982). An excellent study of Aristotle's *Poetics*, with a comprehensive discussion of the differences between ancient and modern aesthetics, can be found in S. Halliwell, *Aristotle's Poetics* (London: Duckworth, 1986). A collection of essays on the same subject also includes a bibliography of earlier works: A. O. Rorty, *Essays on Aristotle's Poetics* (Princeton University Press, 1992).

There are fewer studies on Stoic aesthetics, which is mostly covered in specific essays in larger studies, such as one by H. Karabatzaki in the collection by K. Boudouris. Good overall coverage of Stoic aesthetics is provided in M. A. Zagdoun, *La philosophie stoïcienne de l'art* (Paris: CNRS, 2000), and H.-J. Horn, 'Stoische Symmetrie und Theorie des Schönen in der Kaiserzeit', in *Aufstieg und Niedergang der Römischen Welt. Teil II: Principat*, 1454–72, edited by H. Temporini and W. Haase (Berlin and New York: Walter de Gruyter, 1989). For Cicero's aesthetics, see A. Desmouliez, *Cicéron et son goût: essai sur une définition d'une esthétique romaine à la fin de la république*, Collection Latomus 50 (Brussels: Latomus, 1976). For a collection of essays on Philodemus see

D. Obbink ed., *Philodemus and Poetry: Poetic Theory and Practice in Lucretius, Philodemus, and Horace* (Oxford University Press, 1995).

In addition to the treatment of Neoplatonic aesthetics in the general works cited above, mention should be made of the full recent study by O. Kuisma, *Art or Experience. A Study on Plotinus' Aesthetics* (Helsinki: Societas Scientiarum Fennica, 2003). The most comprehensive study of every possible aesthetic context in Augustine is J.-M. Fontanier, *La beauté selon saint Augustin* (Presses Universitaires de Rennes, 1998). Two works which focus specifically on musical aesthetics and the connection between aesthetics and theology in Augustine are: A. Keller, *Aurelius Augustinus und die Musik: Untersuchungen zu 'De musica' im Kontext seines Schrifttums* (Würzburg: Augustinus-Verlag, 1993); C. Harrison, *Beauty and Revelation in the Thought of Saint Augustine* (Oxford: Clarendon Press, 1992).

Note on the texts and the translations

Our translation of Gorgias' *Encomium of Helen* is based on Diels–Kranz, *Fragmente der Vorsokratiker* vol. II (Berlin: Weidmann, 1952). The translations of Plato in this volume are all based on the Oxford Classical Text, ed. J. Burnet (1902–6), except for the translation of the *Sophist* for which volume I of the new Oxford Classical Text, ed. E. A. Duke and others (1995) has been used. The translated extracts from *Republic* 2, 3 and 10 are taken from Plato, *The Republic*, ed. G. R. F. Ferrari, trans. T. Griffith (Cambridge University Press, 2000), by kind permission of Cambridge University Press.

Our translation from Xenophon is based on the Oxford Classical Text, ed. E. C. Marchant (vol. II, 2nd edition 1921). We have translated the Aristotle selections from the Oxford Classical Texts edition of *De arte poetica liber*, ed. R. Kassel (1965, corr. repr. 1968) and *Politica*, ed. W. D. Ross (1957).

The translations of Philodemus are based on *Filodemo. Il quinto libro della poetica: P.Herc. 1425 e 1538*, ed. C. Mangoni (Naples: Bibliopolis, 1993) and *Philodème de Gadara. Sur la musique. Livre IV*, ed. D. Delattre (Paris: Les Belles Lettres, 2007); the latter also includes a French translation. For Cicero we used the relevant volumes in the Teubner series: *De inventione*, ed. E. Stroebel (Leipzig, 1915); *De oratore*, ed. K. F. Kumaniecki (Leipzig, 1969); *Orator*, ed. P. Reis (Stuttgart, 1963); *De finibus*, ed. C. Moreschini (Munich, 2005); *De natura deorum*, ed. W. Ax (Leipzig, 1933); *Tusculanae disputationes*, ed. M. Pohlenz (Leipzig, 1918); and *De officiis*, ed. C. Atzert (Leipzig, 1963), We also made some use of the recent

Oxford Classical Texts of *De officiis*, ed. M. Winterbottom (1994) and *De finibus*, ed. L. D. Reynolds (1998).

The translations from Seneca are based on *L.Annaei Senecae Ad Lucilium epistulae morales*, ed. L. D. Reynolds (Oxford: Clarendon Press, 1965) and *Sénèque. Des bienfaits*, ed. F. Préchac (Paris: Les Belles Lettres, 1926–7). The translated extracts from Longinus are taken from *Ancient Literary Criticism. The Principal Texts in New Translations*, ed. D. A. Russell and M. Winterbottom (Oxford: Clarendon Press, 1972), by kind permission of Oxford University Press. The most import- ant edition of the Greek text is that of D. A. Russell, *'Longinus'. On the Sublime* (Oxford: Clarendon Press, 1964). To translate Philostratus and Philostratus the Younger we used the Teubner text of Philostratus, ed. C. L. Kayser (1870–1) and the Loeb edition of both works entitled *Pictures (Imagines)*, ed. A. Fairbanks (1931).

The translated extracts from Aristides Quintilianus are taken from A. Barker, ed., *Greek Musical Writings. Vol. 2, Harmonic and Acoustic Theory* (Cambridge University Press, 1989), by kind permission of Cambridge University Press. There is also a Teubner edition of the Greek text by R. P. Winnington-Ingram (1963), and Barker's *Greek Musical Writings* includes a complete translation.

Our selections from Plotinus are translated from the Oxford Classical Text of P. Henry and H.-R. Schwyzer (1964–82). The trans- lations from Augustine *On Order, On True Religion, On Free Choice of the Will, Confessions* and *On the Trinity* are based on the Latin text of the Corpus Christianorum, Series Latina, ed. W. M. Green (1970), K. D. Daur (1962), L. Verheijen (1981) and W. J. Mountain (1968). The extracts from Augustine, *On Music* are translated from M. Jacobsson, ed., *Aurelius Augustinus. De musica liber VI* (Stockholm: Almqvist and Wiksell International, 2003), which also includes an English translation. The translated extracts from Proclus are based on the Teubner texts of the *Commentary on the Timaeus*, ed. E. Diehl (Leipzig, 1903) and the *Commentary on the Republic*, ed. W. Kroll (Leipzig, 1899–1901). The translated extract from the *Anonymous Prolegomena to the Philosophy of Plato* is based on the text of L. G. Westerink (Amsterdam: North Holland Publishing Company, 1962), which includes an English translation.

Apart from the three texts mentioned above – the extracts from Plato's *Republic*, from Longinus and from Aristides Quintilianus – all but one of the Greek texts in this volume were translated by Anne Sheppard. The extract from Gorgias' *Encomium of Helen* and all the Latin texts were translated by Oleg Bychkov. The footnotes explain allusions which might not be familiar to readers of this volume, indicate cross-references between texts and authors and, in a few cases, explain our choice of a particular textual reading or of a particular phrase in translation.

The texts are mostly presented in chronological order, so far as that can be determined. In the case of some authors, such as Cicero, the dates of individual works are known for certain and placing them in chronological order is no problem. With others, such chronological ordering is based on less secure foundations. In the case of Plato, in particular, we have listed works according to the prevailing view of their chronological order, without wishing to be dogmatic about either the correctness of that order or its significance. The *Enneads* of Plotinus have been placed in the order of Porphyry's edition, not according to their chronological order.

The great majority of the texts translated in this volume were copied and recopied in late antiquity and the Middle Ages. Modern critical editions of these texts are based on medieval manuscripts which may not always reproduce the lost original accurately. Readers will notice some use of square brackets in the translations of Aristotle's *Poetics* and Plotinus' *Enneads*. These have been used where the words translated, although printed in most editions of the Greek text, are probably not part of the original text. In Augustine, *On Music* 11.31 square brackets have been used in a different way, for an editorial addition needed to preserve the flow of meaning in the translation. The work of Philodemus survives only on fragmentary papyri; as a result there are a number of gaps in the text, marked in the translation as ellipses and noted in the footnotes.

Some key Greek and Latin terms presented particular problems for the translator, especially when we have translated the same term in the original language with different English equivalents. This issue arose especially in relation to the following terms.

Kalon/honestum

The Greek adjective '*kalos*' (neuter '*kalon*') is a very general term of commendation, used freely in both aesthetic and moral contexts. The English word 'fine' is in some ways the best equivalent and has been used in the translations of Plato's *Ion* and *Hippias Major*. However in translating Plato's *Symposium, Phaedrus* and *Timaeus*, as well as Plotinus and Proclus, 'beautiful' has been used, and the abstract noun *'kallos'* has been rendered as 'beauty'. In Cicero and Augustine, the Latin word *'honestus'* (neuter *'honestum'*, abstract noun *'honestas'*) is used in the same sense as the Greek *'kalos'* and has accordingly been translated by 'excellent', 'noble' or 'fine' so as not to obscure its aesthetic connotations. (See also n.1 to Cicero, *On Moral Ends* 2.14.45.)

To prepon/decorum

The Greek participial phrase *'to prepon'* is widely used in literary and rhetorical contexts to refer to what is 'appropriate' or 'fitting'. In Cicero's Latin *'decorum'* renders the Greek *'prepon'* and so has been translated as 'fitting'. It is important to bring out the aesthetic connotations of this term, often obscured in English translations.

Mousikē/musica

Originally in Greek *'mousikē'* referred to any art which fell within the province of the Muses. Griffiths' phrase 'music and poetry' in Plato, *Republic* 2.376e and elsewhere thus renders the single Greek word *'mousikē'*. However it is clear that Philodemus and Aristides Quintilianus in writing *'On Mousikē'* are primarily concerned with what we would call 'music'. The Latin word *'musica'* has the same range of meaning as the Greek *'mousikē'*, which explains why Augustine in the *De musica (On Music)* discusses topics such as metre and rhythm.

Erōs

The Greek word *'erōs'* and its cognates are used of sexual love and desire. These words play a particularly important role in our passages from Plato's *Symposium* and *Phaedrus* and from Plotinus. We have used 'love', 'desire' or a combination of these two English words, as seemed most appropriate in a given context.

Mimēsis

Following Griffiths' usage in his translation of Plato's *Republic* we have consistently translated the Greek word '*mimēsis*' as 'imitation'.

Nous

In Plato's *Ion* the Greek word '*nous*' has been rendered as 'reason'. In Plotinus and other Neoplatonic authors '*nous*' becomes a technical term within their metaphysics and we have followed standard usage in translating it as 'intellect' in such contexts.

Technē

The Greek word '*technē*' covers what we mean by 'skill' as well as 'art'. We have used whichever of these two English words seemed most appropriate to a given context; in particular 'skill', not 'art', has been used in translating Plato's *Ion* and *Phaedrus*.

Numerosus

This Latin adjective, derived from the word '*numerus*' ('number') is used by Augustine in a technical sense that is broader than the classical meaning of 'related to metre or rhythm'. Therefore we have rendered it as 'having a numeric nature'.

Ratio

This Latin noun, and the related adjective and adverb, '*rationabilis*' and '*rationabiliter*', have a wide range of meanings: from 'computation', 'reason', and 'rationality' to 'proportion' or even 'musical interval'. Various terms have been used in translating the extracts from Augustine, *On Order* and *On Music*, as is indicated in the footnotes to those passages; however, most meanings of '*ratio*' and its derivatives can be expressed by the English 'regular' or 'regularity', which was the term of choice.

GREEK AND ROMAN
AESTHETICS

GORGIAS

Encomium of Helen[*]

8–14

If, however, it was speech that persuaded her and deceived her soul, it is **8**
not difficult to defend her against this too and acquit her of the charge, in
the following way. Speech is a powerful master, which accomplishes most
divine deeds in the most diminutive and imperceptible body. For it can
put an end to fear, take away sorrow, incite joy and augment pity. I will
demonstrate that this is so.

Indeed, a demonstration for the listeners that would form their opinion **9**
is in order. I consider and call every sort of poetry 'speech with metre'.
Those who listen to it shudder with great fear, and are seized by tear-
ful pity and mournful longing; the soul experiences something personal,
through these words, on account of the good or ill fortunes that befall
the affairs and bodies of others. But it is time to turn from one point to
another.

Through words, inspired incantations bring pleasure and drive away **10**
pain. For the power of the incantation, working together with the soul's
power of judgement, enchants, persuades and converts it by witchcraft.
We know of twin arts, witchcraft and magic, that mislead the soul and
deceive the judgement.

So many people have persuaded or do persuade so many others on **11**
so many subjects by composing false discourse! Now if everybody had

---

[*] In this speech Gorgias defends the behaviour of Helen of Troy as having been forced in some
way. One such forceful factor, according to him, is persuasive speech by Paris.

3

the memory of all past things, awareness of all present things, and fore-knowledge of all future things, the same words would not have the same power. However, the way things are now, people do not easily remember the past, or discern the present, or divine the future: hence in most cases most people employ opinion as their soul's counsellor. However, opinion, being slippery and uncertain, subjects those who use it to slippery and uncertain fortunes.[1]

12   ... For what would also prevent Helen, in the same way, from going unwillingly under the influence of speech, as if she were dragged by force? Indeed, although the essence of persuasion is not the same as that of constraint, it has exactly the same power. For the speech that has persuaded the soul that it targeted forces it both to believe what is said and to go along with what is done. And he who persuades, like the one who forces, is guilty of a crime – just as she who is persuaded, like the one who is forced by the power of speech, is wrongly accused.

13   In order to see that persuasion, when it is added to speech, shapes the soul as it wishes, one must look at the following types of discourse: first, at the discourse of astronomers, who, pitting opinions against each other and removing one while instilling another, make the incredible and unclear clear to the eyes of opinion. Second, at the contests which have to take place using the spoken word,[2] where one speech delights and convinces a large portion of the crowd by being skilfully written, not by being honestly spoken. Third, at the philosophical debates, where the exhibited swiftness of thought shows how malleable is the formation of opinion.

14   Now the power of speech has the same effect on the constitution of the soul as the mixture of drugs on the nature of the body. For just as different kinds of drugs purge the body of different humours, and some put an end to disease and others to life, in the same way some kinds of speech distress those who listen to them, while others delight them, some frighten them, others inspire courage, and yet others drug and bewitch the soul by some evil persuasion.

---

[1] Some text is missing at this point and there is a serious textual problem with the next line. We followed the general sense, upon which most commentators agree, not any particular conjecture.

[2] Gorgias means contests that take place in the lawcourts.

PLATO

Ion

533d–536d[1]

SOCRATES: This ability of yours to talk well about Homer, which I spoke **533d** of just now, is not a skill but a divine force which moves you. It is like the force in the stone which Euripides called Magnesian, but which most people call Heraclean.[2] For indeed this stone not only attracts iron rings themselves but also passes its force on to the rings so that they in their **533e** turn can do the same as the stone and attract other rings. Sometimes there is a very long chain of rings and bits of iron, all attached to each other; the force which links them all together comes from that stone. In just this way the Muse herself makes people inspired, and they in turn inspire others, forming a chain of inspiration. For all the good epic poets recite all these fine poems not through skill but because they are inspired. The same goes for the good lyric poets: just as those who celebrate the Corybantic rites[3] are not in their right minds when they dance, so too **534a** the lyric poets are not in their right minds when they compose these fine poems; whenever they embark on harmony and rhythm, they act like Bacchants[4] and are possessed. Just as Bacchants, when possessed, draw

---

[1] In this extract Socrates is in discussion with Ion, a rhapsode. Rhapsodes gave dramatic recitations of Homeric poetry. Socrates is trying to show Ion that his ability to recite Homer and to talk about his work is not due to knowledge.

[2] I.e., the magnet.

[3] The Corybantic rites, in honour of the goddess Cybele, involved frenzied dancing, believed to be therapeutic in treating some kinds of madness.

[4] Worshippers of the god Bacchus, also known as Dionysus.

honey and milk from rivers and are not in their right minds, so the lyric poets' soul does this too, as they themselves say.

534b To be sure the poets tell us that they bring us their poems like bees, gathering them from springs flowing with honey in groves and gardens of the Muses, and they claim that they are winged, like bees; and they tell the truth. For a poet is a light, winged, holy thing, unable to compose until he is inspired and out of his mind, his reason no longer in him; no one can compose poetry or give oracles as long as they have their reason. So each poet can compose fine poems only in the genre to which the Muse has urged him – one dithyrambs, another encomia, another dance-songs, another epic, another poems in iambics.[5] Each of them is bad at all the other genres. This is because it is by divine dispensation, not by skill, that they compose and **534c** utter many fine things about the world, just as you do about Homer. They do this not by skill but through a divine force, since, if it were by skill that they knew how to speak well about one subject, they would also know how to do so about all other subjects. That is why the god takes away these people's **534d** reason and uses them as ministers and givers of oracles and divine prophets so that we who hear them may know that it is not these people, whose reason is not in them, who are saying these things which are so valuable; rather the god himself is the speaker and is addressing us through them.

The best evidence for what I am saying is Tynnichus of Chalcis who never composed any poem worth mentioning, other than the paean which everyone sings. This is almost the finest of all poems and, as he himself **534e** says, simply 'an invention of the Muses'.[6] For in this way the god seems to me to show us, most clearly, so that we are in no doubt, that these fine poems are not human, nor produced by human beings, but are divine and produced by gods, and the poets are nothing but interpreters of the gods, each one possessed by the appropriate deity. As a way of showing this, **535a** the god deliberately sang the finest song through the worst poet. Do you not think what I am saying is true, Ion?

ION: Yes, indeed I do. For your words touch my soul, so to speak, Socrates, and I agree that good poets interpret these messages from the gods for us by divine dispensation.

---

[5] Dithyrambs were lyric poems sung by a chorus. Encomia were songs of praise. The iambic metre was used for poems of invective. Socrates assumes, both here and later, that a different Muse presides over each of the poetic genres which he lists.

[6] The words quoted here are all that survives of the paean, or song in praise of the god Apollo, by Tynnichus, who is known only as its author.

SOCRATES: Then do you rhapsodes in your turn interpret the words of the poets?

ION: That is also true.

SOCRATES: So you are interpreters of interpreters?

ION: Absolutely.

SOCRATES: Come then, Ion, tell me this and do not conceal the answer, 535b
whatever I ask you. When you recite epic verses well and most amaze
your audience – whether you are singing about Odysseus leaping on the
threshold, making himself known to the suitors and pouring arrows out
at his feet, or about Achilles rushing to attack Hector, or singing some
sad passage about Andromache or Hecuba or Priam[7] – are you then in
your right mind? Or are you beside yourself and, under the influence of 535c
inspiration, do you imagine you are present at the events you are describing, whether in Ithaca or at Troy or wherever the story of the epic is actually set?

ION: How clearly you have made this point, Socrates! I shall tell you,
without concealing anything. When I recite a sad passage, my eyes fill
with tears; when it is something frightening or terrifying, my hair stands
on end with fear and my heart jumps.

SOCRATES: What? Suppose a man weeps at sacrifices and festivals, 535d
wearing embroidered robes and golden garlands, without having lost
any of these things, or is afraid when standing among more than 20,000
friendly people, when no one is stripping him of his clothes or doing him
any harm. Should we say, Ion, that such a man is in his right mind?

ION: No indeed, Socrates, certainly not, to tell you the truth.

SOCRATES: Then do you realize that you rhapsodes have exactly this
effect on most of your audience too?

ION: I am very well aware of it. Every time I perform I look down at 535e
them from the stage and see them weeping and looking terrified and
marvelling at what is being said. For I have to pay close attention to
them; if I make them weep, I shall be laughing myself as I take my

7 Socrates here alludes to some very well-known parts of the Homeric poems: the opening of
Odyssey 22, where Odysseus arrives home after his wanderings following the end of the Trojan
War and reveals himself to the suitors who have been paying court to his wife Penelope on the
assumption that he is dead; *Iliad* 22.312 ff., where Achilles attacks Hector and eventually kills
him; and passages such as *Iliad* 6.390–502, where Hector bids farewell to his wife Andromache
before going into battle, *Iliad* 22.405–515, describing the grief of Andromache and of Hector's
parents, Priam and Hecuba, when they see Achilles maltreating Hector's body, and *Iliad*
24.710–59, the lamentations of Hecuba and Andromache over Hector's body.

money but if I make them laugh, I shall be weeping myself because I will lose money.

SOCRATES: Then do you realize that the members of your audience are the last of the iron rings which I said pick up the force from the Heraclean stone? You the rhapsode and actor are the middle ring, and the poet him-

536a self is the first ring; by means of all these rings the god pulls the souls of men whichever way he wants, passing on the force from one link in the chain to the next. Just as with the stone, there is a very long chain of dancers and producers and under-producers, hanging sideways from the rings which hang down from the Muse. One poet is attached to one Muse, another to another – we use the word 'possessed', which is close in

536b meaning; for the poet is held fast. Others are attached to one or another of these primary rings and are inspired by a particular poet: some are pos-sessed and held fast by Orpheus, some by Musaeus,[8] but most by Homer. You, Ion, are one of these; you are possessed by Homer and when anyone performs poems by anyone else, you fall asleep and have nothing to say but when anyone utters a song by this poet, you wake up at once and your

536c soul dances and you have plenty to say. For you say what you say about Homer not by skill, nor by knowledge, but by divine dispensation and possession. Those who celebrate the Corybantic rites[9] hear clearly only the tune which belongs to the god by whom they are inspired; they dance and sing freely to that tune but do not care about the others. In just the same way, Ion, whenever anyone mentions Homer, you have plenty to say,

536d but you have nothing to say about the other poets. You asked me why you have plenty to say about Homer but nothing about the other poets; the reason is that your ability to praise Homer is not due to skill but to divine dispensation.

---

[8] Orpheus was a mythical musician, famous for the power of his song to charm animals, trees and even rocks. Musaeus was another mythical singer, often associated with Orpheus.
[9] Cf. n. 3 above.

Hippias Major

287e–298a[1]

HIPPIAS: I understand, my good friend, and I will tell him[2] in reply what   287e
the fine is. I will never be refuted. You can be sure, Socrates, to tell the
truth, that a fine girl is something fine.

SOCRATES: A fine and noble answer, Hippias, by the Dog![3] If I give that
answer, will I have answered the question quite correctly? Will I never be   288a
refuted?

HIPPIAS: How could you be refuted, Socrates, about something everyone is agreed on? Everyone who hears you will confirm that what you are
saying is correct.

SOCRATES: Well, certainly. Come, Hippias, let me go over what you are
saying for myself. He will ask me a question something like this, 'Go on,
Socrates, answer: consider all the things which you say are fine. What is
the fine itself that explains why these things would be fine?' Will I then
say that if a fine girl is something fine, that explains why these things
would be fine?

---

[1] In the *Hippias Major* Socrates is trying to find a definition of 'the fine' (τὸ καλόν) in discussion
   with the sophist Hippias of Elis. Shortly before our extract begins, at 286c, Socrates has introduced an imaginary disputant whose questions about 'the fine' he could not answer. For most of
   the rest of the dialogue he presents himself as engaged in trying to answer the questions which
   this disputant would put to him.
[2] I.e., the imaginary disputant.
[3] Plato regularly presents Socrates as swearing 'by the Dog', perhaps a way of avoiding a more serious oath.

288b HIPPIAS: Do you think he will still try to refute you on the grounds that what you say is not fine? Will it not be ridiculous if he does try?

SOCRATES: I am sure he will try, my excellent friend; the outcome will show whether he will be ridiculous if he does try. But I want to tell you what he will say.

HIPPIAS: Tell me then.

SOCRATES: 'How sweet you are, Socrates,' he will say. 'Is not a fine mare
288c something fine? Even the god praised mares in the oracle.'[4] What shall we say, Hippias? Would we not have to say that the mare is something fine, the fine mare, at least? How could we dare to deny that the fine is something fine?

HIPPIAS: That is true, Socrates. The god put it quite correctly, for our mares are very fine.

SOCRATES: 'Well,' he will say, 'what about a fine lyre? Is it not something fine?' Should we agree, Hippias?

HIPPIAS: Yes.

SOCRATES: So after this I am pretty sure, judging from what he is like, that he will say, 'My good man, what about a fine pot? Is it not something fine?'
288d HIPPIAS: Socrates, who is this man? How ill-educated he is! He dares to use such vulgar words about a solemn subject.

SOCRATES: He is like that, Hippias. He is not refined but rude; he only cares about the truth. Nevertheless, we must try to answer the man and my own view is as follows: if the pot has been made smooth and round and finely fired, by a good potter, as some fine two-handled pots have, the very fine ones which hold six *choes*[5] – if he is asking about
288e a pot like that, it must be agreed to be fine. How could we say it is not fine when it is?

HIPPIAS: We could not, Socrates.

SOCRATES: 'So,' he will say, 'a fine pot too is something fine? Answer!'

HIPPIAS: I think this is correct, Socrates. Even this utensil is fine if it has been finely made, but as a whole it does not deserve to be judged fine, compared to a mare and a girl, and everything else that is fine.
289a SOCRATES: Well, I understand, Hippias, that when he asks these questions, we should then respond as follows: 'My man, do you not know that

[4] This may refer to a Delphic oracle in which horses are praised but not called fine.
[5] A *choe* (χοή) is a measure of liquid.

10

the saying of Heraclitus[6] is correct, that "the finest of monkeys is base compared to the class of men", and the finest of pots is base compared to the class of girls, as Hippias the sophist says.' Is that not right, Hippias?

HIPPIAS: You have answered absolutely correctly, Socrates.

SOCRATES: Listen then. After this, I am sure that he will say, 'What, Socrates? If someone compares the class of girls with the class of gods, will he not have the same experience as when the class of pots was compared to the class of girls? Will not the finest girl be seen to be base?[7] Does not even Heraclitus, whom you cite, say exactly this, that "the wisest of men will appear to be a monkey in wisdom and fineness and everything else compared to a god"?' Should we agree, Hippias, that the finest girl is base compared to the class of gods?

HIPPIAS: Who could disagree with that, Socrates?

SOCRATES: Then if we agree to that, he will laugh and say, 'Socrates, do you remember the question you were asked?' 'I do,' I will say. 'I was asked what the fine itself is.' 'Then,' he will say, 'although you were asked about the fine, are you answering, as you yourself admit, with something which happens to be no more fine than base?' So it seems, I will say. Or what do you advise me to say, my friend?

HIPPIAS: I advise you to say this. For it is true that the class of men is not fine compared to gods.

SOCRATES: 'Moreover,' he will say, 'if I asked you from the beginning what is fine and what is base, if you answered as you did just now, you would not have answered correctly, would you? Do you really still think that the fine itself, that by which everything else is adorned and seen to be fine, when that form is added to it, is a girl or a mare or a lyre?'

HIPPIAS: But if this is what he is looking for, Socrates, it is the easiest thing in the world to reply by telling him what the fine is, by the addition of which everything else is adorned and seen to be fine. So the man is very foolish and has no understanding of fine things. For if you reply by telling him that the fine which he is asking about is nothing other than gold, he will be at a loss and will not try to refute you. For we all know, I suppose, that anything to which this is added, even

289b

289c

289d

289e

---

[6] Heraclitus of Ephesus was a philosopher of the sixth century BC. Socrates here quotes fr. 82 Diels–Kranz and, shortly afterwards, fr. 83.

[7] I follow P. Woodruff, *Plato. Hippias Major* (Oxford: Blackwell, 1982) in using 'be seen to be' here and in the rest of this extract to capture the ambiguity of the Greek verb φαίνεσθαι which can mean either 'to appear F' or 'to be clearly F'.

if it appears base beforehand, will be seen to be fine when adorned by gold.

SOCRATES: You do not know how stubborn the man is, Hippias, and how unwilling he is to accept anything easily.

290a HIPPIAS: So what, Socrates? He must accept what is said correctly, or be laughed at for not accepting it.

SOCRATES: Not only will he not accept this answer, my good friend, but he will actually make fun of me. He will say: 'You madman, do you think Phidias[8] is a bad craftsman?' And I think I will say, 'No, not at all.'

HIPPIAS: You will be right to say that, Socrates.

SOCRATES: Right indeed. Yet when I agree that Phidias is a good crafts-
290b man, he will say, 'Well then, do you think Phidias did not know about this fine thing you are talking about?' And I will say, 'Why do you ask?' 'Because he did not make Athene's eyes of gold,' he will say, 'nor the rest of her face, nor her feet, nor her hands, as you would expect if something made of gold was going to be finest. He made them of ivory. Clearly he made a mistake about this, through ignorance, not knowing that it is gold, after all, which makes everything fine, wherever it is added.' What answer should we give when he says this, Hippias?

290c HIPPIAS: It is not difficult. We will say that Phidias made the statue correctly. For I think ivory is a fine thing too.

SOCRATES: 'Then why,' he will say, 'did he not make the middles of the eyes out of ivory, but out of stone, finding stone as much like ivory as pos-sible? Is fine stone also a fine thing?' Will we agree, Hippias?

HIPPIAS: We will, at least when it is appropriate.

SOCRATES: 'And is it base when it is not appropriate?' Do I agree, or not?

HIPPIAS: Agree, at least when it is not appropriate.

290d SOCRATES: 'Well then, you clever man,' he will say, 'what about ivory and gold? Do they make things be seen to be fine when it is appropriate and base when it is not appropriate?' Will we deny that, or will we agree with him that he is correct?

HIPPIAS: We will agree to this, at least, that whatever is appropriate for each thing makes it fine.

SOCRATES: 'Then is it appropriate,' he will say, 'when someone is boil-ing the pot we were talking about just now, the fine one, and it is full of fine bean soup, to use a gold stirring spoon or one made of figwood?'

---

[8] Phidias was an Athenian sculptor active in the mid-fifth century BC. One of his most famous works was the gold and ivory statue of the goddess Athene made for the Parthenon at Athens.

HIPPIAS: By Heracles,[9] what kind of man is this, Socrates! Will you not   **290e**
tell me who he is?

SOCRATES: You would not recognize him if I were to tell you his name.

HIPPIAS: But at any rate I already know that he is an ignorant person.

SOCRATES: He is indeed a bane, Hippias. Still, what will we say? Which
stirring spoon is appropriate to the soup and the pot? Is it clearly the one
made of figwood? For it makes the soup smell better, I think, and at the
same time, my friend, it will not break our pot, spill the soup, put out the
fire and deprive those who were going to have a feast of a very noble dish.
That golden spoon would do all these things. So I think we are saying
that the figwood spoon is more appropriate than the golden one, unless   **291a**
you take a different view.

HIPPIAS: Yes, it is more appropriate, Socrates. But for my part, I would
not engage in discussion with someone who asks about things like that.

SOCRATES: Quite rightly, my friend. For it would not be appropriate
for you to be filled up with words like that when you are so finely dressed
and finely shod and have a reputation for wisdom all over Greece. But
getting mixed up with the man does not bother me. So teach me first and   **291b**
answer for my sake. 'If the figwood spoon is really more appropriate than
the golden one,' the man will say, 'would it not be finer, since you agreed,
Socrates, that the appropriate is finer than the inappropriate?' Should we
not agree, Hippias, that the figwood spoon is finer than the golden one?

HIPPIAS: Would you like me to tell you, Socrates, what to say the fine is
so as to extricate yourself from most arguments?

SOCRATES: Certainly. But not before you tell me how to answer. Which   **291c**
of the two spoons I mentioned just now is appropriate and finer?

HIPPIAS: If you like, answer that it is the one made of figwood.

SOCRATES: Now tell me what you were going to tell me just now. For
according to this answer, if I say the fine is gold, apparently gold will turn
out to be no finer than figwood. What do you say the fine is this time?

HIPPIAS: I will tell you. I think you are looking for an answer which says   **291d**
the fine is the sort of thing which will never be seen to be base for anyone
anywhere.

SOCRATES: Certainly, Hippias. Now you have a really fine understanding of the point.

---

[9] Like a character in the comedies of Aristophanes, Hippias expresses his surprise by invoking the
demigod Heracles (Hercules). Cf. for example, Aristophanes, *Acharnians* 284, *Clouds* 184.

HIPPIAS: Listen then. If anyone can say anything against this, you can certainly say I do not understand anything at all.

SOCRATES: Tell me then as quickly as possible, by the gods.

HIPPIAS: I say that it is finest for every man everywhere to be rich, healthy and honoured by the Greeks, and when he reaches old age, hav-
291e ing given his own parents a fine burial when they died, to receive a fine and grand burial from his own children.

. . .

292e HIPPIAS: I am quite sure, Socrates, that what I said is fine for everyone and will be agreed to be so.

SOCRATES: 'And will be fine in the future?' he will say. 'For I suppose the fine is always fine.'

HIPPIAS: Certainly.

SOCRATES: 'Then it was also fine in the past,' he will say.

HIPPIAS: It was.

SOCRATES: 'What about Achilles? Did the visitor from Elis[10] say it was fine for him to be buried after his parents, and fine for his grandfather
293a Aeacus, and for all the others who were the children of the gods, and for the gods themselves?'[11]

HIPPIAS: What is this? Go to heaven![12] These questions the man is asking are blasphemous, Socrates.

SOCRATES: What? It is not actually blasphemous to say these things when someone else asks the question, is it?

HIPPIAS: Perhaps.

SOCRATES: 'Perhaps,' he will say, 'you are the man who says that it is always fine to be buried by your children and to bury your parents. Was not Heracles also included in "everyone" as well as all the people we mentioned just now?'[13]

HIPPIAS: But I did not mean it applied to the gods.
293b SOCRATES: 'Nor to the heroes, it seems.'

[10] I.e., Hippias.
[11] Achilles and Aeacus are offered as counter-examples to Hippias' sweeping general statement. Both Achilles and his paternal grandfather, Aeacus, had one divine parent since Achilles' mother was the sea-nymph Thetis and Aeacus was a son of the supreme god, Zeus. Socrates' point is that it makes no sense to talk of the children of gods burying their parents. There may also be a reference to Achilles' choice between a short and glorious life and a long but undistinguished one, as described in Homer, *Iliad* 9.410–16.
[12] This phrase is a variant on an Aristophanic expression which means 'Go to hell!'
[13] Like Achilles and Aeacus, Heracles, as a son of Zeus, had one divine parent.

HIPPIAS: Not to the ones who were children of gods.

SOCRATES: 'But it applies to those who were not?'

HIPPIAS: Certainly.

SOCRATES: 'So according to your argument, apparently, it is terrible and impious and base for Tantalus and Dardanus and Zethus, but fine for Pelops and the others with similar parentage?'[14]

HIPPIAS: That is what I think.

SOCRATES: 'Then,' he will say, 'you think something you did not say just now, that to bury one's parents and be buried by one's children is base sometimes, for some people; it is still more impossible, it seems, for this to become and be fine for everyone so that this definition has turned out just like the previous ones, the girl and the pot, and in an even more ridiculous way it is fine for some people but not for others. Even today, Socrates,' he will say, 'you cannot yet answer the question what the fine is.' He will rightly reproach me in that kind of way if I answer him like this. He mostly talks to me pretty much like that, Hippias, but sometimes, as if to take pity on my inexperience and lack of education, he himself makes a suggestion and asks me if the fine, or whatever else he happens to be enquiring about, which is the subject of discussion, is such-and-such. 293c 293d

HIPPIAS: What do you mean, Socrates?

SOCRATES: I will tell you. 'My dear Socrates,' he says, 'stop giving answers like this in this way – for they are very silly and easy to refute. Consider whether something like this seems to you to be fine; we touched on it just now in our answer, when we said that gold is fine for the thing for which it is appropriate, but not for the thing for which it is not appropriate, and that everything else is fine if this is added to it. Consider whether this, the appropriate itself – the nature of the appropriate itself – is really the fine.' I usually agree with suggestions like this every time because I do not know what to say. Anyway, do you think the appropriate is fine? 293e

HIPPIAS: In every way, to be sure, Socrates.

SOCRATES: Let us look into it, so as not to be deceived after all.

HIPPIAS: We must look into it.

SOCRATES: Consider then. Do we say that the appropriate is what makes everything which possesses it be seen to be fine when it is present, or what makes it be fine, or neither of these? 294a

---

[14] Tantalus, Dardanus and Zethus were also sons of Zeus while Pelops, Tantalus' son, though a famous Greek hero had mortal parents.

HIPPIAS: I think it is what makes things be seen to be fine. Just as when someone wears fitting clothes or shoes, even if he is ridiculous, he is seen to be finer.

SOCRATES: Then if the appropriate makes things be seen to be finer than they are, would the appropriate be a kind of deception about the fine, and not what we are looking for, Hippias? For I thought we were looking for that by which all fine things are fine. In the same way, excess

294b is that by which all large things are large. For all large things are large because of this and if they are not seen to be so but are in fact excessive, they must be large. So too, we say, what is the fine by which all things are fine, whether they are seen to be so or not? For it cannot be the appropriate since, by your argument, that makes things be seen to be finer than they are and does not let them be seen as they are. We must try to say

294c what it is that makes things fine, as I said just now, whether they are seen to be so or not. For that is what we are looking for, if we are looking for the fine.

HIPPIAS: But the appropriate, Socrates, makes things both be and be seen to be fine, when it is present.

SOCRATES: Then is it impossible for things which are really fine not to be seen to be fine, at least when that which makes them be seen to be fine is present?

HIPPIAS: It is impossible.

SOCRATES: Shall we agree to this, Hippias, that everything which is really fine, in the way of customs and practices, is thought to be fine and

294d is always seen to be fine by everyone? Or on the contrary, are they not recognized? Are they, most of all, the objects of strife and fighting, both in private between individuals and in public between city-states?

HIPPIAS: Rather the latter, Socrates. They are not recognized.

SOCRATES: They would be recognized if 'being seen to be' were added to them, and it would be added if the appropriate was fine and made other things not only be fine but be seen to be fine. So if the appropriate is what makes things be fine, it would be the fine which we are looking for, but not if it is what makes things be seen to be fine.

294e On the other hand, if the appropriate is what makes them be seen to be fine, it would not be the fine that we are looking for. For that makes things be fine, and the same thing could never make fine things both be seen to be, and be, not only fine but anything else. Let us choose whether we think the appropriate is what makes things be seen to be fine, or to be fine.

HIPPIAS: I think it is what makes things be seen to be fine, Socrates.

SOCRATES: Oh dear, discovering what on earth the fine is has slipped away and left us, Hippias, since the appropriate has been clearly seen to be something other than fine.

HIPPIAS: Yes, by Zeus, Socrates. It seems very odd to me.

SOCRATES: Let us not let it go yet, my friend. I am still hopeful that it will become clear what the fine is. 295a

HIPPIAS: Of course, Socrates. It is not hard to find. I am quite sure that if I were to go to a quiet place for a little while and consider by myself, I could tell you with the utmost precision.

SOCRATES: Ah, do not brag, Hippias! You see how much trouble it has given us already: I am afraid it may get angry with us and run away even more. And yet I am talking nonsense, for you will find it easily, I think, 295b when you are alone. By the gods, find it in front of me and look for it along with me, as we did just now, if you want to. If we find it, that will be very fine; if not, I think I will be content with my lot, and you will find it easily when you go away. And if we find it now, of course I will not cause trouble by trying to find out what it was that you discovered by yourself. Now consider just what you think the fine is. I say it is – but pay 295c attention to me carefully and watch that I do not talk nonsense – let us say that whatever is useful is fine. This is what I was thinking of when I made that statement: eyes are fine, we say, not when they seem to be such that they cannot see but when they are able and useful for seeing. Is that not right?

HIPPIAS: Yes.

SOCRATES: So we say the whole body too is fine in this sense, sometimes for running, sometimes for wrestling. The same applies to all animals, to 295d a fine horse or cock or quail, to all equipment and means of transport by land and sea, to boats and to warships, to all instruments, both musical instruments and those belonging to other types of skill and, if you like, to practices and laws. We call almost all of these fine in the same way. In each case we look at its nature, its manufacture and its condition; we say the useful is fine in respect of the way in which it is useful, the object for which it is useful, and the time when it is useful, and that the useless in 295e all these respects is base. You agree with this, Hippias, do you not?

HIPPIAS: I do.

SOCRATES: So are we now right in saying that the useful is fine, more than anything?

HIPPIAS: We are right, Socrates.

SOCRATES: Then that which is able to produce a particular thing is useful for that for which it is able, and the unable is useless?

HIPPIAS: Certainly.

SOCRATES: So ability is fine, and lack of ability is base?

296a HIPPIAS: Yes indeed. There is other evidence for this, Socrates, especially in politics. For in politics to be able in one's own city is finest of all, and not to be able is basest of all.

SOCRATES: You speak well. By the gods, Hippias, is that why wisdom is finest of all and ignorance basest of all?

HIPPIAS: What are you thinking, Socrates?

SOCRATES: Steady on, my friend. I am afraid of what we are saying.

296b HIPPIAS: Why are you afraid, Socrates, when your argument has made really fine progress?

SOCRATES: I wish it had. Consider this with me: would anyone do anything which he did not know how to do and was in no way able to do?

HIPPIAS: Not at all. How could he do what he was not able to do?

SOCRATES: So people who make mistakes, and who produce or do bad things involuntarily, would never do anything if they could not do these things?

HIPPIAS: Clearly.

296c SOCRATES: But those who are able are able by ability; for they are not so by inability, I suppose.

HIPPIAS: No indeed.

SOCRATES: Is everyone who does things able to do the things he does?

HIPPIAS: Yes.

SOCRATES: All men do far more bad things than good, from childhood onwards, and they make mistakes involuntarily.

HIPPIAS: That is so.

SOCRATES: Well then, shall we say that this ability and these useful things which are useful for doing something that tends to the bad are fine, or far from it?

296d HIPPIAS: Far from it, in my opinion at least, Socrates.

SOCRATES: Then, Hippias, the able and the useful is apparently not the fine that we are looking for.

HIPPIAS: Suppose it is able to do good, Socrates, and is useful for that sort of thing.

SOCRATES: Then the idea that the able and useful without qualification is fine has gone away. Is this what our hearts were trying to tell us, Hippias, that the fine is being useful and able to do something for a good end?

HIPPIAS: I think so. 296e

SOCRATES: This, at any rate, is beneficial. Is that not right?

HIPPIAS: Certainly.

SOCRATES: Indeed, fine bodies and fine customs and cleverness and everything which we mentioned just now is fine in this sense, that it is beneficial.

HIPPIAS: Clearly.

SOCRATES: So the beneficial appears to be the fine that we were looking for, Hippias.

HIPPIAS: Absolutely, Socrates.

SOCRATES: But the beneficial is the agent of good.

HIPPIAS: It is.

SOCRATES: The agent is nothing other than the cause. Is that right?

HIPPIAS: That is right.

SOCRATES: Then the fine is a cause of the good.

HIPPIAS: It is. 297a

SOCRATES: But the cause of something, Hippias, is different from that of which it is a cause. For the cause would not cause a cause, I suppose. Consider this: was the cause not seen to be an agent?

HIPPIAS: Certainly.

SOCRATES: Then is it what comes into being, rather than the agent, that is acted upon by the agent?

HIPPIAS: That is so.

SOCRATES: So what comes into being and the agent are different things?

HIPPIAS: Yes.

SOCRATES: Then the cause is not a cause of a cause but of what comes 297b into being because of the cause.

HIPPIAS: Certainly.

SOCRATES: Then if the fine is a cause of good, the good would come into being because of the fine. That, it seems, is why we pursue wisdom and all other fine things, because their product and offspring, the good, is most worthy of pursuit. It looks from what we are discovering as though the fine is a sort of parent of the good.

HIPPIAS: Yes, certainly. Finely said, Socrates.

SOCRATES: Is the following also a fine saying, that the father is not a son, nor the son a father?

297c HIPPIAS: Fine indeed!

SOCRATES: And the cause is not something which comes into being, nor is what comes into being a cause.

HIPPIAS: What you say is true.

SOCRATES: Then by Zeus, my very good friend, the fine is not good, nor is the good fine. Do you think that is possible, following what was said before?

HIPPIAS: No by Zeus, I do not think it is.

SOCRATES: Are we satisfied and would we want to say that the fine is not good and the good is not fine?

HIPPIAS: No by Zeus, I am not satisfied at all.

297d SOCRATES: Yes by Zeus, Hippias! To me this is the least satisfactory of all the arguments we have put forward.

HIPPIAS: So it seems.

SOCRATES: Then it looks as though the situation is not as it appeared just now. We were wrong to think the statement, that the beneficial and the useful and what is able to do some good are fine, was the finest of arguments. On the contrary, this argument is more ridiculous than the previous ones, if that is possible – I mean the arguments in which we thought that the girl and each of the particular things we spoke of before was the fine.

HIPPIAS: So it seems.

SOCRATES: For my part, Hippias, I do not have anywhere else to turn. I am at a loss. Do you have anything to say?

297e HIPPIAS: Not at present but, as I said just now, I am sure that I will find something if I think it over.

SOCRATES: I am so eager for knowledge that I do not think I can wait for you to take your time. I believe I have just had an idea! Look: what about what gives us pleasure, not all kinds of pleasures but those which come through sight and hearing? Could we say this is the fine? How would we

298a fare in the competition then? I suppose, Hippias, that fine people and fine decorations and paintings and sculptures – all the fine ones, that is – give us pleasure when we see them. Fine sounds and all kinds of music and words and stories have just the same effect. So if we could answer that overconfident man as follows, 'My noble friend, the fine is what is pleasant through hearing and sight,' do you not think we would put a stop to his overconfidence?[15]

[15] This last definition may sound promising but in the final pages of the dialogue it too is refuted and, like many Platonic dialogues in which Socrates is looking for a definition, the *Hippias Major* ends inconclusively.

Symposium

206a–212a[1]

206a Then in short, she said, love is the desire to possess the good for ever.

What you say is quite true, I said.

206b Since love is always this desire, she said, what kind of effort and pursuit should be called love? How do people pursue it? What do they do? How does it work? Can you tell me?

If I could, Diotima, I said, I would not be such an admirer of your wisdom and I would not be coming to you to learn precisely this.

I will tell you, she said. It is procreation in beauty, whether in body or in soul.

What you say needs prophetic interpretation, I said. I do not understand.

206c I will tell you more clearly, she said. All human beings, Socrates, are pregnant both in body and in soul, and when we reach a certain age, we naturally desire to procreate. We cannot procreate in ugliness, only in beauty. Yes, the intercourse between a man and a woman is procreation. It is a divine business: this is what is immortal in mortal creatures, preg-
206d nancy and reproduction. They cannot occur in the discordant, and the ugly is discordant with everything divine, while the beautiful is in concord with it. The goddess of beauty presides over giving birth, as Fate and

---

[1] This extract comes from Socrates' praise of love (ἔρως) in the *Symposium*. Socrates reports a dialogue between himself and Diotima, a wise woman from Mantinea.

Eileithyia.[2] That is why, when a pregnant creature approaches beauty, it becomes gracious, glad and relaxed, and it procreates and reproduces; but when it approaches ugliness, it contracts in sadness and pain and turns away and shrinks back and does not reproduce but retains what it has conceived and is distressed. Therefore those who are pregnant and already swollen become very excited about beauty because that which has   **206e** beauty releases them from the great pain of giving birth. For, Socrates, she said, love is not, as you suppose, desire for beauty.

Then what is it?

Desire to reproduce and procreate in beauty.

All right, I said.

Certainly it is, she said. Then what about reproduction? Reproduction is the closest mortals can come to living for ever and being immortal. It   **207a** follows from what we agreed that immortality must be desired as well as goodness, if love is the desire to possess the good for ever. According to this argument, love must also be the desire for immortality.

. . .

Even you, Socrates, could perhaps be initiated in these mysteries of love;   **209e** but the purpose of these lower rites, if one follows them correctly, is to   **210a** reach the final vision of the mysteries and I am not sure if you would be capable of this. I will tell you, she said, and will make every effort to explain. Try to follow, if you can. For, she said, someone who is pursuing this in the right way should begin, when he is young, by pursuing beautiful bodies. First, if his guide leads him in the right way he should love just one body and produce beautiful discourses in that relationship. Then he   **210b** should realize that the beauty in one body is akin to the beauty in another body; if he must pursue beauty of physical form, it is extremely foolish not to consider beauty in all bodies as one and the same. Once he realizes this he becomes a lover of all beautiful bodies and gives up his obsession with just one body, despising that and thinking it unimportant.

After this he becomes aware that beauty in souls is more valuable than bodily beauty, so that it is enough for him if someone is decent in soul even if he has only little of the bloom of beauty. He loves and cares for   **210c** that person, and gives birth to the kinds of discourse which will improve the young.[3] Thus he is compelled to contemplate beauty in practices and

---

[2] Eileithyia was the Greek goddess of childbirth.
[3] I follow Ast and Dover in deleting the words καὶ ζητεῖν.

laws and to see that it is all related, so that he realizes that bodily beauty is something unimportant. After practices, his guide leads him to types of knowledge, so that he sees their beauty too. Looking now at ample

210d beauty, he is no longer slavishly attached to one individual, to the beauty of a little boy or of one person or of a single practice. No longer a base and petty slave, he will instead be turned towards the wide sea of beauty and, contemplating that, he will give birth to many grand and beautiful discourses and thoughts in a boundless love of wisdom. Eventually, having been strengthened and increased there, he will see a unique type of knowledge, knowledge of the kind of beauty I am now going to tell you about.

210e Try to pay attention as much as possible, she said. Anyone who has been educated in love up to this point, contemplating beautiful objects rightly and in order, will now reach the end of the mysteries of love; he will suddenly see something of a wondrous, beautiful nature. This,

211a Socrates, is the object of all the previous labours. First, it always *is*, neither coming into being nor ceasing to be, neither waxing nor waning. Then it is not beautiful in one way and ugly in another, not beautiful at one time and not at another, not beautiful in relation to one thing and ugly in relation to another, not beautiful here and ugly there because it is beautiful in some people's eyes but ugly in the eyes of others. The beautiful will not appear to him as a face or hands or any other bodily feature. It will not appear as a discourse or a type of knowledge, nor as located in any determinate place such as an animal or the earth or the heavens

211b or anywhere else. It is always itself, by itself, with itself, uniform. All other beautiful things participate in it but in such a way that while they come into being and cease to be, it does not increase or decrease at all but remains unaffected.

When someone ascends from things in this world, by loving boys in the right way, and begins to catch sight of that beauty, he has almost reached the end. For this is the right way to pursue the mysteries of love, or to

211c be guided in them by someone else: the lover should begin from beautiful things in this world and ascend continually in pursuit of that beauty. Like someone climbing a ladder, he should go from one body to two, and from two bodies to all beautiful bodies, and from beautiful bodies to beautiful practices, and from practices to beautiful types of learning, and finally from types of learning to that type of learning which studies nothing other than that beauty itself, so that in the end he understands what beauty really is.[4]

That, dear Socrates, said the woman from Mantinea, is where human life should be lived, if anywhere, contemplating beauty itself. If you ever see it, you will not value beauty in gold, or clothing, or beautiful boys and youths. Yet at present when you see beautiful boys and youths you are overwhelmed and, like many others, so long as you can see your beloved and keep company with him, you are ready to give up eating and drinking, if that were possible, and do nothing but gaze at him and keep company with him. Then what do we think it would be like, she said, if it were possible for someone to see beauty itself, pure, unmixed and unalloyed, not tainted by human flesh and colours and lots of mortal non-sense – suppose he could simply see divine beauty itself? Do you think, she said, that would be a bad life for a human being, looking in that direction and gazing at it with the right part of himself[5] and keeping company with it? Do you not realize, she said, that that is the only place where it will be possible for him, looking at beauty with the part that can see it, to bring forth not images of virtue, since he is not in contact with an image, but true virtue, since he is in contact with the truth. Is it the case that when he brings forth true virtue and nurtures it, he becomes loved by the gods and he too is immortal if anyone is?

211d

211e

212a

[4] Reading ἵνα γνῷ, rather than καὶ γνῷ, with Dover and others.
[5] I.e., with the rational part of his soul. The phrase 'the part that can see it' in the next sentence has the same reference.

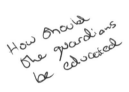

Republic 2–3

2.376e–3.402a[1]

376e 'What should their education be, then? Isn't it hard to find a better education than the one which has been developed over the years? It consists, I take it, of physical education for the body, and music and poetry for the mind or soul.'

'It does.'

'And shouldn't we start their education in music and poetry earlier than their physical education?'

'We should.'

'Do you count stories as part of music and poetry, or not?'

'Yes, I do.'

'And are stories of two kinds – one true, the other false?'

'Yes.'

377a 'Should we educate them in both, starting with the false?'

'I don't understand what you mean,' he said.

'You mean you don't understand that we start off by telling children legends? These, I take it, are broadly speaking false, though there is some truth in them. And we start children on these legends before we start them on physical education.'

'That is right.'

---

[1] In the extracts from *Republic*, Books 2 and 3, Socrates is discussing, first with Adeimantus and then with Glaucon, how the philosopher-rulers of the ideal state should be educated.

'That was what I meant when I said we should start their education in music and poetry before their physical education.'

'You were right,' he said.

'Very well, then. You are aware that it is the beginning of any under-taking which is the most important part – especially for anything young and tender? That is the time when each individual thing can be most eas-ily moulded, and receive whatever mark you want to impress upon it.' 377b

'Yes, of course.'

'Shall we be perfectly content, then, to let our children listen to any old stories, made up by any old storytellers? Shall we let them open their minds to beliefs which are the opposite, for the most part, of those we think they should hold when they grow up?'

'No. We shall certainly not allow that.'

'For a start, then, it seems, we must supervise our storytellers. When 377c they tell a good story, we must decide in favour of it; and when they tell a bad one, we must decide against it. We shall persuade nurses and moth-ers to tell children the approved stories, and tell them that shaping chil-dren's minds with stories is far more important than trying to shape their bodies with their hands. We must reject most of the stories they tell at the moment.'

'Which ones?'

'If we look at our greatest stories, we shall see how to deal with lesser examples as well,' I replied. 'Greater and lesser must have the same stand-ard, and the same effect. Don't you think so?' 377d

'Yes, I do,' he said. 'But I'm not even sure which these "great" stories are you talk about.'

'The ones Hesiod and Homer both used to tell us – and the other poets. They made up untrue stories, which they used to tell people – and still do tell them.'

'Which stories? What is your objection to them?'

'The one which ought to be our first and strongest objection – espe-cially if the untruth is an ugly one.'

'What is this objection?'

'When a storyteller gives us the wrong impression of the nature of gods 377e and heroes. It's like an artist producing pictures which don't look like the things he was trying to draw.'

'Yes,' he said, 'it is right to object in general to that sort of story. But what exactly do we mean? Which stories?'

'I'll start,' I said, 'with an important falsehood on an important subject. There is the very ugly falsehood told of how Ouranos did the things Hesiod says he did, and how Kronos in his turn took his revenge on him. As for what Kronos did, and what his son did to him, even if they were true I wouldn't think that in the normal course of events these stories should be told to those who are young and uncritical. The best thing would be to say nothing about them at all. If there were some overriding necessity to tell them, then as few people as possible should hear them, and in strict secrecy. They should have to make sacrifice. Not a pig,[2] but some large and unobtainable sacrificial animal, to make sure the smallest possible number of people heard them.'

'Yes,' he said. 'Those stories are pretty hard to take.'

'We will not have them told in our city, Adeimantus. When the young are listening, they are not to be told that if they committed the most horrible crimes they wouldn't be doing anything out of the ordinary, not even if they inflicted every kind of punishment on a father who treated them badly. We won't tell them that they would merely be acting like the first and greatest of the gods.'

'Good heavens, no. Personally, I don't think these are at all the right stories to tell them.'

'Nor, in general, any of the stories – which are not true anyway – about gods making war on gods, plotting against them, or fighting with them. Not if we want the people who are going to protect our city to regard it as a crime to fall out with one another without a very good reason. The last thing they need is to have stories told them, and pictures made for them, of battles between giants, and all the many and varied enmities of gods and heroes towards their kinsmen and families. If we do intend to find some way of convincing them that no citizen has ever quarrelled with another citizen, that quarrelling is wrong, then this is the kind of thing old men and women must tell our children, right from the start. And as the children get older, we must compel our poets to tell stories similar to these. As for the binding of Hera by her son, the hurling of Hephaestus out of heaven by his father, for trying to protect his mother when she was being beaten, and the battles of the gods which Homer tells us about,[3] whether these stories are told as allegories or not as allegories,

378a

378b

378c

378d

---

[2] Those initiated into the secrets of the Eleusinian mysteries had to sacrifice a pig.
[3] The story of Hephaestus binding his mother was told by the lyric poet Alcaeus (fr. 349 Lobel–Page).

we must not allow them into our city. The young are incapable of judging what is allegory and what is not, and the opinions they form at that age tend to be ineradicable and unchangeable. For these reasons, perhaps, we should regard it as of the highest importance that the first things they hear should be improving stories, as beautiful as can be.'

'That makes sense,' he said. 'But suppose someone were to go on and ask us what these things are, and what stories we should tell, which ones should we say?'

'Adeimantus,' I said, 'we are not acting as poets at the moment, you and I. We are the founders of a city. It is the founders' job to know the patterns on which poets must model their stories, or be refused permission if they use different ones. It is not their job to start creating stories themselves.'

'True,' he said. 'But what about this question of patterns for stories about the gods? What should these patterns be?'

'Something like this, I should think. They should always, I take it, give a true picture of what god is really like, whether the poet is working in epic, or in lyric, or in tragedy.'

'Yes, they should.'

'Well then, isn't god in fact good? Shouldn't he be represented as such?'

'Of course.'

'The next point is that nothing that is good is harmful, is it?'

'No, I don't think so.'

'Does what is not harmful do any harm?'

'No.'

'Can what does no harm do any evil?'

'No, it can't do that either.'

'But if something does no evil, it couldn't be the cause of any evil, could it?'

'Of course not.'

'Very well. Now, is the good beneficial?'

'Yes.'

'Responsible for well-being, in other words?'

'Yes.'

'In that case the good is not responsible for everything. It is responsible for what goes well, but not responsible for what goes badly.'

'Absolutely.'

'In which case,' I said, 'god, since he is good, could not be responsible for everything, as most people claim. Some of the things that happen to men are his responsibility, but most are not; after all, we have many fewer good things than bad things in our lives. We have no reason to hold anyone else responsible for the good things, whereas for the bad things we should look for some other cause, and not blame god.'

'I think you are absolutely right.'

379d 'In that case,' I said, 'we should not allow Homer or any other poet to make such a stupid mistake about the gods, and tell us that two jars

> Stand in the hall of Zeus, full filled with fates.
> One of the two holds good, the other ill.

Nor that the person to whom Zeus gives a mixture of the two

> Sometimes encounters evil, sometimes good,

whereas for the person to whom he does not give a mixture, but gives evil in its pure form,

> Dread famine drives him over earth's fair face.[4]

379e Nor describe Zeus as

> Of good and evil steward and dispenser.[5]

As for Pandarus' violation of the oaths and the truce, we shall disapprove of anyone who says that Athena and Zeus were the cause of it,[6] or that Themis and Zeus were the cause of the quarrel of the goddesses, and 380a the judgement between them.[7] Nor again must we let the young hear the kind of story Aeschylus tells, when he says:

> For god implants the fatal cause in men,
> When root and branch he will destroy a house.

If anyone writes about the sufferings of Niobe[8] – as here – or about the house of Pelops,[9] or the Trojan War, or anything like that, we must either

---

[4] Socrates here partly quotes and partly paraphrases Homer, *Iliad* 24.527–32.

[5] It is not known where this line of poetry comes from.

[6] See *Iliad* 4.69 ff.

[7] The goddesses Hera, Athene and Aphrodite quarrelled over which of them was the most beautiful. Paris, son of Priam, the king of Troy, was asked to judge between them and gave the prize to Aphrodite, who had promised him Helen as a reward. Paris' abduction of Helen brought about the Trojan War.

[8] The two lines quoted here come from Aeschylus' lost play, *Niobe* (fr. 156 Nauck = fr. 154a15–16 Radt). Niobe, the mother of many children, boasted that she was superior to the goddess Leto, the mother of Apollo and Artemis. In consequence Leto sent her children to destroy the children of Niobe.

[9] Pelops was the father of Atreus and Thyestes, grandfather of Agamemnon and Menelaus.

not allow them to say that these events are the work of a god, or if the poet claims that they *are* the work of a god, then he must find more or less the sort of explanation we are looking for at the moment. He must   380b
say that what god does is right and good, and that these people's punishments were good for them. We must not allow the poet to say that those who paid the penalty were made wretched, and that the person responsible was a god. If poets said that the wicked were made wretched because they needed punishment, and that in paying the penalty they were being helped by god, then we should allow that. But the claim that god, who is good, is responsible for bringing evil on anyone, is one we must oppose with every weapon we possess. We must not let anyone make this claim in our city, if it is to be well governed, nor should we let anyone hear it, whether the hearer be young or old, and whether or not the storyteller   380c
tells his story in verse. These claims, if they were made, would neither be holy, nor good for us, nor consistent with one another.'

'You have my vote for this law,' he said. 'I thoroughly approve.'

'There you are, then,' I said. 'That would be one of the laws about the gods, one of the patterns on which storytellers must base their stories, and poets their poems – that god is not responsible for everything, but only for what is good.'

'Yes,' he said, 'that should do it.'

'What about a second law, or pattern? Do you think god is a magician?   380d
Would he deliberately appear in different guises at different times? Are there times when he really becomes different, and changes his shape into many forms, and other times when he deceives us into thinking that is what he is doing? Or do you think he has a single form, and is of all creatures the least likely to depart from his own shape?'

'I'm not sure I'm in a position to answer that, just at the moment.'

'How about a different question? When things do depart from their own shape, isn't it necessarily true that they either change themselves or   380e
are changed by something else?'

'Yes, it is.'

'Doesn't an external cause of change or motion have least effect on the finest specimens? Think of a body, for example, and the effect on it of food, drink and exertion. Or plants, and the effect of sun and wind and things like that. Isn't the healthiest and strongest specimen least affected?'

'Yes, of course.'   381a

31

'And wouldn't the bravest and wisest soul be least disturbed and altered by an outside influence?'

'Yes.'

'The same, presumably, goes for anything manufactured – furniture, houses and clothes. What is well made and in good condition is least affected by time and other influences.'

'That is so.'

381b 'So anything which is a fine example, whether by its nature or its design, or both, is the most resistant to being changed by an external agency.'

'It looks like it.'

'But god and his attributes are in every way perfect.'

'Of course.'

'So god would be most unlikely to take many shapes as a result of external causes.'

'Most unlikely.'

'Could he, in that case, change and transform himself?'

'Obviously he does,' he said. 'If he changes at all, that is.'

'Does he then turn himself into something better and more beautiful, or into something worse and uglier than himself?'

381c 'If he does change, it must necessarily be into something worse. I don't imagine we are going to say that god is lacking in beauty or goodness.'

'No, you are quite right,' I said. 'And that being so, do you think that anyone, Adeimantus, whether god or man, is prepared to make himself worse in any way at all?'

'No, that's impossible,' he said.

'In which case,' I replied, 'it is also impossible for god to have any desire to change himself. No, each of the gods, it appears, is as beautiful and good as possible, and remains for ever simply in his own form.'

'Yes,' he said, 'I think that must undoubtedly follow.'

381d 'Well, then, my friend, we don't want any of the poets telling us,' I said, 'that

> Disguised as strangers from afar, the gods
> Take many shapes, and visit many lands.[10]

---

[10] Homer, *Odyssey* 17.485–6.

We don't want any of their falsehoods about Proteus and Thetis,[11] nor do we want tragedies or other poems which introduce Hera, transformed into the guise of a priestess, collecting alms for

> The life-giving sons of Argive Inachus.[12]

And there are many other falsehoods of the same sort which we don't
381e
want them telling us – any more than we want mothers to believe them, and terrify their children with wicked stories about gods who go round at night, taking on the appearance of all sorts of outlandish foreigners. That way we can stop them from blaspheming against the gods, and also stop them turning their children into cowards.'

'No, we don't want any of that.'

'Well then,' I suggested, 'though the gods would not themselves change, maybe they nevertheless make it seem to us that they appear in all sorts of different guises? Perhaps they deceive us, and play tricks on us.'

'Possibly.'

'What! Would a god be prepared to deceive us, in his words or his
382a
actions, by offering us what is only an appearance?'

'I don't know.'

'You don't know,' I said, 'that the true falsehood – if one can call it that – is hated by god and man alike?'

'What do you mean?'

'I mean this. No one deliberately chooses falsehood in what is surely the most important part of himself, and on the most important of subjects. No, that is the place, more than any other, where they fear falsehood.'

'I still don't understand,' he said.

'That's because you think I'm talking about something profound,' I
382b
said. 'But all I mean is that the thing everyone wants above all to avoid is being deceived in his soul about the way things are, or finding that he has been deceived, and is now in ignorance, that he holds and possesses the falsehood right there in his soul. That is the place where people most hate falsehood.'

'I quite agree,' he said.

'As I was saying just now, this ignorance in the soul, the ignorance of the person who has been deceived, can with absolute accuracy be called

---

[11] Both Proteus and Thetis were minor sea deities who changed into many different shapes when mortals tried to catch them.
[12] The line comes from a lost play by Aeschylus (fr. 168 Nauck).

true falsehood, whereas verbal falsehood is a kind of imitation of this condition of the soul. It comes into being later; it is an image, not a wholly unmixed falsehood. Don't you agree?'

'I do.'

'The real falsehood is hated not only by gods but also by men.'

'Yes, I think so.'

'What about verbal falsehood? When is it useful, and for whom? When does it not deserve hatred? Isn't it useful against enemies, or to stop those who are supposed to be our friends, if as a result of madness or ignorance they are trying to do something wrong? Isn't a lie useful in those circumstances, in the same way as medicine is useful? And in the myths we were discussing just now, as a result of our not knowing what the truth is concerning events long ago, do we make falsehood as much like the truth as possible, and in this way make it useful?'

'Yes,' he said, 'that is exactly how it is.'

'In which of these ways, then, is falsehood useful to god? Does he make falsehood resemble the truth because he doesn't know about events long ago?'

'No, that would be absurd,' he said.

'So there is nothing of the false poet in god.'

'I don't think so.'

'Is he afraid of his enemies? Would he tell lies for that reason?'

'Far from it.'

'Or because of the ignorance or madness of his friends, perhaps?'

'No,' he said. 'No one who is ignorant and mad is a friend of the gods.'

'There is no reason, then, for god to tell a falsehood.'

'No, none.'

'So the supernatural and the divine are altogether without falsehood.'

'Absolutely.'

'In that case, god is certainly single in form and true, both in what he does and what he says. He does not change in himself, and he does not deceive others – waking or sleeping – either with apparitions, or with words, or by sending signs.'

'That's how it seems to me too,' he said, 'as I listen to what you say.'

'Do you agree then,' I asked, 'that this should be the second pattern for telling stories or writing poems about the gods? They are not magicians who change their shape, either in their words or their actions, and they do not lead us astray with falsehoods.'

'Yes, I agree.'

'So while there is much in Homer we approve of, we shall not approve of Zeus's sending a dream to Agamemnon;[13] nor of Aeschylus, when Thetis says that Apollo, singing at her wedding, "dwelt upon the children" she would have, **383b**

> Their length of life, their freedom from disease,
> And summing up, sang me a hymn of blessing
> For my good luck and favour with the gods.
> My hope was high, for Phoebus was a god,
> And Phoebus' mouth, brimming with mantic art,
> Must speak the truth, I thought. But he who sang,
> He who was present at the feast, the one
> Who said these things, is now the one who killed
> My son.[14]

When anyone talks in this way about the gods, we shall get angry with him, and not grant him a chorus.[15] Nor shall we allow teachers to use his works for the education of the young – not if we want our guardians to become god-fearing and godlike, to the greatest extent possible for a human being.' **383c**

'I entirely agree,' he said, 'with these patterns, and I would want to see them made law.'

'When it comes to stories about the gods, then,' I said, 'this is apparently the sort of thing which from their earliest childhood people must be told – and not told – if they are to show respect for the gods and their parents, and put a high value on friendship with one another.' **386a**

'Yes, I think our views on this are correct,' he said.

'What about courage? If we want them to be brave, aren't these the stories we should be telling them, plus the kind of stories which will minimize their fear of death? Do you think anyone can ever get to be brave if he has this fear inside him?' **386b**

'Good heavens, no.'

---

[13] In *Iliad* 2.1–34 Homer recounts how Zeus sends Agamemnon a dream promising him victory over the Trojans if he attacks immediately. Zeus is deceiving Agamemnon since his real intention is to bring about a Greek defeat and so show the Greeks that they cannot do without Achilles who has withdrawn from the fighting.

[14] These lines come from a lost play by Aeschylus (fr. 350 Nauck). Achilles, Thetis' son, was killed by an arrow shot by Paris but guided by Phoebus Apollo.

[15] That is, not allow his play to be produced.

'How about belief in the Underworld and its horrors? Do you think that makes people fearless in the face of death, makes them choose death in preference to defeat or slavery?'

'Of course not.'

'This is another branch of storytelling, then, where it looks as if we must keep an eye on those who want to tell these stories. We shall have to ask them to stop being so negative about the Underworld, and find something positive to say about it instead. What they say at the moment is neither true, nor helpful to those we want to become warlike.'

386c

'Yes, we shall have to keep an eye on them,' he said.

'Then we shall eliminate all descriptions of that sort, starting with:

> I had rather labour as a common serf,
> Serving a man with nothing to his name,
> Than be the lord of all the dead below.[16]

. . .

387b We shall ask Homer and the rest of the poets not to be angry with us if we strike out these passages, and any others like them. Not that they lack poetic merit, or that they don't give pleasure to most people. They do. But the more merit they have, the less suitable they are for boys and men who are expected to be free, and fear slavery more than death.'

'Absolutely.'

'So we must also discard all the weird and terrifying language used about the Underworld. No more wailing Cocytus, or hateful Styx,[17] or food for worms, or mouldering corpses, or any other language of the kind which makes all who hear it shudder. It may be fine in some other context, but when it comes to our guardians, we are worried that this shuddering may make them too soft and impressionable for our needs.'

387c

'We are right to be worried,' he said.

'That sort of language must go, then?'

'Yes.'

'And our storytellers and poets should use language which follows the opposite pattern?'

'Obviously.'

387d 'Then we shall get rid of weeping and wailing by famous men.'

---

[16] Homer, *Odyssey* 11.489–91. These words are spoken by the ghost of Achilles in the Underworld to Odysseus.

[17] Cocytus (literally 'Wailing') and Styx (literally 'Hateful') were two of the rivers in the Underworld.

'We shall have to,' he said. 'We can't get rid of the other things, and not that.'

'What you *should* ask yourself, though,' I said, 'is whether or not we shall be right to get rid of them. Our view is that a good man does not regard it as a disaster when death comes to another good man, his friend.'

'Yes, that is our view.'

'So he certainly wouldn't lament on his friend's account, as if something awful had happened to him.'

'No, he wouldn't.'

'But we also say that when it comes to living a good life, a good man is the most capable of meeting his own needs, and has less need of other people than anyone else has.' 387e

'True.'

'So he least of all will regard it as a misfortune to lose a son, or a brother, or some money, or anything like that.'

'Yes.'

'And he least of all will grieve over the loss. He more than anyone can take it in his stride when an accident of this kind happens to him.'

'He can indeed.'

'We shall be right, then, to get rid of the heroes' songs of lamentation, putting them in the mouths of women – and not even the best women, at that – and cowards. We want the people we say we are bringing up to be 388a guardians of our country to be appalled at the idea of behaving like this.'

'Yes, we shall be right,' he said.

. . .

'If our young men take these kinds of things seriously, my dear 388d Adeimantus, if they don't laugh at them as the unworthy offerings of storytellers, then, since they are only human, they are hardly going to think it beneath them to behave like this themselves. They won't be appalled at the very idea of speaking or acting in this way. No, they'll be quite unashamed, making not the slightest effort to put a brave face on it, as they give voice to great songs of grief and lamentation over trivial misfortunes.'

'You're absolutely right,' he said. 388e

'But that isn't how they should be behaving, as our reasoning just now showed. And until someone gives us a good reason for believing something different, we must have faith in our reasoning.'

'No, it isn't how they should be behaving.'

'On the other hand, they must not be too fond of laughter either. Abandonment to violent laughter, generally speaking, is a violent agent for change.'

'I agree,' he said.

389a 'So we must not accept it if we are shown men of any importance – still less gods – being overcome by laughter.'

'Particularly not the gods.'

'So we won't accept this sort of thing about the gods from Homer:

> Unquenchable the laughter that arose
> Among the blessed gods. They sat and watched
> Hephaestus bustling up and down the hall.[18]

We mustn't accept this, according to your reasoning.'

389b 'Call it mine, if you like,' he said. 'We certainly mustn't accept it, anyway.'

'Then again, truth is another thing we must value highly: if we were right just now, if lies really are useless to the gods, and useful to men only in the way medicine is useful, then clearly lying is a task to be entrusted to specialists. Ordinary people should have nothing to do with it.'

'Clearly.'

'So if anyone is entitled to tell lies, the rulers of the city are. They may do so for the benefit of the city, in response to the actions either of enemies or of citizens. No one else should have anything to do with

389c lying, and for an ordinary citizen to lie to these rulers of ours is as big a mistake – bigger, in fact – as telling your doctor or trainer lies about the condition of your body when you are ill or in training, or giving a ship's captain misleading information about the ship and its crew, and how you or your fellow-sailors are getting on.'

'Very true,' he said.

. . .

392a 'Well, then,' I asked, 'in our definition of the kind of stories which may and may not be told, what class of stories is left? We have dealt with stories about the gods, and about demigods, heroes and the dead.'

'We have.'

'The final class, then, would be stories about mankind.'

[18] *Iliad* 1.599–600.

'Clearly.'

'And we are not in a position to lay down rules for that just at the moment, my friend.'

'Why not?'

'Because we shall say, I imagine, that writers of poetry and prose both make very serious errors about mankind. They say that lots of people are 392b unjust but happy, or just but miserable, and that injustice pays if you can get away with it, whereas justice is what is good for someone else, but damaging to yourself. We shall stop them saying things like this, and tell them to say just the opposite in their poems and stories. Don't you think so?'

'I'm quite sure we shall,' he said.

'But if you admit I'm right about that, can't I claim that you have admitted what we have been trying to prove all along?'

'Yes,' he said, 'I see how the argument would go.'

'So we can't reach an agreement about mankind, and the kind of stor- 392c ies which should be told, until after we have discovered what sort of thing justice is, and shown that its nature is to be profitable for the person who possesses it, whether or not people *think* he is just.'

'Very true.'

'Let that be enough on the stories. The telling of them, I suggest, is the next thing for us to think about. Then we shall have completely covered both what should be told and how it should be told.'

'I don't understand,' said Adeimantus at this point. 'What do you mean?'

'It's important that you do understand, though,' I said. 'Here's a way of 392d looking at it which may give you a better idea. Aren't all stories told by storytellers and poets really a narrative – of what has happened in the past, of what is happening now, or of what is going to happen in the future?'

'Well, obviously.'

'Don't they achieve their purpose either by simple narrative, or by narrative expressed through imitation, or by a combination of the two?'

'There again, I'm afraid, I still need a clearer explanation.'

'As a teacher,' I said, 'I seem to have a laughable inability to make my meaning clear. I'd better do what people who are no good at speaking do – avoid generalizations, take a particular example, and try to use that 392e to show you what I mean. You know the beginning of the *Iliad*, where the poet says that Chryses asks Agamemnon to let his daughter go, and Agamemnon loses his temper, and then Chryses, when his request is turned down, utters a prayer to Apollo against the Achaeans?' 393a

39

'Yes. I do.'

'In that case, you must be aware that down as far as the lines

> He implored the Achaean lords, but most of all
> Atreus' two sons, the marshals of the host,[19]

the poet speaks in person. He does not attempt to direct our imagination towards anyone else, or suggest that someone other than himself is speaking. But in the lines which follow he talks as if he himself is Chryses, and does everything he can to make us imagine it is not Homer speaking, but the priest. He talks like an old man. The whole of the rest of his narrative is constructed along more or less the same lines – not only events at Troy, but also events in Ithaca, and the whole of the *Odyssey*.'

'Exactly,' he said.

'But it's all narrative – both the individual speeches he delivers and the bits he says in between the speeches?'

'Yes, of course.'

393c 'And when he makes a speech in the character of someone else, can we say that he always makes his own style as close as possible to that of the person he tells us is speaking?'

'No question of it.'

'But making yourself resemble someone else – either in the way you speak or in the way you look – isn't that imitating the person you make yourself resemble?'

'Of course it is.'

'In passages like this, apparently, Homer and the rest of the poets use imitation to construct their narrative.'

'Yes.'

'If there were no passages where the poet concealed his own person, 393d then his whole work, his whole narrative, would have been created without using imitation. To save you telling me again that you don't understand how this can be, I will explain. Imagine Homer told us that Chryses came, bringing his daughter's ransom, as a suppliant to the Achaeans, and in particular to their kings, but then went on to tell the story not in the person of Chryses, but still as Homer. You realize that would be simple narrative, not imitation. The story would go something like this. 393e I'm no poet, so I won't tell it in verse: "The priest came and prayed that

40

the gods might grant to the Achaeans that they should capture Troy, and return home safely, but he asked them to release his daughter in return for the ransom, and out of reverence for the god. When he had finished, the rest of the Achaeans showed him respect, and would have agreed to his request, but Agamemnon lost his temper, telling him to depart immediately, and not come back again; otherwise his priest's staff and the god's garlands would be no protection to him. The priest's daughter would be an old woman living in Argos with him before there was any question of releasing her. He told the priest to go away and stop bothering him, if he wanted to get home safely. The old man was alarmed by Agamemnon's threats, and went away in silence. But after he had left the camp he addressed many prayers to Apollo, calling on the cult-names of the god, reminding him of past favours, and asking his help in return if he had ever, in the building of temples or the sacrifice of victims, given the god a gift which had been a source of pleasure to him. In return for these favours, he prayed that Apollo's arrows might make the Achaeans pay for his tears." That, my friend, is the simple narrative, without imitation.'

    'I see,' he said.

    'In that case,' I said, 'you can also see that you get just the opposite if you omit what the poet says between the speeches, and leave the dialogue.'

    'Yes, I can see that too,' he said. 'That's the kind of thing you get in tragedy.'

    'Exactly,' I said. 'Now I think I can make clear to you what I couldn't make clear before, that one type of poetry and storytelling is purely imitative – this is tragedy and comedy, as you say. In another type, the poet tells his own story. I imagine you'd find this mainly in dithyramb.[20] The third type, using both imitation and narrative, can be found in epic poetry, and in many other places as well. Are you following me?'

    'Yes. I see now what you were getting at.'

    'Now, let me remind you what we have just been saying. We said we had decided *what* stories should be told, but still had to look into the question *how* they should be told.'

    'Yes, I remember that.'

    'So the thing I was really trying to say we should make up our minds about was this. Shall we permit poets to use imitation in their works? Or

394a

394b

394c

394d

---

[20] Dithyramb was a type of lyric poetry sung by a chorus.

partly imitation and partly narrative? In which case, when should they use one, and when the other? Or should they not use imitation at all?'

'Let me make a prediction,' he said. 'You're going to ask whether or not we should allow tragedy and comedy into our city.'

'Possibly,' I said. 'Possibly more than that, even. I don't know yet. But we have set sail, and must go where the wind, or the argument, blows us.'

'You are right,' he said.

394e   'Here's a question for you, then, Adeimantus. Do we want our guardians to be given to imitation, or not? Or does the same principle apply here as applied earlier?[21] The principle was that each individual can only do one thing well. He can't do lots of things. If he tries, he will be jack of all trades, and master of none.'

'Yes, it does apply. Why shouldn't it?'

'Does it apply to imitation as well? Is the same person incapable of imitating many things as well as he can imitate one?'

'Of course.'

395a   'So he's unlikely both to follow one of the worthwhile occupations and also to be a versatile imitator, and given to imitation. After all, the same people aren't even able to be successful in two apparently quite similar forms of imitation such as comedy and tragedy. You did classify both of those, just now, as types of imitation?'

'I did. And you're right. The same people can't be good at both.'

'Nor as reciters and actors either.'

'True.'

'The same people can't even be actors in comedy as well as tragedy.

395b These are all examples of imitation, aren't they?'

'Yes, they are.'

'What's more, Adeimantus, I think man's nature is a currency minted into even smaller denominations than these. This means he can't be good at imitating many different things, nor good at doing the many real things of which the imitations are copies.'

'Very true,' he said.

'So if we stick to our original plan, which was that our guardians should

395c be released from all other occupations, and be the true architects of freedom for our city; and that everything they do must contribute to this

---

[21] Socrates refers to the argument at 369e–370c, recapitulated at 374a–d, just before the discussion of poetry begins.

end, it is essential that they do not do or imitate anything else. If they do imitate anything, then from their earliest childhood they should choose appropriate models to imitate – people who are brave, self-disciplined, godfearing, free, that sort of thing. They should neither do, nor be good at, imitating what is illiberal, nor any other kind of shameful behaviour, in case enjoyment of the imitation gives rise to enjoyment of the reality. **395d** Have you never noticed how imitation, if long continued from an early age, becomes part of a person's nature, turns into habits of body, speech and mind?'

'I certainly have,' he said.

'So imitating a woman, young or old, maybe abusing her husband, or competing with the gods and boasting about her good fortune, or in the **395e** grip of disaster, or grief, or mourning, will not be a legitimate activity for the people we say we are interested in – the ones we wanted to grow up into the right sort of men. They are, after all, men. And still less do we want them imitating a woman who is ill, or in love, or in childbirth.'

'Absolutely not,' he said.

'Nor should they imitate female or male slaves behaving in the way slaves behave.'

'No. Not that either.'

'Nor the wrong sort of men, presumably: cowards, and those whose behaviour is the opposite of what we said just now they *should* imitate – men who insult or ridicule one another, or use bad language, drunk or for that matter sober, and all the other faults which people of this sort are **396a** guilty of in their language and behaviour towards themselves and others. Nor, in my opinion, should they get in the habit of modelling themselves, in their language or behaviour, on people who are mad. They must recognize madness and wickedness in men and women, but none of this is behaviour for them to adopt or imitate.'

'Very true,' he said.

'What about people working in bronze?' I asked. 'Or practising some other art or skill? Or rowing triremes, or calling the time to the rowers, **396b** or any other activity of this type? Should our guardians imitate them?'

'How can they,' he said, 'if they are not even allowed to be interested in any of them?'

'What about horses neighing and bulls bellowing? Will they imitate those? Or the sound of rivers, or the sea breaking on the shore, or thunder, or anything of that sort?'

'No. They are forbidden either to be mad or to behave like those who are mad.'

396c 'If I understand you rightly, then,' I said, 'there is a form of speech and of narrative which is the one the right sort of man would employ when he needed to say something, and then again a second form of speech, quite unlike the first, which would appeal to a man with the opposite kind of nature and upbringing, and which he would employ.'

'What are these forms of speech?'

'I think the decent man, when he comes in his narrative to some saying or action of a good man, will be prepared to report it as if he himself really were the person concerned. He will not be ashamed of

396d an imitation of this sort. He will imitate the good man most when he acts in a responsible and wise manner, and will imitate him less, and less fully, when the good man is led astray by disease or passion, or by drunkenness or misfortune of some kind. When he comes to someone who is unworthy of him, I think he'll refuse to make any serious attempt to resemble one who is his inferior – except perhaps briefly, when the character is doing something good – both because he has had no training in imitating people like this, and because he resents shap-

396e ing and modelling himself on the pattern of his inferiors. Inwardly he treats behaviour of this sort as beneath him – unless of course it's in jest.'

'Very likely,' he said.

'So he'll use the kind of narrative we described a few moments ago, when we were talking about Homer's epics. The way he tells stories will combine both styles, imitation and the other kind of narrative, but with only a small amount of imitation even in a long story. Or have I got it wrong?'

'No,' he said, 'this is bound to be the style of a speaker of this sort.'

397a 'Now, as for the speaker who is not of this sort, the worse he is, the more prepared he will be to use imitation all the time.[22] There is nothing he will regard as beneath him, and so he will take it upon himself, in all seriousness, and at public performances, to imitate all the things we were talking about just now – thunder, the din of wind and hail, of wheels and pulleys, the sound of trumpet, pipe, panpipe, and every musical instru-

397b ment, even the noise of clogs, or sheep, or birds. Will the way this man

---

[22] Reading μιμήσεται rather than διηγήσεται.

44

tells stories consist entirely of imitation, in word and gesture, with maybe a small element of narrative?'

'Again, it's bound to.'

'There you are, then,' I said. 'That's what I meant when I said there were two styles of storytelling.'

'I accept that,' he said. 'There *are* two.'

'Of these two styles the first involves only slight variations. If he uses a musical mode and rhythm which are right for his style, it is pretty well possible for the person who tells stories in the right way – since the variations in his style are very slight – to achieve musical consistency, using a single mode and of course a similarly appropriate rhythm.'   397c

'That is certainly true.'

'What about the style of the other storyteller? Because of the enormous range of variations it contains, won't it need just the opposite treatment – all the musical modes, and every kind of rhythm – if it too is to be told in a way appropriate to it?'

'Undoubtedly.'

'Do all poets, then, and storytellers of all kinds, hit upon one or other of these styles, or some combination of the two?'

'They must,' he said.

'In that case,' I asked, 'what shall our policy be? Shall we allow them   397d all into our city? Or one or other of the pure styles? Or the mixed style?'

'If my view prevails,' he said, 'we shall allow only the pure imitator of the good man.'

'And yet the mixed style is enjoyable as well, Adeimantus. In fact, the one which is the exact opposite of the one you are selecting is by far the most enjoyable, in the opinion of children and their attendants, and of the population at large.'

'Yes, it is the most enjoyable.'

'Possibly, however, you would say that this style is not in tune with our regime. Our men do not have a dual or manifold nature, since each of   397e them performs only one task.'

'No, it is not in tune.'

'Is this the reason, then, why ours is the only city in which we shall find a shoemaker who is only a shoemaker, and not a ship's captain as well as a shoemaker, a farmer who is only a farmer, and not a juryman as well as a farmer, a soldier who is only a soldier, and not a businessman as well as a soldier, and the others the same?'

'Yes,' he said.

398a   'Suppose, then, there were a man so wondrously wise as to be utterly versatile, able to imitate anything. If he came to our city wanting to perform his poems in person, it looks as if we would fall down before him, tell him he was sacred, exceptional and delightful, but then explain to him that we do not have men like him in our city, that it is not right for them to be there. We would pour myrrh over his head, garland him with woollen garlands, and send him on his way to some other city. For our own good, we would content ourselves with a simpler, if less enjoyable,

398b   poet and storyteller, who can imitate the decent man's way of speaking, and model his stories on those patterns which we laid down at the beginning of our attempt to provide an education for our soldiers.'

'Yes, that is certainly what we should do, if it were up to us.'

'Well, my friend,' I said, 'on the poetic and musical side of our education it looks as if we have dealt pretty fully with the section on stories and myths. We have laid down both what stories are to be told and how they are to be told.'

'Yes, I agree,' he said. 'I think we have dealt with that.'

398c   'Well then, does that leave the question of styles of songs and music?'

'Obviously it does.'

'Presumably anyone could now work out the kind of character we need to prescribe for those, to be in harmony with what has been laid down already.'

Glaucon laughed. 'It looks, in that case, Socrates, as if I'm not "anyone." I'm not sure I'd trust myself to make a guess, on the spur of the moment, about the sort of thing we ought to prescribe. Though I have a pretty good idea.'

'What you certainly can say with some confidence, I imagine, is that

398d   music is essentially composed of three elements: words, harmonic mode[23] and rhythm.'

'Yes, I can say that,' he said.

'As far as the words go, then, they are no different from words which are not set to music. Shouldn't they conform to the same patterns we laid down just now, and be in the same style?'

'Yes, they should.'

---

[23] In Greek music, the different modes, or 'attunements', were different scale-like structures underlying melodies. These differences in melodic structure were associated with differences in style, poetic genre, occasion and mood.

'What is more, the mode and rhythm must follow from the words.'
'Of course.'
'And mourning and lamentation were things we said we could do without in our stories.'
'They were.'
'Which then are the mourning modes? You're musical. You tell me.' 398e
'The Mixolydian,' he said. 'The Syntonolydian. That sort of thing.'
'Should these be banned, then?' I asked. 'After all, they are no use even to women – if we want them to be good women – let alone to men.'
'They certainly should.'
'Drunkenness is also something quite unsuitable for our guardians. And so are luxury and laziness.'
'Of course they are.'
'Which of the modes, then, are appropriate to luxury and parties?'
'There are some Ionian modes,' he said, 'and again Lydian, which are called relaxed.'
'Will these be any use to men of a warlike disposition?' 399a
'No,' he said. 'So it looks as if that leaves you with the Dorian and Phrygian.'
'I don't know about modes,' I said. 'Leave me the mode which can most fittingly imitate the voice and accents of a brave man in time of war, or in any externally imposed crisis. When things go wrong, and he faces death and wounds, or encounters some other danger, in all these situations he 399b
holds out to the end in a disciplined and steadfast manner. Plus another mode for someone engaged in some peaceful, voluntary, freely chosen activity. He might be trying to persuade someone of something, making some request – praying to a god, or giving instructions or advice to a man, or just the opposite. He might be listening patiently to someone else making a request, or explaining something to him, or trying to get him to change his mind, and on that basis acting as he thinks best – without arrogance, acting prudently and calmly in all these situations, and being content with the outcome. These two modes, then: one for adversity and one 399c
for freely chosen activity, the modes which will best imitate the voices of the prudent and of the brave in failure and success. Leave me those.'
'Leave you, in other words, with precisely the two I suggested just now,' he said.
'That means we shan't want an enormous range of strings, and every possible mode, in our songs and melodies.'

'No, I think not,' he said.

'In which case we shan't produce any makers of those triangular harps,
399d or regular harps, or all those many stringed instruments which can play
many modes.'

'Apparently not.'

'What about the makers and players of reed instruments? Will you
allow them into your city? Isn't playing a reed instrument more "many
stringed" than anything else? And aren't the instruments which can play
many modes in fact just imitations of the reed-pipe?'

'Yes, obviously they are.'

'That leaves you the lyre and the cithara,' I said.[24] 'They'll be right for
the city. In the countryside, by contrast, there could be some sort of panpipe for our herdsmen.'

'Well, that's certainly the way our reasoning points,' he said.

399e 'There's nothing very radical,' I said, 'in our preferring Apollo and
Apollo's instruments to Marsyas and his instruments.'[25]

'Good heavens, no,' he said. 'I'm sure there isn't.'

'Ye dogs!' I said.[26] 'Without meaning to, we have purged the city we
said was too luxurious.'

'That was sensible of us,' he said.

'Come on, then,' I said. 'Let's purge the rest of it. Our next concern
after mode will be rhythm. We should not pursue complexity, nor do
we want all kinds of metres. We should see what are the rhythms of a
400a self-disciplined and courageous life, and after looking at those, make the
metre and melody conform to the speech of someone like that. We won't
make speech conform to rhythm and melody. Which these rhythms are is
for you to say, as it was with the modes.'

'I really don't know what to say about that,' he said. 'In my experience,
there are three types of rhythm from which metres are woven together,
just as when it comes to tones, there are four elements from which all the
modes are derived. But I have no idea which types imitate which lives.'

[24] The reed-pipe (αὐλός) is compared to a 'many stringed' instrument here because of its versatility. By contrast the lyre and the cithara, which could produce fewer tones and therefore fewer
modes, are regarded as less versatile and so less dangerous.
[25] According to a well-known story, the satyr Marsyas challenged the god Apollo to a musical
competition in which Marsyas played the reed-pipe while Apollo played the cithara. Marsyas
lost and was flayed alive by Apollo.
[26] Plato regularly presents Socrates as swearing 'by the Dog', perhaps a way of avoiding a more
serious oath. Cf. *Hippias Major* 287e (p. 9).

48

'That's something we can ask Damon about,' I said. 'He can tell us   **400b**
which metres are appropriate to meanness of spirit, arrogance, madness
and other faults of character, and which rhythms should be left for those
whose character is the opposite. I seem to remember, though I can't be
sure, hearing him use terms like "composite enoplion"; then there were
"dactyls", and "heroic metre", which he arranged, somehow or other, so
that upbeat and downbeat were made equal as it turns into short or long at
the end. Then there was the "iambic", I seem to remember, and another
he called "trochaic", with their long and short syllables. For some of them,   **400c**
I think he condemned or approved the pulse of the metrical feet as much
as the rhythms themselves. Or possibly it was the two together, I can't be
sure. All these questions, as I say, can be referred to Damon.[27] It would
take us a long time to decide them. Or do you think we should try?'

'God forbid.'

'But that gracefulness and want of grace can follow on from what is   **400d**
rhythmical and unrhythmical, that is something you can decide.'

'Of course.'

'But then if rhythm and mode follow language, as we said just now,
and not the other way round, what is rhythmical must follow and imitate fine language, while what is not rhythmical follows the opposite. The
same with harmony and discord.'

'Yes, rhythm and mode certainly should follow language,' he said.

'What about manner of speaking,' I asked, 'and what is actually said?
Don't they follow from the nature of the speaker's soul?'

'Of course.'

'And the other things follow from manner of speaking?'

'Yes.'

'In that case, all these things – the right way of speaking, the right
attunement, grace and rhythm – follow from a good nature. I don't mean   **400e**
the good nature which is the polite name we give to stupidity[28] but the

---

[27] Damon was a fifth-century musical theorist, associated by Plato with the sophists. Metre in
classical Greek poetry is based on length of syllable, not on stress-accent. One long syllable
(marked –) is the equivalent of two short ones (marked ∪) and different types of metre have
different proportions between the divisions ('upbeat' and 'downbeat') of the metrical foot: 2:2 or
equal as in dactyl (– ∪ ∪) and spondee (– –); 2:1 or double as in iamb (∪ –) and trochee (– ∪),
for example. The enoplion (or 'martial') rhythm was used for processional and marching songs;
heroic metre is the metre of Homeric epic, the dactylic hexameter, in which dactyls and spon-
dees can be substituted for each other.

[28] The Greek word εὐήθεια, here translated literally 'good nature', usually meant 'simplicity' or
'stupidity'.

true intelligence which consists in a character which is rightly and properly constituted.'

'Exactly,' he said.

'So if the young are to perform their proper function, aren't these the qualities they should be everywhere aiming at?'

'They are.'

401a 'Painting is full of these qualities, I imagine, as is any skill of the same sort. So are weaving, embroidery, building – the manufacture of any household object, in fact – even the condition of our bodies and of all things that grow. All these contain gracefulness and want of grace. Want of grace or rhythm, and wrong attunement, are close relatives of wrong speech and a wrong nature, while their opposites are close relatives and imitations of the opposite, the self-disciplined and good nature.'

'Precisely,' he said.

401b 'Is it only the poets we have to keep an eye on, then, compelling them to put the likeness of the good nature into their poems, or else go and write poems somewhere else? Don't we have to keep an eye on the other craftsmen as well, and stop them putting what has the wrong nature, what is undisciplined, slavish or wanting in grace, into their representations of living things, or into buildings, or into any manufactured object? Anyone who finds this impossible is not to be allowed to be a craftsman 401c in our city. That way our guardians will not be brought up among images of what is bad, like animals put out to graze on bad pasture. We don't want them browsing and feeding each day – taking in a little here and a little there – and without realizing it accumulating a single large evil in their souls. No, we must seek out the craftsmen with a gift for tracking down the nature of what is fine, what has grace, so that our young can live in a healthy environment, drawing improvement from every side, whenever things which are beautifully fashioned expose their eyes or ears 401d to some wholesome breeze from healthy regions and lead them imperceptibly, from earliest childhood, into affinity, friendship and harmony with beauty of speech and thought.'

'Yes, that would be by far the best way for them to be brought up,' he said.

'Aren't there two reasons, Glaucon, why musical and poetic education is so important? Firstly because rhythm and mode penetrate more deeply into the inner soul than anything else does; they have the most powerful effect on it, since they bring gracefulness with them. They make a

person graceful, if he is rightly brought up, and the opposite, if he is not. **401e**
And secondly, because anyone with the right kind of education in this
area will have the clearest perception of things which are unsatisfactory –
things which are badly made or naturally defective. Being quite rightly
disgusted by them, he will praise what is beautiful and fine. Delighting
in it, and receiving it into his soul, he will feed on it and so become noble
and good. What is ugly he will rightly condemn and hate, even before he   **402a**
is old enough for rational thought. And when rationality does make its
appearance, won't the person who has been brought up in this way recognize it because of its familiarity, and be particularly delighted with it?'

'Yes,' he said. 'If you ask me, that certainly is the point of a musical
and poetic education.'

Republic 10

10.595a–608b[1]

595a   'There are many reasons,' I said, 'why I feel sure we have gone about founding our city in the right way, but I am thinking particularly of poetry.'

'What in particular about poetry?'

'Our refusal to accept any of the imitative part of it. Now that we have distinguished the elements of the soul from one another, it is clearer than ever, in my view, that imitative poetry is the last thing we should allow.'

595b   'Why do you say that?'

'Between ourselves – I'm sure you won't denounce me to the writers of tragedy and all the other imitative poets – everything of that sort seems to me to be a destructive influence on the minds of those who hear it. Unless of course they have the antidote, the knowledge of what it really is.'

'What do you have in mind when you say that?'

'I'd better explain,' I said, 'though the affection and respect I have had

595c   for Homer since I was a child makes me very reluctant to say it. He seems to me to have been the original teacher and guide of all these wonderful tragedians of ours. All the same, no man is worth more than the truth. So, as I say, I had better explain myself.'

'You certainly had.'

[1] By the beginning of *Republic*, Book 10, the description of the ideal state and its philosopher-rulers is complete. Socrates returns to the topic of poetry and presents additional arguments for excluding most of it from the state he has described.

'Listen, then. Or rather, answer.'

'Ask away.'

'Can you give me any idea what exactly this thing "imitation" is? Speaking for myself, I don't really understand what it aims to be.'

'In which case, of course I'm *bound* to understand it.'

'That wouldn't be so very unusual,' I said. 'People who don't see well **596a** are often quicker to see things than people whose eyesight is better.'

'That's true,' he said. 'But even if something does occur to me, I'm not going to summon up much enthusiasm for saying so with you here. You'd better rely on your own eyes.'

'Very well. Would you like us to follow our usual procedure in starting the enquiry? We generally postulate a certain form or character – a single form or character, always – for each plurality of things to which we give the same name. Do you follow that?'

'Yes, I do follow it.'

'In which case, let's take any plurality you care to name. For example, I **596b** take it there are many couches, if you like, and many tables.'

'Of course.'

'But when it comes to forms for these pieces of furniture, there are presumably two. A single form of a couch, and a single form of a table.'

'Yes.'

'Don't we usually say also that for each type of furniture the person who makes it looks at the appropriate form? Then one will make the couches we use, another will make the tables, and so on with other kinds of furniture. But the form itself is presumably not the work of any of the craftsmen. How could it be?'

'It couldn't.'

'Now, turn your attention to a maker of a different kind. What name are you going to give him?'

'What kind of maker is that?' **596c**

'The kind who can create all the objects which the individual crafts-men can create.'

'It's a clever man you're talking about. Remarkably clever.'

'Wait till you hear the rest of it. This same craftsman is not only cap-able of making any sort of furniture. He can also create all the things that grow out of the earth. He produces all living creatures – including him-self – and on top of that produces heaven and earth, the gods, everything in heaven, and everything under the earth in Hades.'

596d   'A complete and astonishing genius, you mean.'

'Don't you believe me?' I said. 'Tell me this. Do you think it's altogether impossible for there to be a craftsman of this kind? Or do you think that in one way there *could* be a creator of all these things, though in another way there couldn't? Can't you see that there is a way in which you would be capable of creating all these things for yourself?'

'What way is that?'

'There's nothing very difficult about it,' I said. 'This kind of workmanship is often – and easily – practised. I suppose the quickest way is if you 596e   care to take a mirror and carry it around with you wherever you go. That way you'll soon create the sun and the heavenly bodies, soon create the earth, soon create yourself, other living creatures, furniture, plants, and all the things we've just been talking about.'

'Yes,' he said. 'I could create them as they appear to be. But not, I take it, as they truly are.'

'Good. That's exactly the point. Isn't that just the kind of craftsman a painter is?'

'Indeed it is.'

'Of course you can say the things he creates are not real. Yet there is a sense in which the painter does create a couch, isn't there?'

'Yes. The painter too creates a couch as it appears to be.'

597a   'What about the carpenter who makes a couch? Didn't you just say he creates a particular couch, but not the form or character which we say is what a couch is?'

'Yes, I did.'

'Then if he does not create what a couch is, he can't be creating the real thing. Something like the real thing, but not itself the real thing. So if you were to say that it fully is – this thing made by a carpenter who makes couches, or by any other craftsman – you probably wouldn't be telling the truth.'

'No. Or not in the opinion of those who occupy themselves with arguments of this sort, at any rate.'

'In which case, let's not find it at all surprising if the carpenter's couch, too, is in fact rather shadowy by comparison with truth.'

597b   'No, we shouldn't find that surprising.'

'Now,' I said, 'This imitator of ours. When we ask our question "Who exactly is he," would you like us to use the same examples?'

'Yes, if you like.'

'Very well. We have these three sorts of couch. There's the one which exists in the natural order of things. This one, I imagine we'd say, was the work of a god. Or would we say someone else?'

'No, I don't think we would.'

'Then there's the one made by the carpenter.'

'Yes,' he said.

'And then the one made by the painter, isn't there?'

'Let's take it there is.'

'Painter, carpenter, god, then. Three agents responsible for three kinds of couch.'

'Yes, three.'

'Now, either from choice or because there was some necessity for him not to produce more than one couch in the natural order of things, god has made only this one couch – what a couch is, just that. Two, or more than two, of these were never brought forth by god, nor could they be.' **597c**

'Why not?'

'Because if he made even two, then another would make an appearance in its turn – the one whose form both the others possessed. And this one would be what a couch is, rather than the two.'

'Correct,' he said.

'God was aware of this, I imagine, and wanted to be the true creator of the true couch. Not just any old maker of any old couch. That's why he gave it an essentially unique nature.' **597d**

'Probably.'

'So do you want us to call him its natural creator, or something of that sort?'

'We'd certainly be justified in calling him that, given that he has created both this and everything else in its essential nature.'

'What about the carpenter? Shouldn't we call him a craftsman who makes couches?'

'Yes, we should.'

'And the painter? Is he too a craftsman and creator of such things?'

'Certainly not.'

'What are you going to say he does to a couch, then?'

'I think the most reasonable description would be to say that he is an imitator of what those craftsmen make.' **597e**

'Very well,' I said. 'So you call "imitator" the maker of the product which is two removes from nature, do you?'

55

Continues

'I do indeed,' he said.

'In that case, this is what the writer of tragedies, if he is an imitator, will be. Someone whose nature it is to be two removes from the king and the truth. And the same with all other imitators.'

'It looks like it.'

'So, we are in agreement about the imitator. Now, tell me something about the painter. Do you think, in each case, he is trying to imitate the thing itself, the one which exists in the natural order of things? Or is he trying to imitate the work of craftsmen?'

'He is trying to imitate the work of craftsmen,' he said.

'As it is? Or as it appears to be? Can you make your definition a little more precise?'

'What do you mean?'

'I mean this. When you look at a couch from the side or from the front, or from anywhere else, does the couch itself change? Or does it stay the same, and merely look different? And the same with other things.'

'Yes, that's how it is,' he said. 'It looks different, but it's really the same.'

'Well, that's the point of my question. In each individual case, what is the object of painting? Does it aim to imitate what is, as it is? Or imitate what appears, as it appears? Is it imitation of appearance, or of truth?'

'Of appearance,' he said.

'In that case, I would imagine, the art of imitation is a far cry from truth. The reason it can make everything, apparently, is that it grasps just a little of each thing – and only an image at that. We say the painter can paint us a shoemaker, for example, or a carpenter, or any of the other craftsmen. He may know nothing of any of these skills, and yet, if he is a good painter, from a distance his picture of a carpenter can fool children and people with no judgement, because it looks like a real carpenter.'

'Of course it can.'

'I suppose the thing we have to remember in all these cases is this. When someone tells us, in any particular context, that he has met a man who has knowledge of all these crafts, and of all the things each individual practitioner of them can know, and that this man's knowledge is in every respect more accurate than anyone else's, the answer we should give someone like this is that he is some sort of simpleton, who has apparently come across a magician and imitator, and been taken in by him.

He has decided this man is an expert, because he himself is incapable of distinguishing knowledge from ignorance or imitation.'

'Absolutely true.'

'Very well,' I said. 'Now, our next question concerns both tragedy and its mentor, Homer. It arises out of the claim that the tragedians know about all the arts, that they know about everything human – as it relates to virtue and vice – and everything divine as well. The good poet, they say, if he is to do a good job of creating the things he does create, must necessarily create them with knowledge. He could not create it otherwise. So the questions we have to ask are these. Are the people they have come across imitators? Have they been deceived by them? Don't they realize, when they look at their works, that these are two removes from the real thing, and easy for someone who does not know the truth to create? After all, it is appearances, not realities, they are creating. Or is there some truth in what these people say? Do good poets really have knowledge of the things the general public thinks they write so well about?'

'Yes,' he said. 'Those *are* the questions we have to ask.'

'Do you think, then, assuming someone had the ability to create both things – the object of the imitation *and* its image – that he would allow himself to show any enthusiasm for the production of images? Would he make this his chief aim in life, his proudest possession?'

'No, I'm sure he wouldn't.'

'If he really knew about the things he imitates, I imagine, he'd be much keener on action than on imitation of it. He'd try to leave many fine actions as memorials to himself, and be much more interested in having poetry written in honour of him than in writing poetry in honour of others.'

'I'm sure he would. In terms of prestige and benefit, there's no comparison.'

'Very well, then. For most subjects, we needn't ask Homer or any of the other poets to justify himself. We needn't ask if any of them has any medical knowledge, rather than just being an imitator of medical language. Or which patient any poet, old or new, is ever said to have made healthy, in the way Asclepius[2] did. Or what students of medicine he left behind him, as Asclepius left his descendants. Nor need we ask the poets

598e

599a

599b

599c

[2] Asclepius, son of Apollo, was a great healer, regarded in Greek tradition as the patron of medicine.

about most of the arts. We can forget about them. But when it comes to
the greatest and finest of the things Homer tries to tell us about – mili-
599d tary command, the founding of cities, a man's education – then I think
we *are* entitled to be curious. "My dear Homer," we can say to him, "if
you are not two removes from truth in this matter of goodness – not a
maker of images, what we defined as an imitator – if you are even at one
remove from truth, and if you were capable of distinguishing the behaviour which makes men better or worse in private life or in public life, then
tell us which city has ever been better governed because of you. Sparta is
better governed because of Lycurgus, and so are many other cities, great
599e and small, because of many other individuals. What about you? Which
city says that *you* are its great law-giver, or attributes its success to you?
Italy and Sicily say it is Charondas. We say it is Solon. Which city says it
is you?" Will he be able to name a city?'

'No, I don't think so,' said Glaucon. 'Even Homer's most devoted sup-
porters don't make that claim.'

600a 'Is any war in Homer's day recorded as having been won by his leadership or strategy?'

'No.'

'Do we find a number of ingenious contributions to the arts, or other
human activities, attributed to him? That's what you'd expect to find in
the life of a wise man. The kind of thing we are told about Thales of
Miletus, for example. Or Anacharsis the Scythian.'

'No, absolutely nothing of that sort.'

'Well then, in his private life, if not in public life? Does Homer have the
reputation of being a formative influence on people during his lifetime?
600b Did they love him for his company, and hand down some "Homeric" way
of life to their successors? Take Pythagoras. Not only was Pythagoras
himself very much loved for this reason, but even to this day his successors call their way of life "Pythagorean," and can be easily identified as
Pythagoreans.'

'No,' he said, 'there's nothing of that kind told about him either. As
far as education and culture go, Socrates, Homer's disciple Creophylus
might well strike us as even more absurd than his name,[3] if the stories
600c about Homer are true. It is said that Creophylus showed not the slightest
interest in the man himself when he was alive.'

---

[3] Creophylus is said to have been an epic poet and a relative of Homer. His name means 'meat-tribe'.

'Yes, I've heard that story,' I said. 'But if Homer really had been able to educate men and make them better, Glaucon – because he had knowledge of these things, and not just the ability to imitate them – do you think he could have failed to gain himself a lot of disciples, and be respected and loved by them? Think of Protagoras of Abdera, Prodicus of Ceos, and any number of others. They have this ability to persuade any of their contemporaries who takes private lessons from them that he will not be capable of managing either his own household **600d** or his own city unless they themselves take charge of his education. So greatly are they loved for this wisdom that their disciples all but carry them around on their shoulders. If Homer had been capable of helping men on the path towards goodness, would his contemporaries have allowed him and Hesiod to roam the world giving recitations? Wouldn't they have grabbed hold of them as something more valuable than gold, and compelled them to come home, and live with them? **600e** And if they couldn't persuade them, wouldn't they themselves have acted as their attendants wherever they went, until they had completed their education?'

'I think you're absolutely right, Socrates,' he said.

'In that case, shall we say that all artists, starting with Homer, are imitators of images of goodness and the other things they create, without having any grasp of the truth? As we've just been saying, the painter will create what *looks* like a shoemaker, though he himself knows noth- **601a** ing about shoemaking and the kind of people who look at his painting know nothing about it either. They judge things by their colours and shapes.'

'Exactly.'

'The same goes for the poet, too, I take it. We can say that he colours his pictures of all these skills with his words and phrases, and that the only thing he knows anything about is imitation. The result is that people like himself, people who judge things on the basis of language, think that what he has to say seems excellently said – whether he is using his metre, rhythm and harmony – to describe shoemaking, or generalship, or any- thing else. Such is the power of bewitchment naturally possessed by the **601b** tools he uses. And yet a poet's words, when stripped of the colours pro- vided by his art, and taken by themselves – well, I think you know what they're like. You've seen them, after all.'

'Indeed I have.'

'It's like the faces of people who have youth without beauty,' I said. 'Like looking at them when they lose their bloom of youth.'

'Exactly,' he said.

. . .

602c 'And this sort of imitation,' I said, 'really and truly is connected with something twice removed from the truth, isn't it?'

'Yes.'

'Then here is another question. What part of a person does it have its effect on?'

'What kind of thing do you mean?'

'I'll tell you. If we rely on our eyesight, presumably, the same thing does not look the same size close to and far off.'

'No, it doesn't.'

'And the same things can look crooked and straight to people look-ing at them first in water and then out of water. Or concave and convex, because of our eyes' variable perception of colours or shades. Our souls **602d** are clearly full of this kind of confusion. Things like shadow-painting,[4] conjuring, and all the other arts of the same kind rely on this weakness in our nature to produce effects that fall nothing short of witchcraft.'

'True.'

'Isn't that why measuring, counting and weighing proved to be a won-derful help to us? They meant we were not ruled by what *looked* bigger or smaller, or more, or heavier, but by the thing which did the calculating or the measuring – or the weighing, for that matter.'

'Naturally.'

602e 'And these operations, of course, are the function of the rational elem-ent in the soul.'

'Yes, the rational element.'

'Quite often this element makes its measurements, indicates that one group of things is bigger or smaller than another – or the same size – but simultaneously finds that the same group of objects presents exactly the opposite appearance.'

'Yes.'

'But didn't we say it was impossible for one thing to have opposite opinions about the same things at the same time?'[5]

---

4 Shadow-painting was a technique for giving the impression of depth in two dimensions.
5 A reference back to a much earlier passage of the *Republic*, 4.436b.

'We did. And rightly.'

'In which case, the part of the soul whose opinions conflict with the measurements cannot be the same as the part whose opinions agree with the measurements.' 603a

'No, it cannot.'

'Well, the part which puts its trust in measurement and calculation will be the best part of the soul.'

'Of course.'

'And the part which disagrees with this part will be one of the weaker elements in us.'

'Bound to be.'

'This was the point of agreement I wanted to reach when I said painting – and imitation in general – operates in an area of its own, removed from the truth, and that it associates with the element in us which is far removed from intelligence – a liaison and friendship from which nothing 603b healthy or true can result.'

'Precisely,' he said.

'An inferior art, then, imitation. And its union with what is inferior produces inferior offspring.'

'That's the way it looks.'

'And is that only imitation in things we see?' I asked. 'Or is it also imitation in things we hear – what we call poetry?'

'Poetry as well, I would guess.'

'Well,' I said, 'let's not trust to guesswork alone, and the analogy with painting. Let's turn directly to the actual part of our thought which 603c poetic imitation has to do with, and see whether that is something trivial or something important.'

'Yes, that is what we should do.'

'We can put it to ourselves like this. Imitation, we say, imitates men performing actions freely or under compulsion. As a result of their actions, they believe they have done well or badly, and in all these situations they feel pain or pleasure. There wasn't any more to it than that, was there?'

'No.'

'Now, is a man's attitude consistent in all these activities? Or is it the 603d same with actions as it was with vision? Then he was in a state of civil war, and held opposite opinions about the same things within himself. Is he at odds with himself in the same way when it comes to his actions? Is he at war with himself? Come to think of it, though, that isn't a question which is still waiting to be answered. We answered all those questions quite satisfactorily in the earlier part of our discussion, when we agreed that there were countless contradictions of this kind, that the soul was full of them.'[6]

'Correct,' he said.

'Yes, it was correct,' I said. 'But there was something we left out then **603e** which I think we now have to explain.'

'What is that?'

'What we said then, I think, was that if something happens to a good man – losing a son, perhaps, or something else of great value – he will more easily endure it than anyone else would.'[7]

'He certainly will.'

'The question we now have to ask ourselves is whether he will feel no pain at all. Or if that is impossible, will he nonetheless observe some moderation in his grief?'

'Yes,' he said, 'that seems closer to the truth.'

604a 'Right. In that case, tell me something else about him. Do you think he will put up a better fight and resistance against his grief when he is being observed by his equals, or when he is on his own, in a deserted place, all by himself?'

'I should think there'll be a big difference when he is being observed,' he said.

'Yes. When he is on his own, I imagine, he will not be ashamed to say all sorts of things which he would be embarrassed if anyone else heard him saying. And he'll do all sorts of things which he wouldn't be prepared to have anyone see him doing.'

'That is so,' he said.

'Are reason and established custom the things which encourage him to **604b** resist, while what drags him back to his grief is his misfortune itself?'

'Yes.'

'And when a human being has opposing impulses, relating to the same thing, at the same time, we say these must necessarily be two different elements.'

'Yes, of course.'

'Is one element prepared to follow custom wherever custom leads?'

---

[6] Another reference to *Republic* 4, this time to 439c–441c.
[7] Cf. *Republic* 3.387d–e (p. 37).

'And where would that be?'

'Custom says, presumably, that in misfortune the best thing is not to be upset, but to be as calm as possible – for a number of reasons. In the first place, it is not clear how much is good and how much bad in situations of this sort. Second, if we look to the future, it does no good to take things hard. Third, nothing in human affairs is worth taking that seriously. And fourth, grieving gets in the way of the thing which ought, in these situations, to come to our assistance as swiftly as possible.' 604c

'What thing do you mean?' he asked.

'Reflection on what has happened,' I replied. 'People should accept the way things have fallen out the way they accept the fall of the dice, and then make their plans in the way reason prescribes as best for them. They shouldn't spend their time howling, clutching hold of the part which is hurt, like children who have fallen over. They should always accustom their souls to concentrate straight away on curing and repairing 604d the damaged and injured part. They should use healing to do away with lamentation.'

'Yes,' he said, 'that would certainly be the right attitude to take towards misfortune.'

'So it's the best element, we say, which is prepared to use this kind of rational calculation as a guide.'

'Clearly.'

'Whereas the element which draws us towards mourning and the recollection of our sufferings, which can never get its fill of these things – won't we describe this as irrational, lazy and a friend to cowardice?'

'Yes, we will.'

'This element, the fretful element, is highly susceptible to all sorts 604e of varied imitation. The calm, thoughtful character, on the other hand, unchanging and true to itself, is hard to imitate, and not a simple matter to understand if it is imitated – particularly in public, when you get a diverse collection of people in the theatre. What is being imitated is quite unfamiliar to them.'

'Absolutely.' 605a

'The imitative poet's nature is obviously not adapted to this element in the soul, nor is his wisdom framed to appeal to it. Not if he's going to be popular with the general public. His concern is with the fretful, variegated character, because that is the one which is easy to imitate.'

'Obviously.'

'So we'd be justified now in taking him and putting him on a par with
the painter. His products, like the painter's, are inferior by comparison
605b with the truth, and he resembles him also in associating with an inferior
part of the soul, not with the best part. By rights, therefore, we ought
not to admit him into a city which is going to be well governed, since it
is an inferior part of the soul that he arouses and feeds, and by making
this strong destroys the rational part. It's the same with a city. If you give
power to those who are bad, and hand the city over to them, you destroy
those who are better. In exactly the same way, we shall say, the imitative poet sets up a bad regime in the soul of each individual, gratifying
605c the senseless part of it, the part which cannot distinguish larger from
smaller, and which regards the same things at one time as large and at
another time as small. He is nothing but an image-maker, and he stands
far removed from the truth.'

'He does indeed.'

'However, we haven't yet brought our most serious accusation against
imitative poetry. Its ability to corrupt even good people – with a very few
exceptions – is surely a disgrace.'

'Of course it is, if that really is what it does.'

'Listen, and see what you think. The best of us, I imagine, when we
hear Homer or one of the tragic poets imitating some hero in a state of
605d grief as he drags out a long speech of lamentation, or even breaks into
song, or starts beating his breast ... well, you know how it is. We enjoy it,
and surrender ourselves to it. We follow and share the hero's sufferings,
treat them as real, and praise as an excellent poet the person who most
affects us in this way.'

'Yes, I know how it is. How could I fail to?'

'And yet when some misfortune affects one of us personally, you're
aware how we pride ourselves on doing the exact opposite – if we can
605e have the strength to remain silent, and endure. We seem to regard this as
men's behaviour, and what we praised in the poetic context as women's
behaviour.'

'Yes, I'm aware of that,' he said.

'Is praise of that sort justified, then – if you see a man behaving in a
way you wouldn't dream of behaving yourself, a way you'd be ashamed to
behave, and are not repelled by it, but take pleasure in it and praise it?'

'Heavens, no,' he said. 'That kind of praise sounds quite unreasonable.'

606a 'Yes, it does,' I said. 'At least, it does if you look at it like this.'

'Like what?'

'Think about it. Here we have this element which in one situation – in our private misfortunes – is forcibly held in check, though it has this hunger which can only be satisfied by weeping and wholesale lamentation, since these are the satisfactions this kind of thing by its nature desires. Then in another situation this same part is fulfilled and gratified by the poets, and what is by nature the best part of us, inadequately educated by reason or habit, abandons its watch over grieving of that kind. It says **606b** the sorrows it is watching are another's, and if someone else, who claims to be a good man, is grieving inappropriately, there is nothing for us to be ashamed of in applauding him and pitying him. We believe there is a positive benefit, which is pleasure, and would not be prepared to lose that by rejecting the whole poem. It is given to few people, I suspect, to work out that the pleasure they take in what happens to others necessarily carries over into what happens to them. If they allow the faculty of pity to grow strong, by feeding it on the sorrows of others, it is hard to restrain it when it comes to their own sorrows.'

'Very true,' he said.   **606c**

'The same argument applies to laughter, doesn't it? If there are jokes you wouldn't dream of making yourself, but which you very much enjoy when you hear them in the comic theatre, or even in private company – if you don't regard them as the wrong sort of jokes, or hate them, isn't what you are doing the same as with the things you pity? That element in yourself which wanted to make jokes, but which you kept in check by means of reason because you were frightened of being thought a buffoon, you now release. You don't realize that giving it its head in this way results in your playing the comedian, over and over again, in your own life.'

'Exactly.'

'Doesn't it apply also to sex, anger, and all the desires, pains and pleas- **606d** ures in the soul which we say accompany any of our actions? Isn't the effect of poetic imitation on us the same? It feeds and waters these things, when they ought by rights to wither away. And it makes them our rulers, though if we want to be better and happier rather than worse and more wretched, they ought to be ruled by us.'

'I have to agree with you,' he said.

'In that case, Glaucon, when you come across Homer's admirers saying **606e** that this is the poet who has educated Greece, that he is worth studying both for our general education and for the management of human affairs,

607a that we should learn from him and follow this poet in the arrangement and conduct of the whole of our own lives, then by all means show them the warmth of friendship and affection. They are, after all, excellent people within their limitations. By all means agree that Homer is highly poetic, and first among tragic writers, but be aware that the only poetry we can accept into our city are hymns to the gods and verses in praise of good men. If you accept the honeyed Muse, in song or poetry, pleasure and pain will be twin kings in your city in place of established custom and the thing which has always been generally accepted as best – reason.'

'Very true,' he said.

607b 'Well, since we've brought up the subject of poetry again, let our defence be this. Since that is what she is like, it was not unreasonable of us to banish her from our city. Reason demanded it. And let us say to her, if she looks like accusing us of being harsh or uncultured, that there is a long-standing antagonism between poetry and philosophy. The "howling dog" which "yelps against its master," "great in the empty eloquence

607c of fools," "the mob of wise men who have mastered Zeus," "how subtle thinkers are but beggars yet," and countless other passages, are evidence of their long-standing opposition.[8] And if, despite this, imitation, the poetry which is for pleasure, has any argument to show that she should be included in a well-governed city, let our reply be that, left to ourselves, we would gladly allow her back. We know how beguiling we ourselves find her. But it is wrong to abandon what we believe to be true. Don't

607d you find that as well, my friend? Don't you find her beguiling, especially when it is through Homer that you behold her?'

'Yes, very.'

'So is she entitled to make her return – but only after having defended herself, in lyric or some other metre?'

'Absolutely.'

'And I suppose we might allow those of her defenders who have no gift for poetry, but are lovers of poetry, to speak in prose on her behalf, and tell us she is not only pleasurable but also a good thing – for polit-

607e ical regimes and individual human lives. We'll be good listeners, since I imagine it will clearly be to our advantage if she is shown to be a good thing as well as pleasurable.'

'How can it not be to our advantage?' he said.

---

[8] The sources of these quotations are not known.

'And if they can't tell us that, my dear friend, then we must do what lovers do when they have fallen in love with someone and decided their love is not a good thing. They stay away. It may be a struggle, but they stay away nonetheless. It's the same with us. The love of imitative poetry has grown in us as a result of our being brought up in these wonderful regimes of ours, and this will predispose us to believe that she is as good **608a** and as true as possible. But while she remains incapable of making this defence, we shall recite to ourselves, as we listen to her, this argument we have put forward, as a kind of charm to prevent any relapse into our childish but popular passion. And this will be the spell we shall recite, that this kind of poetry is not something to be taken seriously, as something important, with some bearing on the truth. The listener should be on his guard against it if he is concerned about the regime within him, **608b** and his views on poetry should be the ones we have put forward today.'

Phaedrus

243e–251a[1]

243e SOCRATES: So consider, my fine lad, that the previous speech belonged
244a to Phaedrus the son of Pythocles, from Myrrhinus; but the speech which
I am going to deliver belongs to Stesichorus, the son of Euphemus, from
Himera. It must go like this: 'False is the tale'[2] which says that when a
lover is there, one should favour the non-lover because the former is mad
while the latter is sane. If it were simply the case that madness is an evil,
that would be right enough; but in fact the greatest benefits come to us
through madness, granted by a divine gift. For indeed the prophetess at
244b Delphi and the priestesses at Dodona[3] have conferred very many benefits
on Greece, both to individuals and to states, when possessed by madness, but have done little or nothing when sane. If we were to mention the
Sibyl[4] and all the others who by the use of inspired prophecy have made
many predictions for many people and so set things right for the future,
we would spend a long time saying things which are clear to everyone.

...

---

[1] Socrates and Phaedrus are discussing both rhetoric and love. Socrates has delivered a speech
   arguing that lovers should not be favoured, because they are mad. Stesichorus was a Greek poet
   of the sixth century BC who, according to legend, was struck blind for speaking ill of Helen of
   Troy but recovered his sight when he composed a 'palinode', or recantation.
[2] These words are a quotation from Stesichorus' palinode.
[3] Delphi was the site of the most famous oracle of Apollo in the ancient world. Dodona was the site
   of an oracular oak-tree sacred to the supreme Greek god, Zeus.
[4] A mythical prophetess.

The third kind of madness[5] is the possession and madness which comes   **245a**
from the Muses. It takes hold of a tender and virgin soul, awakening it
and rousing it to frenzy in songs and other kinds of poetry, and it edu-
cates future generations by glorifying countless deeds performed by the
men of old. As for the man who comes to the doors of poetry without the
madness of the Muses, convinced that skill will make him a satisfactory
poet, he lacks fulfilment himself and the poetry of the sane and sober is
eclipsed by that of the mad.

…

The whole account of the fourth kind of madness comes to this: when-   **249d**
ever someone sees beauty here, he is reminded of true beauty,[6] he grows
wings and once his wings have grown he is eager to reach up to it, but
he cannot; he looks upwards like a bird and does not care about things
below, opening himself to the accusation of madness. This is the best of   **249e**
all the inspired states, both in itself and in its origins, both for the one
who has it and for the one who associates with it. It is because he shares
in this madness that one who loves the beautiful is called a lover. For as I
have said, every human soul by its nature has seen a vision of reality, or it
would not have entered into life as a human being. However it is difficult   **250a**
for some souls to use their experiences in this world as a means of recol-
lecting those realities; it is difficult for all those who saw what was there
at that time only briefly, and for those who were unfortunate when they
fell into this world so that they were turned towards injustice by some
of the company they kept and forgot the holiness they had seen at that
time. There remain a few who can remember well enough. These souls,
when they see a likeness of the realities of that world, are amazed and no
longer in control of themselves, but they do not understand what is happening to them because they cannot see well enough. The likenesses in   **250b**
this world of justice and self-control and all the other qualities prized by
souls hold no lustre. Just a few people, using their own weak faculties, go
to their images and behold with difficulty the original of what has been
represented.

---

[5] The first two kinds of madness, mentioned in the omitted passage, are prophetic madness and
the madness of those suffering from an inherited curse (such as Orestes or Oedipus), whose
madness reveals a cure for their suffering.
[6] Plato alludes here, and in what follows, to his theory of recollection (ἀνάμνησις). According to
this theory, when we perceive things in the world of sense-experience we are reminded of the
divine world of Platonic Forms which our souls experienced before they became embodied.

Beauty, on the other hand, could be seen shining brightly when we followed Zeus and when others followed other gods in a joyful dance; at that time we saw a blessed sight and vision and were initiated into that mystery which it is right to call most blessed. We were complete when we celebrated it, with no experience of all the evils which awaited us in the future. We were initiated in complete, simple, calm, happy sights, seeing the vision in a pure, radiant light, pure and unmarked by what we now carry around and call a body, imprisoned in it like a shell.

Let that be a tribute to memory; I have spoken at some length now, because of my longing for what was then. As for beauty, as I said, it shone brightly in that higher world and when we came here we grasped it by the clearest of our senses because it gleams most clearly. For sight is the keenest of our bodily senses. It does not see wisdom and all the other desirable qualities – for wisdom would arouse terrible love and desire if it reached our sight and offered such a clear image of itself. As things are, it fell to beauty alone to be brightest and most desirable. Those who are not newly initiated or who are corrupt do not move rapidly from here to there, to Beauty itself: they gaze at its namesake here, not revering it when they see it but abandoning themselves to pleasure and trying to behave like four-footed beasts and beget children; in their insolence they feel neither fear nor shame at pursuing unnatural pleasure. But whenever the man who is newly initiated, and who saw many of the sights at that earlier time, sees a godlike face or a bodily shape that imitates Beauty closely, first of all he shudders and feels some of the fear of that earlier time; then he looks at it and reveres it as a god. If he were not afraid of being thought completely mad, he would sacrifice to his beloved as if to a statue of a god.

264c

SOCRATES: But I think you would agree to this, at least: every speech should hold together as a self-contained body, like a living creature. It should lack neither hand nor foot but should have a beginning, a middle, and an end, composed in a manner appropriate to each other and to the whole.

Timaeus

28a–29b[1]

So whenever the craftsman looks continually at what is always the same,   **28a**
using something like this as his model, and reproduces its form and character, everything he makes must be fine and beautiful; whenever he looks   **28b**
at what has come into being, using a model that has come into being,
what he makes is not beautiful. As for the world as a whole – let us call it
the cosmos or whatever other name would be most acceptable – we must
first ask the fundamental question that should be asked about everything
to begin with, namely, whether it always existed, with no beginning, or
whether it has come into being, beginning from some starting-point. It
has come into being, for it is visible and tangible and corporeal: all such
things are perceptible and perceptible things, grasped by opinion along   **28c**
with sense-perception, clearly come into being and have been produced.
We say that what has come into being must be produced by some cause.

    It is hard work to discover the maker and father of this universe and
it is impossible to tell everyone about him when he has been discovered.
However we should at least consider this question: which model was used
by the one who fashioned the universe? Was it a model which is always the   **29a**
same and unchanging or a model which has come into being? If this world
is beautiful and its craftsman is good, clearly he was looking at the eternal
model; on the other hand, if it is what one should not even mention, he

---

[1] This passage comes from the beginning of Timaeus' account of the origin of the world, produced by a divine craftsman.

was looking at something which has come into being. It is clear to all that he was looking at the eternal, for the world is the finest and most beautiful thing that has come into being and he is the best cause. Having been produced in this way, the world has been fashioned according to a model which can be grasped by reason and understanding and which is always 29b the same. Since this is the case, this cosmos absolutely must be an image of something else.

Sophist

235c–236c[1]

ELEATIC STRANGER: Following the previous method of classification I think I see two kinds of imitative art here too; but I do not think I can yet tell clearly to which of them belongs the type we are looking for.   235c 235d

THEAETETUS: First explain the distinction between the two kinds you mention.

ELEATIC STRANGER: I see one kind, concerned with likenesses, which I call 'eikastic'. This is the kind used when someone produces an imitative copy following the proportions of the model in length, width and depth, as well as using suitable colours for everything.   235e

THEAETETUS: What? Do not all imitators try to do this?

ELEATIC STRANGER: No, not those who sculpt or paint something large. For you should realize that if they were to reproduce the exact proportions of the limbs, the upper parts would seem smaller than they ought to, and the lower parts would seem larger, because we see the   236a former from a distance but the latter from nearby.

THEAETETUS: Yes, to be sure.

ELEATIC STRANGER: Is it not the case that craftsmen nowadays neglect the truth and give their images not the real proportions but those which seem to be beautiful?

THEAETETUS: Absolutely.

---

[1] In the *Sophist* the Eleatic Stranger and Theaetetus are trying to define what a sophist is. The suggestion that sophists are imitators leads them to discuss kinds of imitative art.

ELEATIC STRANGER: Is it not right, then, to call the first kind of image a likeness, since it is at least like the model?

THEAETETUS: Yes.

ELEATIC STRANGER: And the part of the imitative art concerned with this should be called 'eikastic', as we said before?

THEAETETUS: It should.

236b ELEATIC STRANGER: Well then, what about something which appears to resemble the beautiful but only because it is seen from a viewpoint that is not beautiful? If one became able to see such large things accurately one would see that the object is not even like what it is claimed to resemble. What shall we call this? Should we not call it an appearance since it appears to be like its model but is not really like it?

THEAETETUS: What else?

236c ELEATIC STRANGER: Does this part include a great deal of painting and of the whole imitative art?

THEAETETUS: Of course.

ELEATIC STRANGER: Would we not be quite right to call the art which produces an appearance, rather than a likeness, 'phantastic', that is, concerned with appearances?

THEAETETUS: Certainly.

ELEATIC STRANGER: These, then, are the two kinds of image-making I was talking about, eikastic and phantastic.

XENOPHON

Memoirs of Socrates

3.10.1–8

Whenever Socrates had a discussion with any professional artists, he was helpful to them too. On one occasion he called on the painter Parrhasius and had a discussion with him.

'Does painting produce a likeness of what is seen, Parrhasius?' he asked. 'You imitate hollows and heights, dark and light, hard and soft, rough and smooth, young bodies and old, using colours to give a likeness.'

'That is true,' he replied.

'And indeed when you make likenesses of beautiful figures, since it is not easy to come across one person who is blameless in all respects, you draw on many models, combine the most beautiful aspects of each and so make bodies appear entirely beautiful.'

'Yes, that is what we do,' he said.

'Well then,' said Socrates, 'do you imitate the character of the soul, the most appealing, pleasing, likeable, desirable and lovable part of us? Or can this not be imitated?'

'How could it be imitated, Socrates?' he said. 'It has neither symmetry nor colour nor any of the qualities you mentioned just now, and it is not even visible at all.'

'Well then, can people look at others in a friendly or hostile way?' he asked.

'I think they can,' said Parrhasius.

'Can this then be imitated in the expression of the eyes?'

75

'I agree,' he said.

'Do those who are concerned about the good and bad fortune of their friends have the same expressions on their faces as those who are not?'

'No, by Zeus, they do not,' he said. 'For they beam at good fortune and scowl at bad fortune.'

'So is it possible to represent this too?' he asked.

5   'Yes indeed,' he said.

'Furthermore, the qualities of being grand and liberal, common and mean, self-controlled and prudent, undisciplined and vulgar, are displayed in people's expressions and gestures, whether they are standing still or moving.'

'That is true,' he said.

'So these things can be imitated too?'

'Yes indeed,' he said.

'Do you think it is pleasanter,' he asked, 'to see people who exhibit beautiful, good and lovable characters or those whose characters are ugly, wicked and hateful?'

'By Zeus, it makes a great difference, Socrates,' he said.

6   On another occasion Socrates called on the sculptor Clito and had a discussion with him.

'Clito,' he said, 'I see and understand that you sculpt runners, wrestlers, boxers and pancratiasts¹ of different kinds. The appearance of being alive is what most enchants people who look at statues: how do you produce that?'

7   When Clito was at a loss and took time to answer, Socrates said, 'Do you make the statues appear more alive by making the work look like the figures of living people?'

'Yes indeed,' he said.

'So do you make the parts of the body appear more like the real thing and more convincing by modelling them as concave or convex, compressed or expanded, tautened or relaxed, according to the posture?'

8   'Yes, to be sure,' he said.

'Does not imitating the emotions of people in action also give a certain pleasure to the spectators?'

'I suppose so,' he said.

---

¹ The pancration was a combination of boxing and wrestling.

'So you need to model the eyes of fighters so as to look threatening and imitate the facial expression of those who are rejoicing in victory?'

'Very much so,' said Clito.

'In that case,' he said, 'the sculptor must represent the activity of the soul in his figures.'

ARISTOTLE

Poetics

1.1447a–19.1456b

1 Let us discuss poetry in general and its species. We must discuss **1447a** what each species of poetry can do, how plots should be put together to produce a fine piece of work, the number and nature of the component parts and everything else that belongs to the same field of enquiry. Let us begin in the natural way, with first principles.

Epic, tragedy, comedy, dithyramb[1] and most music for the pipe or the lyre are all, in general, types of imitation. They differ from each other in three ways: in the media used, in the objects of imitation, and in the mode or manner of imitation. Some people use colours and shapes to make imitative likenesses of various things (some achieve this through art, others through practice), while others use the voice[2] as the medium of imitation. Similarly all the arts I have mentioned use rhythm, words and melody as the media of imitation, either separately or together. For example, music for the pipe or the lyre and any other arts that can produce the same effect, such as music for pan-pipes, use only melody and rhythm, while dancing uses rhythm by itself, without melody, for dancers imitate characters, emotions and actions by the rhythm of their movements. To date there is no general name for the arts which use only unaccompanied words or just words and metre, whether a mixture of metres or one particular type **1447b**

---

[1] Dithyramb was a type of lyric poetry sung by a chorus.
[2] Aristotle is probably referring here to the use of the human voice to mimic the noises made by animals and birds.

of metre. For we have no general name covering the mimes of Sophron and Xenarchus and Socratic dialogues,[3] nor any name for all imitations in verse, whether in iambic trimeters or elegiacs or any other such metre. Admittedly, people link the composition of poetry to a particular metre and so refer to some writers as elegiac poets and to others as epic poets, calling them 'poets' not because they produce imitations but because, in a general way, they use verse. Even if they use verse to convey medical matters or natural philosophy, people are used to calling them 'poets'. Yet Homer and Empedocles[4] have nothing in common except the metre they use; that is why it is right to call the former a poet and the latter a natural philosopher rather than a poet. Similarly, even if someone produced an imitation by mixing all the metres together, as Chaeremon did when he composed the *Centaur* as a medley of all the metres,[5] he should still be called a poet. So much for definitions of these points.

There are some types of poetry, such as dithyramb, nomic poetry,[6] tragedy and comedy, which use all the media I have mentioned, namely rhythm, music and metre. They differ in that dithyramb and nomic poetry use all the media at the same time while tragedy and comedy use different media in different parts. These, then, are what I mean by differences between the arts as regards the media of imitation.

1448a 2 The objects of imitation are people doing things. These people must be either good or bad (for just these two categories almost always apply to character since all differences in character are differences in badness or goodness); they must be either better than we are, or worse, or just like us. Compare painting: Polygnotus portrayed people as better than we are, Pauson portrayed them as worse, and Dionysius portrayed them as like us.[7] Clearly each of the types of imitation mentioned above will exhibit these differences and will be distinguished by imitating different objects in this way. These dissimilarities may also be found in dancing and in music for the pipe or the lyre, and also in connection

---

3 Sophron and his son, Xenarchus, from Sicily, wrote prose mimes, presenting scenes from daily life, in the fifth century BC. Prose dialogues in which Socrates appeared as a character were written not only by Plato and Xenophon but also by other followers of Socrates such as Aeschines the Socratic.
4 Empedocles (*c.* 492–432 BC) used the Homeric hexameter to expound his philosophical theories.
5 Chaeremon was a tragic poet, active in the mid-fourth century BC. Little is known about his *Centaur*.
6 Nomic poetry, like dithyramb, was a type of choral lyric.
7 Polygnotus, Pauson and Dionysius were all painters of the fifth century BC.

with words and unaccompanied verse. For example, Homer represents people as better than we are, Cleophon represents them as like us, while Hegemon of Thasos, the inventor of parodies, and Nicochares, the author of the *Deiliad*, represent them as worse.[8] The same applies to dithyrambs and nomic poetry, for example in the difference between Timotheus' imitation of the Cyclopes and that of Philoxenus.[9] There is exactly the same difference between tragedy and comedy, for the latter aims to represent people as worse than those of the present day and the former as better.

3   In addition, there is a third difference, in the mode of imitating each of these objects. For it is possible to imitate the same objects, in the same media, sometimes by telling a story – either becoming someone else, as Homer does, or speaking in one's own person, without change – or else dramatically, with all the characters actively doing things. As we said at the beginning, imitation differs in these three ways, the media, the objects and the mode. As a result, in one way Sophocles is the same kind of imitator as Homer, since they both represent people as good, but in another way he is the same kind as Aristophanes, since they both imitate characters dramatically, in action. Some people say that is why their works are called 'dramas', because they imitate people doing things.[10] That is also why the Dorians claim to have invented both tragedy and comedy. The Megarians claim comedy: those in mainland Greece say that it originated when they had a democracy, and those in Sicily also lay claim to it because Epicharmus, the Sicilian comic poet, was much earlier than Chionides and Magnes. Some of the Dorians in the Peloponnese claim tragedy.[11] In each case they regard the names as evidence. For they say that they call outlying villages *komai* while the Athenians call them

[8] There was a fourth-century BC tragic poet named Cleophon, but Aristotle may be alluding to an otherwise unknown epic poet here. Hegemon wrote epic burlesques in the late-fifth century BC. Nicochares may be the same as the comic poet of that name; his *Deiliad* (a title perhaps derived from δειλός 'cowardly' by analogy with *Iliad*) may also have been an epic burlesque.

[9] Timotheus (*c.* 450–360 BC) and Philoxenus (*c.* 435–380 BC) were both famous lyric poets. Philoxenus' portrayal of the Cyclops Polyphemus was said to be a caricature of Dionysius I, tyrant of Syracuse. Aristotle is presumably contrasting a more serious treatment of Polyphemus by Timotheus with the satirical treatment by Philoxenus but the Greek text is defective here and we cannot be sure just what point Aristotle is making.

[10] The word here translated 'doing' is the Greek verb δρᾶν, which is etymologically connected with the word 'drama'.

[11] Chionides and Magnes were, according to Aristotle, the earliest Athenian comic poets. The Greeks in Megara, in Sicily and in the Peloponnese were all Dorians, speaking a different Greek dialect and observing some different religious festivals from the Athenians.

demes; they claim that comic actors are so called not from *komazein*, 'to
revel', but because they wandered among the *komai*, the villages, when
they were driven out of the city in disgrace. They also say that their word
for 'to do' is *dran* while the Athenian word is *prattein*.

1448b

That is my account of the number and nature of the differences
between types of imitation.

4   In general, there seem to be two causes of poetry, both of them
natural.[12] For imitation is natural to human beings from childhood
onwards and humans differ from other animals in being particularly
imitative and in learning initially by imitation; all human beings enjoy
imitation. We can see this from what happens in practice: we enjoy looking at particularly accurate images of things which we find distressing
to see in real life, such as the shapes of the lowest species of animals or
dead bodies. This is because not only philosophers but all other people
too greatly enjoy learning, even if their capacity for it is limited. That is
why people enjoy seeing images, because, when they look at them, they
have the opportunity to learn and to work out what each thing is, saying,
for example, 'This is so-and-so.' For if one happens not to have seen the
thing before, the image will give pleasure not as an imitation but because
of the workmanship or the colour or for some other reason of this kind.
Imitation is natural to us and so are melody and rhythm (for clearly
metres are segments of rhythm). So from the beginning, those who had
the greatest natural aptitude for these things gradually developed them
and their improvisations gave rise to poetry.

Poetry split up according to the character of the poets: the more serious imitated fine actions and those of fine people, while the more trivial
imitated those of the base, at first composing poems of invective while
the others composed hymns and poems of praise. We cannot name any
author of a poem of this kind before Homer, although probably there
were many of them, but from the time of Homer onwards we know of
poems such as his *Margites* and others like that.[13] The iambic metre came
to be used in these poems, since it suited them; the reason why it is now
called 'iambic' is that the poets used this metre to compose *iamboi*, lampoons, against each other. So some of the poets of old composed heroic

[12] The 'two causes of poetry' are probably the two natural tendencies Aristotle goes on to mention,
the tendency to imitate and the tendency to use melody and rhythm.
[13] The *Margites* was a humorous narrative poem, attributed in antiquity to Homer.

poetry and others lampoons. Just as Homer was the supreme poet dealing with serious subjects (for he alone produced poems which are not only well constructed but are also dramatic imitations) so too he was the first to adumbrate the form of comedy, by dramatizing the ridiculous instead of composing invective. For the *Margites* is to comedy what the *Iliad* and the *Odyssey* are to tragedy. Once tragedy and comedy had appeared, poets turned towards each of these forms in accordance with their own natures: some became comic poets rather than composers of lampoons, while others became tragedians rather than epic poets because the new genres were grander and more prestigious than the old.

 This is not the place to investigate whether or not tragedy is suffi-ciently developed with respect to its formal elements, by examining it both in itself and in its relation to the audience. Tragedy originated in improvisation, as did comedy – tragedy in improvisation by the leaders of the dithyramb, and comedy in improvisation by the leaders of the phallic songs which are still customary in many cities even today. Tragedy grew gradually to maturity and people developed all its features as they came to light. After many changes, it stopped altering since it had attained its true nature.

 Aeschylus was the first to increase the number of actors from one to two; he also made the choral parts less important and gave speech the leading role. Sophocles introduced a third actor and scene-painting. Tragedy also became grander: starting with slight plots and ridiculous language, at a late stage it developed away from satyr-play[14] and became more dignified; the metre became iambic trimeter instead of trochaic tet-rameter. For at first they used trochaic tetrameter because the poetry was satyric and more suited to dancing, but when the spoken word was intro-duced nature herself found the right metre. Iambic trimeter is the metre closest to speech; we can see this from the fact that we very often say things in iambic trimeter in talking to each other, but seldom say things in dactylic hexameters and, when we do so, we depart from the natural tone of conversation. There was also an increase in the number of epi-sodes. Let us pass over how all the other aspects of tragedy are said to have been embellished, for it would probably be a large undertaking to go through them in detail.

14 Satyr-plays were mythological burlesques written and produced by tragic playwrights, for per-formance after a set of three tragedies at the festival of the City Dionysia. The chorus was com-posed of satyrs, lascivious and drunken followers of Dionysus, part-human and part-animal.

5   Comedy is, as we have said, an imitation of those who are worse than we are – not worse in every way but only in being ridiculous: the ridiculous is a species of the base and ugly. For the ridiculous is an error or ugliness which does not involve pain or harm; for example, a funny face is ugly and distorted, but not with pain. We know about the changes in tragedy and who was responsible for them, but not about comedy because at first it was not taken seriously. For the archon granted a chorus for comedy only at a late stage; before that they were volunteers.[15] Comedy already had some of its features by the time of the first recorded comic poets and we do not know who introduced masks, prologues, a number of actors and so on. Plot construction originally came from Sicily [with Epicharmus and Phormis][16] to begin with; in Athens Crates was the first to give up the lampoon form and begin to compose generalized stories and plots.

1449b

Epic poetry goes with tragedy in so far as it is an imitation of good characters in verse; however it differs from tragedy in that it uses just one type of metre and is in narrative form. It also differs in length: tragedy tries as far as possible to keep within one revolution of the sun, or not much more, while epic differs in being unrestricted in time – yet at first poets treated time in the same way in tragedy and in epic. Some of their parts are the same, while others are peculiar to tragedy. That is why someone who knows about good and bad tragedy also knows about epic, for the characteristics of epic are also found in tragedy, but not all the characteristics of tragedy are found in epic.

6   We will discuss the art of imitation in hexameters and comedy later.[17] Let us discuss tragedy, picking up the definition of its essence that emerges from what has been said. Tragedy, then, is an imitation of a good, serious action, complete and exhibiting magnitude, using language that has been made pleasurable in different ways in separate sections of the work, in dramatic, not narrative, form, by means of pity and fear bringing about the purification of such emotions. By 'language that has been made pleasurable'

---

[15] The archon, the magistrate who acted as the Athenian head of state, selected the poets to compete in an Athenian dramatic festival and allocated each one a wealthy citizen who had to pay for the costs of the production, especially the costume and training of the chorus.

[16] Epicharmus and Phormis were early Sicilian writers of comedy; cf. 1448a (p. 81). The names probably do not belong here as they do not fit in to the construction of the sentence in Greek.

[17] Epic poetry ('the art of imitation in hexameters') is discussed in chs. 23ff. (1459a ff.; pp. 102–6). Comedy was discussed in the second book of the *Poetics* which no longer survives.

I mean language which has rhythm and melody [or song], and by 'in different ways in separate sections' I mean that some parts of the play are composed using verse alone while others use song.

Since actors perform the imitation, it follows first of all that designing the spectacle must be a component part of tragedy; then so must song and language, since these are the media in which the actors perform the imitation. By 'language' I mean the actual composition of the verses; it is quite obvious what is meant by 'song'. Tragedy is an imitation of an action, and action is performed by agents who must have some definite qualities of character and intellect (for we say that actions are of a particular kind because of the character and intellect of the agents [– there 1450a are two natural ways of explaining actions, intellect and character –] and that people succeed or fail with reference to their actions). The plot is the imitation of the action – for by 'plot' in this sense I mean the organization of the events in the play, by 'character' I mean that according to which we say the agents are people of a particular kind and by 'intellect' I mean everything they say when demonstrating a point or putting forward a general view. Therefore tragedy as a whole must have six parts, which give it its characteristics. These are: plot, character, language, intellect, spectacle and song. Two of these parts are the media of imitation, one is the mode, three are the objects, and there are no other parts besides these. Virtually all poets, one might say, use these parts, for every play has spectacle, character, plot, language, song and intellect.[18] The most important of these is the structured arrangement of the events in the play, for tragedy is an imitation not of people but of actions and life. [Both success in life and its opposite have to do with action, and the goal of human life is doing something, not just being a certain sort of person. We describe people as being of a certain sort by reference to their characters, but we call them successful or unsuccessful by reference to their actions.] The people in a play do not act in order to imitate character; rather character is included along with and because of the actions. So the events and the plot are what the tragedy is there for, and that is the most important thing of all. Furthermore, there could not be a tragedy without action, but there could be one without character. For the tragedies of most of the modern playwrights lack character and in general there are many poets of this kind. Compare the relationship between Zeuxis

---

[18] The precise text and interpretation of this sentence are uncertain.

and Polygnotus in painting:[19] Polygnotus is good at depicting character but Zeuxis' painting lacks character. Moreover, if someone puts together a series of speeches portraying character, which are well expressed and convey intellect effectively, that will not do what tragedy, by definition, does; a tragedy with a plot and a structured arrangement of events will fulfil its function much better even if it uses these other elements less well. In addition, the most attractive things in tragedy, reversals of fortune and recognitions, are parts of the plot. Another indication is that beginners in writing poetry get language and character right before they are able to arrange events in a structured way; the same may be said of almost all the early poets.

The plot, then, is the fundamental principle and, as it were, the soul of tragedy; character comes second. The situation is much the same in painting, for if someone were to apply the most beautiful colours at random, it would give less pleasure than if he outlined an image in black and white. Tragedy is an imitation of an action and it is mainly because of the action that it is an imitation of the people engaged in it. Intellect comes third. This is the ability to say what can be said in a given situation and what is appropriate to it. Doing this in speeches is the function of politics and rhetoric: the playwrights of old made their characters speak like statesmen while those of the present day make theirs speak rhetorically. Character is the sort of thing which reveals the nature of choice [i.e., what the speaker chooses or avoids, in cases where that is not obvious]. That is why speeches in which there is absolutely nothing which the speaker is either choosing or avoiding do not have character. Intellect is shown in what they say when they either demonstrate that something is, or is not, the case, or put forward some general statement. Language comes fourth. By 'language' I mean, as I said before, verbal expression, which is practically the same thing in both verse and prose. Of the remaining parts which are there to give pleasure, song is the most important; spectacle is attractive but is the least artistic and the least akin to poetry, since the effect of tragedy does not depend on a performance and actors, and the production of visual effects owes more to the stage-designer's art than to the poet's.

1450b

---

[19] Cf. n. 7 above. Zeuxis was another famous painter, active in the late-fifth and early-fourth century BC.

7 Having given these definitions, let us next discuss what the structured arrangement of the events should be like, since this is the first and most important part of tragedy. We laid down that tragedy is an imitation of a complete, that is, whole action, exhibiting a certain magnitude (there can be a whole without magnitude). A whole is that which has a beginning, a middle and an end. A beginning is that which in itself does not necessarily come after something else, but something else naturally exists or occurs after it. An end is the opposite: that which in itself naturally exists after something else, either necessarily or for the most part, but there is nothing else after it. A middle is that which in itself comes after something else and after which another thing follows. Therefore well-constructed plots should not begin or end just anywhere, but should have these characteristics.

Now, to be beautiful, an animal or anything else made up of parts should not only have those parts well ordered but should also not be of a random size. Beauty is a matter of size as well as order. That is why a very small animal would not be beautiful, for our vision becomes confused as it comes close to taking no perceptible time; nor would a very large one such as an animal a thousand miles long, for it could not be seen all at once and anyone looking at it would lose their sense of its unity and completeness. Therefore just as both objects and animals should be of a size which is easy to view as a whole, so too plots should be of a length which is easy to remember. The limits of length determined by the dramatic competitions and by perception are not relevant to the art of poetry; if a hundred tragedies had to be performed, they would time the performances by the clock which is what they say used to be done on other occasions.[20] The limits which accord with the actual nature of the thing are that the longer a plot is, the more beautiful it is, provided it remains clear as a whole. As a rule of thumb, an adequate limit of length is 'long enough for a sequence of events in accordance with probability or necessity to produce a change from bad fortune to good, or from good fortune to bad'.

8 A unified plot is not, as some people think, a plot about one person. For innumerable things happen to one person, and not all of them form a unity. Similarly one person performs many actions and they do not

1451a

[20] The text here is puzzling and probably corrupt. There may be a reference to the practice of allocating a limited time for litigants' speeches in the Athenian courts, measured by a water-clock.

make up a single action. That is why all the poets who have composed a *Heracleid* or a *Theseid* or poems like that seem to be making a mistake; they think that because Heracles was one man, his story too is bound to be one story.[21] Homer especially shows his superiority in his fine understanding of this point, whether by art or by instinct: when he composed the *Odyssey* he did not include everything which happened to Odysseus, such as being wounded on Mount Parnassus or pretending to be mad when the Greek fleet mustered against Troy, neither of which necessarily or probably implies the other.[22] Instead he constructed the *Odyssey* about a single action in the sense I am talking about. The same is true of the *Iliad*. Just as in the other imitative arts an imitation is unified if it imitates one object, so too the plot, as an imitation of an action, should imitate one action, and that a whole one; the parts should be arranged in such a way that the transposition or removal of any one section disrupts and dislocates the whole, for if it makes no evident difference whether something is present or absent, that thing is not a part of the whole.

9 It is clear from what has been said that the poet's task is to relate not what happened but the sort of thing that would happen, i.e., what is possible according to probability or necessity. The difference between the historian and the poet is not that one uses verse while the other does not (it would be possible to put the work of Herodotus into verse and it would be just as much history in verse as in prose). The difference is that the historian relates what happened while the poet relates the sort of thing that would happen. That is why poetry is more philosophical and more serious than history, for poetry tends to make universal statements while history makes particular ones. By 'a universal statement' I mean one which tells us what sort of thing a particular kind of person would probably or necessarily do or say; poetry aims at the universal, though it gives the characters names. By 'a particular statement' I mean, for example, what Alcibiades did or what happened to him. In the case of comedy, this is now clear: the comic playwrights construct their plot from a series of probable events and then supply any names they like; they do not write about particular individuals as the lampooners did. In

1451b

[21] The demigod Heracles (Hercules) and Theseus, legendary king of Athens, were two of the best-known early Greek heroes.
[22] The story of Odysseus being wounded by a boar while hunting is told in *Odyssey* 19.393–466 but is not part of the poem's main plot. The story that he attempted to avoid joining the Greek expedition against Troy by pretending to be mad does not appear in Homer at all.

tragedy the playwrights use real names, because the possible is convincing. We are reluctant to believe that something which never happened is possible but anything which has happened is clearly possible, for it would not have happened if it were impossible. Nevertheless in some tragedies only one or two of the names are well known and the others are invented. In some, such as Agathon's *Antheus*,[23] none of the names is well known; in this play both the events and the names have been made up, and yet it gives just as much pleasure.

So one need not try at all costs to cling to the traditional stories which form the subject matter of tragedies. Indeed, it would be ridiculous to try to do this, since even the well-known stories are well known only to a few but nevertheless give pleasure to everyone. It is clear from all this that the poet should be a maker of plots rather than of verses, inasmuch as he is a poet or maker,[24] because he makes imitations and what he imitates are actions. Even if in fact he writes about things which really happened, he is nonetheless a poet, for there is nothing to prevent some things which really happened from being the sort of thing that would probably happen [and that can happen] and, as a poet, he is concerned with them as probable.

Of simple plots and actions, the episodic ones are the worst. By 'an episodic plot' I mean one in which the sequence of episodes is neither probable nor necessary. Bad poets make plots like this of their own accord and good poets make them on account of the actors; for in trying to succeed in the dramatic competition, they extend the plot beyond its potential and are often compelled to distort the sequence of events.

The imitation is not only of a complete action but also of events which **1452a** arouse fear and pity. These emotions are most likely to be aroused when things happen unexpectedly but because of each other. This will be more surprising than if things happen spontaneously or by chance, since even chance events seem most marvellous when they appear to have happened by design. For example, the statue of Mitys at Argos killed the man who was responsible for Mitys' death by falling on him as he looked at it; we do not think that things like this happen at random. So plots of this kind must be finer.

---

[23] Agathon was a famous Athenian tragedian of the later-fifth century BC. Nothing is known about his play, *Antheus*.
[24] The Greek word ποιητής means both 'poet' and 'maker'.

10   Some plots are simple, others complex, since the actions of which the plots are imitations are naturally of these two kinds. By 'a simple action' I mean one which is continuous and unified in the sense defined, where the change of fortune takes place without reversal or recognition. By 'a complex action' I mean one where the change of fortune is accompanied by recognition or reversal or both. These must arise from the actual structure of the plot, so that they are a necessary or probable consequence of what happened earlier, for there is a great difference between happening as a result of something and happening after it.

11   A reversal of fortune occurs when the course of events changes to the opposite, as described, and that, as we have been saying, in accordance with probability or necessity. For example, in the *Oedipus*, the man who comes to bring Oedipus good news and free him from fear about his mother reveals Oedipus' true identity and so does the opposite; and in the *Lynceus*, Lynceus is being led off to be killed and Danaus is following to kill him but, as a result of earlier actions, it comes about that Danaus dies and Lynceus is saved.[25]

Recognition, as the name indicates, is a change from ignorance to knowledge, tending either to affection or to enmity, on the part of people marked out for good or ill fortune. The finest type of recognition is that which occurs at the same time as a reversal of fortune, as happens in the *Oedipus*. There are other types of recognition too, for a recognition of the kind described may involve inanimate objects, even unimportant ones, and one can also recognize whether someone has done something or not. But the kind of recognition which has the most to do with the plot and the action is the one I mentioned first, for this kind of recognition and reversal of fortune will involve either pity or fear, and tragedy is by definition an imitation of actions that arouse these emotions; moreover recognitions of this kind lead to a happy or unhappy ending.

Since recognition involves more than one person, in some cases only one person will recognize the other, when it is clear who the former

---

[25] Aristotle is alluding here, as also in ch. 18 (1455b), to the *Lynceus* by the fourth-century tragedian, Theodectes. Lynceus was the husband of Hypermestra, one of the fifty daughters of Danaus. Danaus ordered his daughters to kill their husbands. Hypermestra was the only one to disobey: she spared Lynceus and bore him a son, presumably keeping both Lynceus and the child secret. It seems that in Theodectes' play the child must have been found and his parentage discovered; apparently Danaus condemned Lynceus to death but a reversal of fortune took place and Danaus died while Lynceus survived.

is, but in others each has to recognize the other. For example, Orestes recognized Iphigenia from the sending of the letter, but there had to be a second recognition for Iphigenia to recognize Orestes.[26]

So reversal of fortune and recognition are two parts of the plot, and suffering is a third. Reversal of fortune and recognition have been explained. Suffering is an action which involves destruction or pain, such as deaths on stage, extreme physical pain, woundings and things like that.

12   We mentioned earlier the parts of tragedy which should be treated as its formal elements. In respect of quantity, i.e., the separate sections into which it is divided, a tragedy has the following parts: prologue, episode, finale and choral part. The choral part is divided into entry-song and ode. All tragedies have these, and some also contain songs by the actors and dirges. The prologue is the whole section of a tragedy before the entry of the chorus, an episode is the whole section of a tragedy between complete choral songs, and the finale is the whole section of a tragedy after which there is no choral song. Of the choral part, the entry-song is the first whole utterance of the chorus, an ode is a choral song which does not use anapaestic or trochaic metre, and a dirge is a lament shared between the chorus and the actors. We mentioned earlier the parts of tragedy which should be treated as its formal elements, and these are the separate sections into which a tragedy is divided in respect of quantity.

13   What should one aim at and beware of in constructing plots? What is the source of the tragic effect? These are the next points to discuss, following on from what has just been said. The construction of the finest tragedy should be complex, rather than simple; it should imitate events which arouse pity and fear, since that is the distinctive feature of this kind of imitation. It is clear first of all that decent men should not be shown passing from good fortune to ill fortune, since this arouses neither pity nor fear but disgust. Nor should wicked men be shown passing from ill fortune to good fortune as this is the least tragic of all, since it has none of the requisite effects: it fails to arouse human feeling, and is not pitiable or fearful either. Nor again should a very bad man fall from good fortune to ill fortune. Such an arrangement would arouse our human feeling   1453a

[26] In Euripides' *Iphigenia in Tauris* Orestes recognizes his long-lost sister Iphigenia when, not knowing who he is, she gives him a letter to deliver to her brother. Iphigenia in her turn accepts that the man to whom she has given the letter really is Orestes only when he shows knowledge of their home.

but not pity or fear, since we feel the former for someone who does not deserve his misfortunes and the latter for someone like ourselves – that is, pity for someone who does not deserve what happens to him, and fear for someone like ourselves; so this situation will arouse neither pity nor fear. There remains the person in between. This is the kind of person who is not outstandingly good and upright, who passes to ill fortune not through vice or wickedness but because of an error,[27] someone of great reputation and good fortune, like Oedipus or Thyestes[28] or distinguished men from that kind of family.

It follows that the well-formed plot should be simple, not double as some people say; it should involve a change not to good fortune from ill fortune but on the contrary from good fortune to ill fortune, not through wickedness but because of a serious error made by the kind of person discussed, or by someone better than that rather than worse. We can see this from what happens in practice: at first the poets recounted any story that came to hand, but nowadays the finest tragedies are composed about a few families, such as those of Alcmaeon, Oedipus, Orestes, Meleager, Thyestes, Telephus[29] and any others to whom terrible things have happened or who have done terrible deeds. The finest tragedy from an artistic point of view has this kind of plot structure. That is why those who criticize Euripides for doing this in his tragedies, most of which end in ill fortune, are making the same mistake. Euripides' practice is correct, as has been said. The greatest proof is this: on the stage and in the dramatic competitions, such plays are regarded as the most tragic, if they are well presented, and even if Euripides does not organize the rest of the play well, he is nevertheless regarded as the most tragic of the poets.

Second comes the kind of plot structure which some people put first; this is the one which has a double structure, like the *Odyssey*, and ends with opposite outcomes for the good and bad characters. Such a plot is thought to come first because of the weakness of audiences. The poets follow the spectators' lead and write what the public wants. The pleasure

---

[27] 'Error' translates the Greek word ἁμαρτία. There has been much discussion over whether Aristotle here is referring to an intellectual error (a mistake, due to ignorance) or to a moral failing of some kind.

[28] Thyestes unwittingly ate the flesh of his own children, served up to him by his brother Atreus because Thyestes had committed adultery with Atreus' wife.

[29] Alcmaeon had killed his mother, Eriphyle, to avenge his father's death. Orestes killed both his mother, Clytemnestra, and her lover, Aegisthus, to avenge the death of his father, Agamemnon. Meleager and Telephus killed their uncles.

given by this kind of plot belongs to comedy rather than tragedy, for in comedy the characters who are worst enemies in the story – Orestes and Aegisthus, for example – leave the stage as friends in the end and no one kills anybody.

14 Pity and fear may be aroused by the spectacle on stage, but also by the actual structure of the events. The latter is preferable, and the sign of a better poet. The plot should be put together in such a way that, even without seeing the events take place, anyone who hears about them shudders with fear and feels pity at what happens. This is how someone who heard the plot of the *Oedipus* would react. To produce this effect by means of spectacle is rather inartistic and needs external aids. Those who use spectacle to produce something which is merely monstrous, without arousing fear, have nothing to do with tragedy; for one should not seek every kind of pleasure from tragedy but only the pleasure which belongs to it. Since the poet should produce the pleasure derived from pity and fear by means of imitation, clearly this must be entwined with the events.

1453b

What kinds of events, then, appear frightening or pitiable? Let us consider this next. In such actions people must do something either to friends and relatives, or to enemies, or to people who are neither friends nor enemies. If an enemy is doing something to an enemy, what he is doing or going to do does not arouse any pity, except in respect of the actual suffering. The same applies to those who are neither friends nor enemies. The poet should look for situations in which the suffering arises among friends and relatives, as when a brother kills or is going to kill or do something else of that kind to a brother, or a son to a father, or a mother to a son, or a son to a mother. It is not possible to undo the traditional stories, I mean, for example, Clytemnestra being killed by Orestes and Eriphyle being killed by Alcmaeon, but the poet should invent for himself and make good use of the traditional material.

Let us explain more clearly what we mean by 'making good use of'. Sometimes the characters act with knowledge and understanding of what they are doing; the playwrights of old presented them like this and so did Euripides when he portrayed Medea killing her children.[30] Sometimes, on the other hand, a character acts but does the terrible deed in ignorance

---

[30] In Euripides' *Medea* Medea kills her own children to take revenge on their father, Jason, for leaving her and marrying the daughter of the king of Corinth.

and then later recognizes the relationship, like Sophocles' Oedipus. In this case the terrible deed is outside the action of the play, but it can take place within the play itself, as in the case of Astydamas' *Alcmaeon* or Telegonus in *Odysseus Wounded*.[31] A third possibility, in addition to these, is when someone is going to do something irreparable through ignorance but recognizes it before he does the deed. There are no other possibilities, for one must either act or not act, either knowingly or in ignorance. Of these, the worst is the case where someone is going to act knowingly and then does not act. That is disgusting and not tragic, since there is no suffering involved. For that reason, no character behaves like that, **1454a** except occasionally, for example when Haemon does not kill Creon in the *Antigone*.[32] Taking action comes second. It is better to act in ignorance, and then recognize what one has done afterwards, for that is not disgusting and the recognition astounds the audience. The best kind of case is the last, for example when Merope in the *Cresphontes* is going to kill her son, but does not kill him and recognizes him, or when the same thing happens to sister and brother in the *Iphigenia* or when the son in the *Helle* recognizes his mother just as he is about to give her up.[33]

For this reason, as I said earlier, tragedies are about a few families. It was chance rather than art that guided the poets in their search and led them to discover how to produce effects of this kind in their plots; so they are compelled to go to the families in which sufferings of this kind occurred. That is enough about the structured arrangement of events and what plots should be like.

15   In the representation of character there are four things to aim at. The first, and most important, is that the characters represented should be good. Speech or action will have character if, as was said earlier, it reveals the nature of choice; it will have good character if the choice is good. This is possible in every class of person. For there can be a

---

[31] Astydamas was a fourth-century tragedian. In the usual version of the story of Alcmaeon, Alcmaeon kills his mother deliberately but it seems that in Astydamas' version he killed her unwittingly. In *Odysseus Wounded*, a lost play by Sophocles, Telegonus, Odysseus' son by Circe, killed his father, whom he had never seen, in a raid on Ithaca.

[32] In Sophocles' *Antigone* 1231–7, a messenger describes how Haemon, distraught at the death of Antigone, first tried to kill his father, Creon, and then killed himself, in remorse.

[33] The *Cresphontes* was a lost play by Euripides in which Merope tried to kill the stranger who came to claim a reward for killing her son, Cresphontes, but discovered in time that the stranger was in fact Cresphontes himself. Aristotle summarizes the plot of Euripides' *Iphigenia in Tauris* in ch. 17 (1455b; p. 98); cf. also n. 26 above. The *Helle* and its plot are unknown.

good woman, and a good slave, although the former is perhaps inferior and the latter generally low. Secondly, characters should be suitable. For example, the character represented may be brave, but it is not suitable for a woman to be brave, or clever, in this way. Thirdly, they should be lifelike. This is different from making the character good and suitable, in the way that term was used earlier. Fourthly, they should be consistent. Even if the subject of the imitation is someone inconsistent and that kind of character is attributed to him, nevertheless he should be consistently inconsistent.

Menelaus in the *Orestes* is an example of unnecessary wickedness of character. The lament of Odysseus in the *Scylla* and the speech of Melanippe are examples of the inappropriate and unfitting. *Iphigenia at Aulis* is an example of inconsistency, for Iphigenia the suppliant is quite different from the later Iphigenia.[34]

One should always look for the necessary or the probable in the representation of character, just as much as in the structuring of events: it should be either necessary or probable that this kind of person says or does things like this, just as it should be necessary or probable that one thing happens after another.

(Clearly the resolutions of plots too should emerge from the plot itself and not from the artifice of a *deus ex machina*, as in the *Medea* or in **1454b** the proposal to sail away in the *Iliad*.[35] Such artifice should be used for things outside the play, either earlier events which a human being could not know or later events which have to be foretold or reported. For we attribute omniscience to the gods. There should be nothing irrational in the actual events, or, if there is, it should be outside the tragedy, as in Sophocles' *Oedipus*.)

Since tragedy is an imitation of people who are better than we are, we should imitate good portrait-painters. For they portray individual

[34] Menelaus behaves in a cowardly way in Euripides, *Orestes* 682–716. The *Scylla* was a dithyramb by Timotheus (cf. n. 9 above) in which Odysseus lamented the loss of his companions who were eaten by the monster Scylla. In Euripides' lost play, *Melanippe the Wise*, the heroine argued against the popular idea of monsters, displaying the kind of cleverness which Aristotle dismisses as unsuitable for a woman. In Euripides' *Iphigenia at Aulis*, 1211–52, Iphigenia pleads for her life when she discovers that she is to be sacrificed to Artemis but later (1368–1401) she accepts her fate.

[35] At the end of Euripides' *Medea* Medea escapes from Corinth in the chariot of the Sun-god. In *Iliad* 2.109–210 Agamemnon tests the fighting spirit of the Greek army by proposing that they abandon the siege of Troy; the army is only too keen to go but is prevented by the intervention of the goddess Athene.

features and although they make people lifelike, they depict them as finer than they really are. So too when the poet represents people who are inclined to be angry or lazy or other such things, he should depict them as having such characteristics and yet being decent people, just as Homer portrayed Achilles as a model of stubbornness and yet good.

One should look out for these points and, in addition, for those which belong to the perceptions necessarily accompanying poetry, for one can often go wrong in these too. I have said enough about them in my published works.[36]

16   I have already explained what recognition is. The first type of recognition, the least artistic and the one which playwrights use most because they cannot think of anything better, is recognition by means of signs. These signs may be birthmarks, such as 'the spear that the Earth-born bear' or stars like those used by Carcinus in his *Thyestes*,[37] or acquired after birth; some of the latter are physical marks such as scars, while others are external tokens like necklaces and the use of the boat in the *Tyro*.[38] These too can be used with more or less success: for example, Odysseus was recognized by means of his scar in one way by the nurse and in another way by the swineherds. All recognitions of that kind, which are used merely for confirmation, are not very artistic, but those which arise from a reversal of fortune, like the recognition in the bathscene, are better.[39]

Second come recognitions which are manufactured by the poet and are therefore inartistic. For example, Orestes in the *Iphigenia* reveals his own identity; for Iphigenia is recognized by means of her letter, but Orestes says himself what the poet wants him to say, not what the plot requires. This, therefore, is quite close to the fault already mentioned, for it would

---

[36]   The reference to 'my published works' is probably to Aristotle's lost dialogue, *On Poets*. It is not clear what Aristotle means by 'those which belong to the perceptions necessarily accompanying poetry'.

[37]   According to legend, the 'Earth-born' sprang from the dragon's teeth sown by Cadmus, founder of Thebes. Their descendants had a birthmark in the shape of a spearhead. Carcinus was a fourth-century tragedian; we do not know the plot of his *Thyestes* but we do know that a star-shaped birthmark was a characteristic of Thyestes' family (cf. also n. 28 above).

[38]   In Sophocles' lost play, *Tyro*, the boat in which Tyro set her twin sons by Poseidon adrift functioned as a recognition token.

[39]   In *Odyssey* 19.386–475 ('the bath-scene'), Odysseus' old nurse, Eurycleia, unexpectedly recognizes him by a scar when she washes his feet, while in *Odyssey* 21.188–224 Odysseus reveals his identity to the herdsmen Eumaeus and Philoetius and shows them the scar simply to confirm what he has already told them.

have been possible for him to bring some tokens too.[40] Another example is the 'voice of the shuttle' in Sophocles' *Tereus*.[41]

The third kind of recognition is by means of memory, when someone sees something and realizes its significance. For example, in Dicaeogenes' **1455a** *Cyprians* the man bursts into tears when he sees the painting and in the tale told to Alcinous, Odysseus weeps when he hears the lyre-player and is reminded of Troy. In both cases recognition follows.[42]

The fourth kind is recognition as a result of reasoning. For example, in the *Choephoroe* Electra reasons: 'Someone like me has come; no one except Orestes is like me; therefore Orestes has come.'[43] Another example is what Polyidus the sophist suggested about Iphigenia: he said it was likely that Orestes reasoned that his sister had been sacrificed and now it was his turn.[44] Another is in Theodectes' *Tydeus*, when he reasons that in coming to find his son he is perishing himself. Yet another is in the *Sons of Phineus*: for when the women see the place, they reason that they are fated to die there, since that was where they were exposed.[45]

There is also a composite kind of recognition which arises from false reasoning by the audience, for example in *Odysseus the False Messenger*. The idea that Odysseus can bend the bow and no one else can is invented by the poet as a premise, as is his claim that he will recognize the bow, which he has not seen; the audience infer, wrongly, that he will reveal his identity by bending the bow when in fact he does so simply by recognizing it.[46]

The best type of all is recognition arising from the events themselves, when great surprise comes about through probable events, as in

---

[40] See n. 26 above.

[41] Tereus raped Philomela, his wife Procne's sister, and attempted to keep his crime secret by cutting out her tongue. However she told her story by weaving a tapestry which showed what had happened.

[42] We know nothing about the plot of the *Cyprians* by Dicaeogenes, a fourth-century tragedian. In *Odyssey* 8.485–586 Odysseus' weeping when he hears a lyre-player in Alcinous' palace singing about the fall of Troy leads to his telling Alcinous who he is and to the account of his adventures in *Odyssey* 9–12.

[43] Aeschylus, *Choephoroe* 168–234.

[44] It is not clear whether this alludes to a play by Polyidus or to a piece of literary criticism.

[45] For Theodectes, see n. 25 above. We know nothing about his *Tydeus* or about the *Sons of Phineus*.

[46] We know nothing about the play, *Odysseus the False Messenger*, and Aristotle's account is hard to follow. In *Odyssey* 21, Odysseus reveals his identity by stringing the bow, which only he can do. It appears that in the play Odysseus on his return to Ithaca brought a false report of his own death; the audience were led to expect him to establish his identity by stringing the bow, but instead he was accepted simply because he recognized it.

Sophocles' *Oedipus* and in the *Iphigenia*; for her wish to send a letter is probable.[47] It is only recognitions of this type that occur without contrived signs and necklaces. Recognitions as a result of reasoning are the second-best type.

17 A poet should compose plots and work them out in language by putting things before his mind's eye as much as possible. For in that way, by picturing them very vividly, as if he were present at the actual events, he can find what is appropriate and is least likely to overlook incongruities. The criticism made of Carcinus is evidence for this. For Amphiaraus was coming back from the temple, which would have escaped notice if it had not been seen, but fell flat on the stage, because the audience did not like it.[48] One should also, as far as possible, work plots out by using gestures. For, given the same natural ability, those who are actually experiencing emotions are the most convincing: someone who is distressed most authentically portrays distress, and someone angry most authentically portrays anger. That is why poetry is produced by someone with natural talent or by a madman; the former is adaptable while the latter is beside himself.[49]

The poet should set out the story of the play in general terms, whether
1455b it has been used before or whether he is inventing it himself, and then divide it into episodes and extend it. As an example of what I mean by 'considering the story in general' consider the *Iphigenia*: 'A girl was sacrificed and disappeared without the knowledge of those who performed the sacrifice; she was settled in another land in which it was the custom to sacrifice strangers to the goddess and she became the priestess of this rite. Later it happened that the priestess' brother arrived (the fact that the oracle told him to go there, and for what purpose, are outside the plot). When he arrived he was captured and was going to be sacrificed but revealed his identity either as in Euripides' play or as in Polyidus, saying – as was probable – that not only his sister but he too must be sacrificed. So he escaped.' After this the poet should put in the names and construct the episodes. He should take care that the episodes are

[47] Cf. n. 26 above.
[48] Cf. n. 37 above. We know nothing else about the scene referred to here.
[49] If the manuscript text here is correct, Aristotle is tacitly accepting Plato's view of poetic inspiration as a kind of madness. There is however quite a strong case for understanding Aristotle as disagreeing with Plato on this point. In that case the text needs to be emended so as to mean 'poetry is produced by someone with natural talent *rather than* by a madman'.

relevant to the plot: for example, in the case of Orestes such episodes are the fit of madness which led to his capture and his escape by means of the purification.[50]

In plays the episodes are short but in epic they are used to increase the length of the poem. The story of the *Odyssey* is quite short: a man is away from home for many years, kept under observation by Poseidon and all alone; the situation at home is that his goods are being used up by his wife's suitors and plots are being laid against his son; he himself arrives in distress and, after revealing his identity, he attacks and destroys his enemies without being killed himself. This is what is proper to the story; the rest is episodes.

18   Every tragedy has a complication and a resolution. What is outside the play, and often some of what is inside, are the complication; the resolution is the rest. By 'complication' I mean everything from the beginning up to and including the part just before the change from good to ill fortune; by 'resolution' I mean the part from the beginning of the change to the end. For example, in Theodectes' *Lynceus* the complication consists of events before the play, the seizure of the child and the disclosure of the parents, and the resolution is everything from the murder charge to the end.[51]

There are four types of tragedy (just as there are four component parts): complex tragedies which depend entirely on reversal of fortune and recognition; tragedies of suffering, for example, the plays about Ajax and Ixion; tragedies of character, for example, the *Phthiotides* and the *Peleus*; and, fourth, simple tragedies, for example, the *Phorkides*, the *Prometheus* and all the plays set in the Underworld.[52]   **1456a**

The poet should try to include all the component parts, if possible, but if not, he should include most of them and the most important, especially given the way people carp at poets nowadays: since there were

---

[50]   The play by Euripides is once again *Iphigenia in Tauris*. On Polyidus, cf. n. 44 above.

[51]   Cf. n. 25 above.

[52]   There were a number of plays about the heroes Ajax and Ixion, including Sophocles' *Ajax*. There were also several plays about Prometheus, including the *Prometheus Bound* attributed to Aeschylus. The other titles listed by Aristotle here belong to lost plays by Sophocles, Euripides and Aeschylus. The phrase 'simple tragedies' is a conjecture, at a point where the manuscript text does not make sense. The reference to 'four component parts' of tragedy is puzzling; I have taken it that the next paragraph is about the component parts, rather than the four types of tragedy, but this is not clear in the Greek.

99

poets in the past who were good at every part, they expect individual poets to surpass the particular excellence of each of them.

It is right too to say that tragedies are the same or different principally on the basis of their plots, that is, according to whether the complication and resolution are the same. Many poets are good at complication but bad at resolution; one should keep control of both.

One should bear in mind what I have often said and not compose a tragedy out of a body of material suitable for an epic – by 'epic' I mean something involving many stories – as if, for example, someone dramatized the whole story of the *Iliad*. For in epic, because of its length, the parts take on the size that suits them but in plays things turn out quite contrary to what one would expect. There is evidence for this in the fact that everyone who has dramatized the sack of Troy as a whole, not just part of it as Euripides did, or the story of Niobe, not in the way Aeschylus did, has either been hissed off the stage or done badly in the competition; even Agathon was hissed off for this alone.[53]

In reversals of fortune and simple plots poets aim with remarkable skill at the effects they want; this is tragic, and also arouses human feeling. This happens when a clever scoundrel, such as Sisyphus, is deceived, or someone brave but unjust is defeated. This is also probable; as Agathon said, it is probable that many improbable things should happen.

One should regard the chorus as one of the actors; it should be a part of the whole and participate in the action, not as in Euripides but as in Sophocles. In other dramatists, the songs have no more to do with the plot than with any other play; that is why the chorus sings interludes. Agathon was the first to introduce this kind of thing. Yet what is the difference between singing interludes and transferring a speech or a whole episode from one play to another?

19 The other elements of tragedy have been discussed; it remains to consider language and intellect. Intellect may be left to the *Rhetoric*, for it belongs more to that discipline. Under intellect come all the effects to be produced by speech. These include proof and disproof, the production of emotions (for example, pity, fear, anger and so on) and making

1456b

[53] Several dramatists wrote plays, now lost, entitled *The Sack of Troy*. Euripides dealt with just part of the story in the *Trojan Women* and in *Hecuba*. Niobe, mother of a large number of children killed by the gods Apollo and Artemis, was the subject of a famous play by Aeschylus, now lost. On Agathon, cf. n. 23 above; we do not know which play of his Aristotle refers to here.

a thing look important or unimportant. It is clear that, in plots too, one should follow the same principles when it is necessary to produce effects of pity or fear, importance or probability. The only difference is that in the plot these effects must be obvious without explanation, whereas in speech they must be produced by the speaker and come about through what he says. Indeed, what would the speaker's function be, if the necessary effects were obvious without his saying anything?

As for language, one type of enquiry concerns forms of speech. Knowledge of this belongs to the art of performance and to the expert in that field: I mean questions such as what is a command, a prayer, a statement, a threat, a question, an answer and so on. Knowledge or ignorance of these matters does not give rise to any critical censure of poetry which is worth taking seriously. Who would regard the point censured by Protagoras as a real fault? According to Protagoras, Homer thinks he is uttering a prayer but is in fact giving an order when he says, 'Sing, goddess, of the wrath ...',[54] since telling someone to do or not do something is an order. Let us leave that aside, as a subject which belongs to another field.

21.1457b

21 Metaphor is the transfer of a term which belongs to something else, either from genus to species or from species to genus, or from species to species or by analogy. By 'from genus to species', I mean, for example, 'My ship stands here'[55] since lying at anchor is a species of standing. An example of transfer from species to genus is 'Indeed Odysseus has performed 10,000 good deeds'[56] since 10,000 is a large number and is used here instead of 'many'. An example of transfer from species to species is 'drawing off the life with bronze' and 'cutting off water with edged bronze'; here 'drawing off' means 'cutting' and 'cutting' means 'drawing off' since they are both species of 'taking away'.[57] By 'analogy' I mean when B is to A as D is to C, since the poet will say 'D' instead of 'B' and 'B' instead of 'D'. Sometimes poets add the term to which the one replaced is related. I mean, for example, that the cup is to Dionysus as the shield is to

1457b

---

[54] These are the opening words of Homer's *Iliad*.
[55] Homer, *Odyssey* 1.185.   [56] Homer, *Iliad* 2.272.
[57] Empedocles frr. 138 and 143 Diels–Kranz. The first phrase refers to a man being killed with a bronze weapon, the second to water being drawn off in a bronze vessel.

Ares. So the poet will call the cup 'Dionysus' shield' and the shield 'Ares' cup'.[58] Again, old age is to life as evening is to day. So the poet will call evening 'the old age of the day', or will use Empedocles' phrase,[59] and call old age 'the evening of life' or 'the sunset of life'. Sometimes there is no word for one of the four related terms but nonetheless it can be expressed by a comparison. For example, scattering seed is called 'sowing' but there is no term for the scattering of light by the sun. Yet this stands in the same relation to the sun as sowing does to seed; hence the expression 'sowing the god-created flame'.[60] It is also possible to use analogical metaphor in a different way, using the transferred term and denying one of its attributes; for example, one might call the shield not 'the cup of Ares' but 'the wineless cup'.

23.1459a–24.1460b

1459a 23 Let us now consider the art of imitation in narrative verse. Clearly the plots should be constructed dramatically, as in tragedy; that is, they should be concerned with one whole, complete action, with a beginning, middle parts and an end, so that the work produces its proper pleasure, like a single, whole living animal. They should not be put together like histories in which the writer must describe not one action but one period of time, showing everything that happened at that time, whether to one person or more, with each of these events related to the others by chance. Just as two events may take place at the same time, like the naval battle at Salamis and the battle of Himera against the Carthaginians, without in any way tending towards the same end, so too in consecutive times one event may happen after another, with no single end result. Most epic poets construct their plots like this. So, as we have already said, Homer's remarkable superiority to the rest is evident in this respect too: he does not try to portray the whole war even though it had a beginning and an end, for the plot would be too big and not easy to view as a whole or, if it was kept to a moderate length, it would be too complex and varied. As it is, he picks out one part of the story and uses many other parts as episodes, diversifying the poem with the Catalogue of Ships, for example,

---

[58] Timotheus fr. 21 Page (*PMG* 797).
[59] The text here is uncertain and we cannot be sure just which phrase Aristotle is attributing to Empedocles.
[60] The source of this quotation is not known.

and other episodes.[61] Other epic poets, like the poets who composed the   **1459b**
Cypria or the *Little Iliad*, compose poems about one man or one period
of time or one action with many parts. For that reason the *Iliad* and the
Odyssey each supply material for only one tragedy, or at most two, while
the *Cypria* supplies material for many and the *Little Iliad* for [more
than eight, such as *The Adjudication of Arms*, *Philoctetes*, *Neoptolemus*,
Eurypylus, *Beggary*, *Spartan Women*, *The Sack of Troy*, *The Departure of
the Fleet*, *Sinon* and *Trojan Women*.]

24   Epic should have the same types as tragedy: simple, complex, based
on character, or based on suffering. The parts are the same, apart from
song and spectacle. Epic too needs reversals of fortune, recognitions and
scenes of suffering, and its intellect and language should be of fine quality. Homer was the first to use all these elements and he does so in an
exemplary way. Each of his two epics has a different structure: the *Iliad*
is simple and based on suffering, while the *Odyssey* is complex (there are
recognitions throughout) and based on character. In addition Homer is
utterly superior in language and intellect.

Epic differs from tragedy in the length of its plot structure and in its
metre. Length has been adequately defined; one should be able to take in
the beginning and the end in one view. This will be the case if the plot
structures are shorter than those of the ancient epics and comparable in
length to the number of tragedies put on at one sitting.[62] Epic has a distinctive way of considerably extending its length: in tragedy it is impossible
to imitate many parts happening at the same time since one can imitate
only the part which is on stage and being performed by the actors. In epic,
on the other hand, because it is narrated, one can deal with many things
happening at the same time and these – as long as they are relevant – make
the poem more impressive. So epic has the advantage as regards grandeur, variety of interest for the audience and diversity of episodes; lack of
variety quickly palls and makes tragedies be hissed off the stage.

The heroic metre[63] has been found by experience to be suitable for
epic. If anyone were to compose a narrative imitation in any other metre,
or in many metres, it would be obviously inappropriate. The heroic

---

61 The Catalogue of Ships at *Iliad* 2.484–779 belongs to the beginning of the Trojan War rather
    than to its tenth year, in which the main action of the *Iliad* takes place.
62 Three tragedies were normally performed one after the other on one day.
63 I.e., the dactylic hexameter.

metre is the most stately and weighty of the metres. (That is why it is especially receptive of metaphors and foreign words, for narrative imitation is extravagant compared to other types.) The iambic trimeter and the trochaic tetrameter are metres of movement, the former for dancing and the latter for action. It would be even odder if someone were to mix them, as Chaeremon did.[64] That is why no one has composed a long narrative structure in any metre other than the heroic; as we said, nature itself teaches us to choose what is suitable.

1460a

Homer deserves praise for many reasons and in particular because he is the only poet who knows just what he should do in his own person. The poet should say very little in his own person; that is not what makes him an imitator. The other epic poets perform in their own person throughout and imitate little and seldom. Homer however, after a brief prelude, immediately introduces a man or a woman or some other character; none of his figures lacks character, all exhibit it. Although one should aim at astonishment in tragedy, there is more scope in epic for the irrational, which is the most important source of astonishment, because one is not looking at the agent. The scene of the pursuit of Hector would appear ridiculous on the stage – the Greeks standing by and not pursuing and Achilles shaking his head to stop them[65] – but in epic it escapes notice. Astonishment gives pleasure: the evidence for this is that everyone makes additions when telling a story, in the belief that they are giving pleasure.

Homer, in particular, has taught the other poets the right way to tell lies, that is, by using false inference. For people think that, if the truth or occurrence of one thing (the antecedent) implies the truth or occurrence of something else (the consequent), then the truth of the consequent implies the truth of the antecedent. But this is a fallacy. That is why if the antecedent is false but the truth of the antecedent would imply the truth or occurrence of the consequent, the poet should put in the consequent. Because we know that the consequent is true, our mind falsely infers that the antecedent is also true. An example of this can be found in the bath-scene in the *Odyssey*.[66]

Probable impossibilities are preferable to unconvincing possibilities. Stories should not be constructed from irrational parts; preferably they

[64] See n. 5 above.   [65] See *Iliad* 22.131–207.
[66] The fallacy in question is the fallacy of affirming the consequent. For the 'bath-scene' (*Odyssey* 19.386–475) see n. 39 above. Cf. also Aristotle's discussion of *Odysseus the False Messenger* in ch. 16 (1455a; p. 97) and n. 46.

should contain nothing irrational but if they do, it should be outside the plot: the *Oedipus*, for example, has this sort of irrationality in Oedipus' not knowing how Laius died. The irrationality should not occur within the play, like the report of the Pythian games in the *Electra* or the man who comes from Tegea to Mysia without speaking in the *Mysians*.[67] So it is ridiculous to say that the plot would have been ruined otherwise, since one should not construct plots like that in the first place. If the poet does put in an irrationality, and it seems that it could have been presented more rationally, that is absurd as well. It is clear that the irrationalities in the *Odyssey* about Odysseus being put ashore on Ithaca[68] would be intolerable if a bad poet had composed them; as it is, Homer sweetens and obscures **1460b** the absurdity by his other good qualities.

Language should be elaborated in parts where there is no action and which display neither character nor intellect, for excessively brilliant language obscures both character and intellect.

26.1461b–1462b

26 The question might be asked whether epic or tragic imitation is **1461b** superior. If the less vulgar is superior and what is addressed to a superior audience is always less vulgar, it is quite obvious that the art which imitates everything is vulgar. On the assumption that the audience does not understand what the performer does not supply in person, they make lots of movements, like second-rate pipe-players spinning round if they have to imitate throwing a discus or dragging the chorus-leader around if they play Scylla.[69] Tragedy is like that. This is also what earlier actors thought about those who came after them: Mynniscus used to call Callipides a monkey, because he overacted, and people thought the same about Pindarus. The whole art of tragedy is related to epic as these actors are to **1462a** the earlier ones. So people say that epic is addressed to a decent audience who have no need of gestures, while tragedy is addressed to a low audience; if it is vulgar, clearly it must be inferior.

---

[67] In Sophocles, *Electra* 680–763 there is a false report of Orestes' death in a chariot race at the Pythian games; since the Pythian games were founded much later, Aristotle probably regards the anachronism as irrational. Both Aeschylus and Sophocles wrote plays entitled *Mysians*, now lost, in which Telephus could not speak to anyone because he had killed his uncle.

[68] In *Odyssey* 13.116–25 the Phaeacians put Odysseus ashore while he is asleep.

[69] Cf. n. 34 above.

Now, first of all, this criticism applies not to poetry but to performance, since it is also possible to overdo the gestures when reciting epic, like Sosistratus, or when singing, like Mnasitheus of Opus. Secondly, not all movement should be ruled out, any more than all dancing, but only the movement of the low; this is the criticism that was made of Callipides and is now made of others too, on the grounds that they imitate women who are not respectable. Moreover, tragedy produces its particular effect even without movement, just as epic does, for it is clear from reading it what a tragedy is like. So if it is superior in all other respects, this objection does not necessarily apply to it.

Also, tragedy has all the elements which epic has (it can even use its metre) and music [and spectacle] as well, as a significant component which produces pleasure in a most vividly perceptible way. It also has vividness both when read and when performed; furthermore, the end of the imitation is attained in a shorter space: what is more compressed gives greater pleasure than a story diluted by being spread over a great length of time – I mean, for example, if someone were to turn Sophocles' *Oedipus* into an epic as long as the *Iliad*.

1462b

Again, the imitation practised by the epic poets is less unified: the evidence for this is that any epic imitation supplies material for many tragedies. As a result, if they deal with a single plot, it either appears curtailed, when it is presented briefly, or else watery and diluted, when it follows the length appropriate to the metre of epic – I mean, for example, if an epic is made up of a number of actions. The *Iliad* and the *Odyssey* have many parts of this kind which also have magnitude in themselves; and yet the structure of these poems is as good as it could possibly be and as far as possible they are an imitation of a single action.

If, then, tragedy excels in all these aspects and also in artistic effect (for epic and tragedy produce not any chance pleasure but the one that has been described), clearly it must be superior to epic because it attains its end more successfully.

So much for tragedy and epic, the number and differences of their types and component parts, the causes of their success and failure, and criticisms of them and how to answer them.

Politics 8

7.1341b–1342a

We accept the classification of tunes made by some of the philosophers; **1341b**
they say that some are relevant to character, some to action and some to
high excitement and that there is a musical mode naturally appropriate
to each of these, one mode for one tune, another for another. At the same
time, we say music should be used not just for one beneficial purpose
but for several: it should be used both for education and for purification
(as for what we mean by 'purification', the term is used without qualification at this point but we will explain it more clearly in the *Poetics*[1]);
thirdly, music should be used for entertainment, for relaxation and recreation after intense effort. Clearly all the modes should be used but they **1342a**
should not all be used in the same way: the modes most relevant to character should be used for education while the modes relevant to action and
excitement should be used when we are listening to others performing.
The emotions which are strongly felt by some souls are present in all to
a greater or lesser degree – for example, pity and fear, and also excitement. Indeed some people are possessed by agitation of this kind; we see
the effect of sacred music on them when they use the tunes which cause
frenzy in the soul and are restored to health, finding, as it were, a cure
and purification. Those who are inclined to pity, fear and emotions in
general must have the same experience, and so must others in so far as

---

[1] Cf. *Poetics* 1449b (p. 84). The mention of 'purification' (κάθαρσις) there is regrettably brief
however.

107

something of the kind happens to each of them; they all experience a sort of purification and relief accompanied by pleasure. In the same way tunes relevant to action give people harmless enjoyment.

So those who enter competitions in music for the theatre should be allowed to use modes and tunes of this kind. Now, there are two groups of people in the audience: the free and educated on the one hand and, on the other, the vulgar, made up of artisans, labourers and other people of that kind; the latter too must be allowed competitions, spectacles and things like that as recreation. Their souls are, as it were, perverted from their natural disposition; so too there are deviant modes and tunes which are high pitched and use smaller intervals than normal. Each group takes pleasure in what is naturally appropriate to it. That is why those who enter competitions must be permitted to use this kind of music directed at this group in the audience. For education, however, as has been said, tunes and modes relevant to character should be used.

PHILODEMUS

On Poems 5

X.21–XII.9

... I accept entirely that a good poet differs from the one who merely writes well. For one can take an irrational story or subject and elaborate it poetically; there have been some poets like that. But the one who is also selective about his subject matter is thought to be a consummate good poet ...[1]

I accept that some who play the pipe are not good pipe-players and that this fact corresponds to my distinction between one who merely writes well and the good poet, and he is not quibbling when he brings in the musicians as witnesses that he is speaking the truth. He claims that making this distinction divides the matter in hand into two, and that the actual composition of poetry would be more, not less, important. I understand this to be the same as saying that perfect composition is more valuable than wealth of thought.[2]

XIII.32–XV.17

Neoptolemus[3] was wrong to separate stylistic arrangement from thought, while saying that it is neither more nor less important, as we have noted.

---

[1] The next, fragmentary sentence mentions Homer and Sophocles. There follows a gap in the papyrus of almost twenty lines before the continuous text resumes.

[2] It is not certain just whom Philodemus is criticizing here; it may be Heraclides Ponticus, a philosopher of the fourth century BC. As elsewhere, Philodemus objects to his opponent's separation of the form of poetry from its content.

[3] Neoptolemus of Parium, a philosopher of the third century BC, wrote important works on poetry and literary criticism, much used by the Roman poet Horace in composing his *Art of Poetry*.

He absurdly subdivides poetic art into (a) the person who has the skill and ability to write poetry, (b) the poem, and (c) poetry.[4] How could that be? He ought rather to call the examples of composition 'poetry' or, better still, to call the 'poems' works and their 'poetry' something like the webs the poet weaves, and the one who has the skill and works with it 'a poet'. If he calls the working 'poetics', when that is the name of the art, he does not know what he is talking about. And it is ridiculous to say that 'the poet' is a subdivision of this. His statement that only the subject matter belongs to 'poetry' is also astonishing, since the 'poem' and everything in general belong to 'poetry'. For a piece of 'poetry' is also a 'poem' – the *Iliad*, for example – but the first thirty lines of this are a 'poem' but not 'poetry'. Equally astonishing is the claim that only the stylistic arrangement is part of the 'poem' and not the thoughts[5] ... actions and presentation of character. If he says something has been perfectly composed in respect of style, here too, by Zeus, it cannot have been perfectly composed without these other features; it seems to me that the arrangement of the action belongs with the arrangement of the style. I pass over the fact that both the subject matter and the arrangement also belong to 'the poet'; he is the one who composes all of them.

XVI.28–XVII.31

I turn now to the adherent of Stoicism.[6] I would not deny that, as a composer of treatises, he is contradictory, hasty and verbose, and what he says is false. What about his contrasting the kind of poetry which is neither good nor bad with good and bad poetry, as if this was a clever idea? What about his calling poetry which has good arrangement and worthwhile thought 'good'? He defines worthwhile thought as 'mostly when poems present good thoughts and deeds' or as the thought in poems that aim at education – but no poet has ever written or will ever write poems that contain such thoughts.[7] But he claims that he accepts as good not only that sort of thing but also poems in which the poets discover their

[4] For Neoptolemus, the term 'poem' apparently referred to style, form and versification, 'poetry' to subject matter and meaning.
[5] A word is missing in the papyrus at this point.
[6] Some lines are missing at this point. It has been suggested that the Stoic attacked by Philodemus here is Ariston of Chios, a philosopher of the third century BC, but this is far from certain.
[7] Philodemus' point here seems to be that for a Stoic such a poet would have to be a Stoic 'wise man', but the Stoics themselves said such wise men were either very rare or did not exist.

own explanations of the subject matter; according to this argument, he says, we will even say some of the poems of Antimachus are educational.[8]

XXXIII.24–XXXIV.33

Imitating Homer and similar traditional poets well would seem not to make Homer and his like worthwhile poets, since they did not imitate themselves. This does not grasp the common notion of good poetry nor do we understand this to be the excellence of poetry[9] ... Someone could say that justice is the imitation of Aristides, goodness the imitation of Phocion, wisdom the imitation of Epicurus, political skill the imitation of Pericles, painting the imitation of Apelles and so on,[10] and the opposite would apply to bad qualities. That makes the judgement of a fine poem completely arbitrary and undefined. Imitating Homer and Euripides and similarly admired poets in all things would not seem sensible. Perhaps we will not even be able to recognize poetry which has imitated these poets appropriately, if we do not know what 'the appropriate' is. But those who offer this explanation will think nothing more ridiculous than that claim. For we shall enquire what it is that makes some poets admired and in what respects they should rightly be imitated.

---

[8] Antimachus of Colophon was an epic poet, active around 400 BC. Ancient literary critics often contrasted him unfavourably with Homer. Following Asmis in *Apeiron* 23 (1990) 168–9, I take it that Philodemus' opponent here regarded Antimachus' poetry as educational because he offered edifying explanations of the myths he recounted.

[9] The next few lines of the papyrus are not fully legible.

[10] Aristides 'the Just' and Phocion, like Pericles, were famous Athenian politicians of the fifth or fourth centuries BC. Apelles was a famous fourth-century BC painter.

On Music 4

Col. 78.3–45[1]

The statement that the parts of the soul must be in proportion with the emotions and with the body is stupid and confused and the extra phrase, 'still more with each other', is completely confused. It is impossible to have a clear conception of the parts of the soul as being in proportion with each other ...[2]

Music is no more able to move the emotions than anything else which pleasantly tickles our senses. Some say that we are tamed by music because our souls are softened and their ferocity is removed, but we should regard these people as very silly indeed. Our reason teaches us that nature has not produced any of the terrible things invented by our folly, none of whose products is very important. It is only reason that can tame us perfectly, when it is perfect, and offer proportionate relief when it is progressing towards perfection.

Cols. 91.3–92.5

Since we have shown it to be completely false that music imitates the emotions that Diogenes has mentioned and that their imitation in music

[1] Here, as in all but the last of the extracts from *On Music*, Philodemus is attacking the views of Diogenes of Babylon, a Stoic philosopher of the third–second century BC.
[2] About fifteen lines here are fragmentary or missing.

produces any benefit as regards virtue, any more, indeed, than imitation in any of the arts which are ten thousand times more imitative, we shall not accept ...[3]

It is also unnecessary to spend time on what follows. Let us grant that 'what is most important for the impulse[4] towards the beautiful is enjoying and liking the right things' and, leaving aside what comes in between, 'enjoying things in moderation' and that 'by means of pleasure music brings us to enjoy things as we should'; however, we hold that music no more 'develops our affinity to pleasure' than fine cooking or perfumery do.

Cols. 115.44–117.35

Sense-organs which are similarly disposed do not agree that an object is bitter and then disagree over whether it is painful or pleasurable; they make the same judgement. In the case of these senses, at least, it is possible for perceptions of quality to vary according to their predispositions, but in the case of organs of hearing there is no difference at all; these all have the same grasp of the same tunes and experience similar pleasures.[5] So as regards enharmonic and chromatic music[6] people disagree, not about the irrational perception of quality, which is not subject to reason, but about how to interpret that perception. Some people, like those close to Diogenes, claim that the former is dignified, noble, simple and pure while the latter is unmanly, vulgar and slavish; others call the former harsh and masterful and the latter gentle and persuasive – both attribute qualities which neither type of music possesses. Others again, who take a more scientific view, tell us to pick out the aural qualities in both types of music since, according to them, nothing which is attributed to either of them properly belongs to it, at least, I repeat, if we consider the nature of hearing. Similar points apply to rhythms and to music for lyric poems ...[7]

---

[3] About twenty-five lines here are fragmentary, missing or not readily capable of translation.

[4] 'Impulse' (ὁρμή in Greek) is a technical term in Stoic philosophy of action.

[5] As an Epicurean, Philodemus believes that sensations occur when atoms given off by an object make contact with the atoms of our sense-organs. Such sensations are immediately pleasurable or painful. In touch and taste, our perceptions vary depending on the state of the atoms in the sense-organ but he claims that this is not the case for hearing.

[6] The terms 'enharmonic' and 'chromatic', used by Aristoxenus in the fourth century BC and in later Greek musical theory to distinguish different harmonic structures, seem to be used here more generally to distinguish two types of music with different ethical characteristics.

[7] About ten lines here are fragmentary or missing.

For this reason the musician who seeks the kind of understanding by which he will be able to discover the dispositions of the different sense-organs is looking for knowledge of things which do not exist – and he is passing on advice about this to no purpose – since no tune which, as a tune, is not subject to reason can rouse a soul 'from immobility when it is at rest'[8] or 'lead it to the natural disposition in its character', nor can it 'soothe it and calm it down when it has been agitated and moved in one direction or another', nor is it 'able to turn it from one impulse to another' nor 'strengthen or weaken its existing disposition'. For music is not something imitative, as some people imagine in their dreams, nor does it, as Diogenes claims, have qualities which resemble qualities of character since these cannot be imitated. According to him, music 'completely displays all the qualities of character so as to include magnificence and humility, courage and cowardice, moderation and boldness': it no more exhibits these than cookery does!

Cols. 121.22–122.36

Now, changing the subject, I turn to one of Diogenes' conclusions, that 'from its origins the tune naturally has something which makes us move and stirs us to action'. If he says it has been introduced by Providence for this purpose, this is not the right moment to examine the question, but if he claims this is true of a tune in the same way as it is of fire, which we say is naturally capable of burning because it has a nature which is capable of burning, he is uttering falsehoods which should not even be thought of. To moved to action is to have an impulse and to make a choice but the tune does not even urge us on, as they claimed, and is not thought to produce acts of choice ...[9]

In his definition of the tune he said it 'naturally made us move'. He seems to be drawn to such a stupid suggestion by the fact that particular musical instruments are closely associated with rowers on ships, in the old days with those who were gathering the harvest or making wine and with many other workers completing arduous tasks. According to him, Ptolemy did this for those who were launching his ship.[10] But in fact those

---

[8] Here, and in what follows, Philodemus is partly quoting Diogenes of Babylon.

[9] About four lines here are fragmentary or missing.

[10] It appears from the parallel passage at col. *41*.25–8 that Diogenes referred to an anecdote about Ptolemy I Soter, king of Egypt 305/4–282 BC, who gave orders to the pipe-player Ismenias to ease the launching of his ship by playing music for the workers.

who provide the music do not do this because the tunes make people move and stir them to action, nor is that the reason why the workers complete their task in a given amount of time and achieve less without music. The real reason is that they stop paying attention to their labours and perform them with a light heart because of the admixture of pleasure. Even if we do not accept the story that Orpheus charmed rocks and trees by his outstanding ability to sing and play at the same time (even today we are used to talking about him in this exaggerated way) – even if, like the Stoic, we envisage him, like a pipe-player on a warship,[11] in charge of a team of builders, we will say this for the reasons given above, not for the nonsensical reasons given by Diogenes.

Col. 124.1–28

We only have Diogenes' word for it that the poem of Crexus,[12] although quite well put together, seems much more dignified with the addition of the tune and that the hymns sung at Ephesus[13] and those sung by the choruses at Sparta will have quite a different effect if the tune is taken away. He thought these examples sufficient to show that music moves us more than words do. He has not considered that there is an easy response to this. One answer will be that the tune makes no further contribution to dignity and rational representation of the divine but only adds pleasure for the ear; another will be that the change occurs because of the additional honour which our minds bestow on gods and men, not because of the tune; yet another, perhaps, will be that this is indeed what happens but the meaning of the poem is actually erased when it is sung.

Cols. 136.27–137.13

Diogenes writes that there is an analogy between music and poetry as regards imitation and, particularly, invention. He could not show this to

[11] The pipe-players on a Greek warship (a 'trireme') gave the time to the rowers. It appears from this passage and from the parallel at col. *41.21–5* that Diogenes rationalized the story of Orpheus charming rocks by his music, following a version in which it was builders, not stones, who responded to his playing.
[12] Crexus introduced musical accompaniment in the dithyramb, a type of choral song.
[13] The festival of the goddess Artemis at Ephesus included contests in music and poetry.

be the case as regards imitation; as regards invention there is no more analogy between music and poetry than between music and the other arts. In so far as the tune is written down and then reproduced in performance, I grant that there is some analogy with literature. Why object to his concerning himself with that kind of analogy? If ... as regards singing and playing the cithara ...[14] let us also grant that there is an analogy with performance by an actor or an orator. But let us say that if music has a clear affinity in all respects with intuitive grasp and reflective understanding, it seems necessary to us that not only those arts but also painting and sculpture should be eagerly practised, for they too have analogies to these qualities of mind and possess several characteristics related to understanding, as do many other arts.

Col. 142.1–35

Unless they want to say things comparable to what one can find in Cleanthes[15] who says: 'The examples offered by poetry and music are of permanent value' and 'The discourse of philosophy has sufficient ability to proclaim matters both divine and human but when written in prose it lacks language appropriate to divine grandeur, whereas epic and lyric poetry, and rhythms, come as close as possible to the truth of contemplation of the divine.' It is difficult to find a more ridiculous statement! It is not the case that thoughts are of no benefit, nor that when they are set to music stimulation comes from both sources – for indeed considerable stimulation comes from the thoughts on their own – nor does it become stronger when there is a musical accompaniment. Someone trying to be fair will say the stimulation is equal; however someone strictly correct will say it is weakened and that there are many reasons for this, including the pleasure, the distraction produced by that and by the loudness and particular characteristics of the sounds, the fact that the words are uttered in continuous sequence rather than following their natural division and the places and situations in which we are listening.

---

[14] A word is missing before 'as regards singing and playing the cithara' and the best part of a line is missing after these words.
[15] One of the earliest Stoic philosophers (331–232 BC) who wrote a famous 'Hymn to Zeus'.

CICERO

On Rhetorical Invention

2.1.1–3

1   Once upon a time the people of Croton, when they abounded in wealth of all kinds and, according to the common opinion, shared the good fortune of the most successful nations of Italy, wanted to adorn the temple of Juno, which they cared for most piously, with outstanding paintings. For this purpose they employed Zeuxis of Heraclea, hired for a high price. At the time it was considered that he far surpassed all other painters. Now he also painted many other pictures: some of them survived down to our own time because of the sanctity of the shrine. In addition, he announced his wish to paint an image of Helen, in order to capture the supreme example of female beauty in his picture. This was welcome news to the people of Croton, who had often heard that he far exceeded others in painting the female body. They thought that, if he applied great effort in the area where he was most talented, he would leave them a celebrated work of art in that temple. Nor were they disappointed in their expectations. For Zeuxis immediately asked them who their most beautiful girls were. In their turn, they immediately led the man to the palaestra and showed him many very handsome[1] boys. For the inhabitants of Croton at one time greatly excelled in physical strength and handsome appearance, and to great acclaim brought home most glorious victories from athletic competitions. Now while he was greatly admiring the bodily beauty of

1

2

---

[1] Cicero uses the term *dignitas* for male beauty, just as he does in *On Duties* 1.36.130 (p. 138).

the boys, they said to him: 'These boys have maiden sisters who live here. So you can tell by looking at them how good-looking their sisters are.' 'So please bring me,' said he, 'the most beautiful of those girls, while I am painting what I promised you, so that true likeness may be transferred

3   into a lifeless copy from the living original.' Then the people of Croton, by public decision, gathered the girls in one place and gave the painter the opportunity to choose the girls he wanted. He picked five. Many poets immortalized their names, because they had received a stamp of approval from the artist who was supposed to have been the most reliable judge in matters of beauty. At the same time, he did not believe that he could find in one body all that he thought was required for beauty, since nature did not give a perfect finish to any individual within one kind. And so, as if she would have nothing to give to the others if she lavished it all on one, nature bestows or withholds different gifts, depending on the individual.

On the Ideal Orator

3.25.96–26.101

25 A speech is adorned, first of all, by giving it a general character **96** through, as it were, its own particular colour and flavour. For to make a speech serious or pleasant, erudite, noble, admirable, or polished, to add just enough feeling and passion, is not a task of particular segments: it is something that shows in the whole body. However, a further sprinkling, as it were, of flowers of speech and ideas does not have to be distributed evenly over the whole oration, but should be concentrated so as to create the impression of gems sparkling throughout ordinary ornaments. One **97** must, then, choose the general character of speech that would capture the attention of the audience most, and that would not only delight, but also delight without saturation ... It is difficult to explain why those things **98** that arouse most pleasure in our senses, and most acutely move them at first sight, are also the fastest to repel us through aversion and satiation. For the most part, how much greater is the beauty of colour and fresh-ness of variety in recent paintings compared to old ones! Nevertheless, although they captivate us at first glance, pleasure does not linger, while at the same time we are riveted to ancient depictions with their rough and old-fashioned look. In singing, how much more sweet and delicate are modulations and falsetto notes compared to more austere and stable tones! At the same time, if they occur frequently, not only those of severe taste, but the whole crowd voices its displeasure.

99 The same is apparent in other senses: thus our delight in ointments with an intensely sweet scent is short-lived compared to those that are moderately fragrant; what has a subtle smell[1] is praised higher than that which reeks of saffron, and even in the case of touch there is a certain limit to the pleasurableness of softness and smoothness. But what about taste, the most voluptuous sense of all, which is more sensitive to sweetness than the other senses? How quickly does it reject and cast off that which is excessively sweet! Who can enjoy sweet drink or food for a long time? At the same time, one easily avoids saturation in both if they tease **100** the sense only lightly with pleasurable sensation. In this way even the greatest pleasure borders on aversion in all experiences. Therefore it should not surprise us that the same is observed in speech. For whether it is a poet or a rhetorician, in either case we observe that if a speech is flowing, striking, ornate, pleasant, but at the same time steady, without interruption or variety – no matter what bright colours are used to adorn this speech or poetic creation – it cannot keep us in a continuous state of delight. And the swiftness with which the orator's or poet's curls and make-up become offensive is due to the fact that, while our senses become satiated by extreme pleasure naturally, and not through the intellect, as regards written and spoken words the vice of over-ornamentation is detected not only by the ear, but also by the judgement of the mind.

101 **26** For this reason, while I do not mind comments such as 'great!' and 'brilliant!' about my own speech, I do not like to hear 'pretty!' or 'charming!' too often. And although I would welcome, as a frequent remark, 'it could not be better!', this reaction of admiration and highest praise during a speech should be tempered by some background shading, so as to allow what is highlighted to stand out in the foreground.

3.45.178–46.181

178 **45** But just as nature itself fashioned many other things in this remarkable manner, so it did for speech: i.e., those things that are most useful also have much dignity, and often even much elegance. This state of the whole world and nature, as we see it, is for the sake of its preservation and wholesomeness: i.e., that the heavens are of a spherical shape; that

[1] A compromise translation between the readings *ceram* (smell of 'wax', contained in the MSS) and *terram* (smell of 'earth' restored from other sources).

the earth is positioned in the centre where it is held by its own natural tendency; that the sun circles around the earth, sinking to the sign of the winter solstice[2] and then gradually ascending to its counterpart; that the moon receives the sunlight as it advances and retires; that the five stars[3] complete similar courses around the earth, except moving by uneven paths. This arrangement is of such a nature that the slightest change in **179** it would make it impossible for it to hold together, and of such beauty that it would be impossible to think of a more elegantly decorated shape. Now let us look at the form and shape of the human being or even of the other animals. You will find no body part attached without some important function, yet the whole form is put together, as it were, in an artful fashion and not haphazardly. **46** And what about trees? Their trunks, branches and leaves exist precisely for the purpose of maintaining and preserving their nature, and at the same time no part ever lacks charm. Let us leave nature alone and look at the crafts. What is more func- **180** tional in a ship than the concave sides of the hull, the bow and stern, the sails, the sailyards and masts? And at the same time they have so much elegance in their external shape that they seem to have been designed not only for their useful function, but also for the purpose of providing aesthetic pleasure. Columns hold up temples and porches: at the same time, there is as much dignity in them as utility. The gabled roof of the Capitol and other buildings was designed because it was necessary, not for its elegance. However, after its objective had been achieved, i.e., to allow rainwater to run off the roof on both sides, its usefulness for the temple resulted in the dignified appearance of the gable-roof. So now, even if the Capitol were to be erected in the heavens where there could not possibly be any rain, it seems that it would lose its dignified look without its gabled roof. The same phenomenon is also observed in all **181** elements of speech, i.e., that utility and functionality is accompanied by some charm and elegance.

3.50.195–51.198

50 Nor should one be surprised by how well an uneducated crowd **195** perceives these things when listening: some amazing power of nature is also present here, as in all other areas. For all possess a certain inner

---

[2] Capricorn.   [3] I.e., wandering stars, or planets.

sense that allows them, without any training in art or artistic principles, to make a judgement about the principles in various arts and whether something corresponds to them. This happens even regarding paintings and statues and other artefacts, although we are less adequately equipped by nature for the appreciation of these things. But the trend is much more prominent as regards the judgement of words, metres and musical tones: indeed, these belong to the common sensory domain of which, **196** thanks to nature, no one is completely deprived. As a result, it is not only artfully composed words that move everyone, but also metres and musical tones. How many people are really knowledgeable in the art of metres and musical scales? At the same time try to make even the smallest mistake in these matters, e.g., cut a sound a bit shorter or protract it a bit longer, and the whole theatre roars in indignation! And does not the same happen regarding the musical tones in singing, when not only choruses but even soloists singing out of tune are hooted off the stage by the ordinary crowd?

197   **51** It is amazing how much of a difference there is between an expert and an uneducated person in terms of performance, and yet how little in terms of judging it! Indeed, artistic skill has a natural origin,[4] and it does not seem to achieve anything if it fails to draw on its natural sources to move and delight us. And nothing is so akin to our natural feelings as metres and musical tones, which excite us, set us on fire, but also calm us down and relax us, and incline us to both joy and sadness.[5] They achieve their greatest power in songs and chants: a fact that was well known, it seems to me, to our most learned king Numa and our ancestors, as can be gleaned from the use of string instruments and pipes during solemn feasts and the verses of the Salii. However the point was most widely **198** recognized by the ancient Greeks ... Now just as the crowd hears a fault in a verse, in the same way it senses anything lame in a speech. However, while there is no mercy for the poet, they make allowances for us orators. Nonetheless, while they maintain silence, they still notice that something that we said is unfitting or imperfect. Granted that those ancients (just as we see some speakers doing even today), when they could not compose a well-rounded period – for, indeed, we acquired the ability or the

---

[4] Cf. Augustine, *On True Religion* 30.54 (pp. 220–1).
[5] This idea is very common to the ancient theory of music: cf., for example, Plato, *Republic* 3.398–9 (p. 47).

courage to employ these only recently – used only three or two, or even just one word per clause. Still, even in their rhetorical infancy they were able to maintain that natural quality which the human ear demands, i.e., that their clauses be of equal length and that they use regular breathing intervals.

Orator

7 **2** However, in creating an imaginary perfect orator I will picture such as perhaps has never existed. For I do not seek to name a particular great

8 orator, but to describe that unsurpassable ideal … For I maintain that, no matter how beautiful a thing of any kind is, it cannot eclipse in beauty the prototype of which it is an impression, as in the case of an artistic impression of some face. This ideal cannot be perceived by the eyes, ears or any other sense, but we grasp it in our mind. So we can imagine something that is more beautiful than those paintings that I mentioned, or the statues of Phidias, which in our actual visual experience have no rivals

9 in their kind. Nor did this artist, when he was working on the images of Jupiter or Minerva, have a visual prototype in front of him of which he could make a likeness, but some exquisite form of beauty was present in his own mind. It is through contemplating this form of beauty and focusing on it attentively that he could direct his artistic hand towards creating its likeness.[1]

    3 Accordingly, just as in sculpture and painting there is something perfect and excellent whose contemplated shape serves as a point of reference in creating the images of those things that are not themselves visible to the eye, in the same way we conceive in our minds the ideal of

---

[1] Here Cicero modifies Plato's theory of art as an imitation of real objects and presents it as an imitation of an idea in the mind of the artist. Cf. Seneca, *Letter* 65 (p. 142).

perfect eloquence, but with our ears we perceive only its copy. Plato – a   **10**
formidable authority and master not only in the area of thought but also
of speech – calls these forms of things 'ideas', denies that they ever come
to be, and maintains that they exist always and reside in our reason and
intellect. Other things arise, decline, are in a flux and unstable, and cannot exist in the same state for a long time. Therefore, whatever is to be
discussed rationally and methodically must be reduced to the ultimate
form and type of its kind.

21.70–22.74[2]

21 However, the foundation of eloquence, just as of other things, is wis-   **70**
dom. For just as in life, so in a speech nothing is more difficult than to
discern what is fitting. The Greeks call this *prepon*, and we rightly call
it *decorum* (the fitting); much excellent advice exists about it, and it is a
subject that is very well worth knowing. Indeed, not knowing it leads to
errors not only in life, but very often also in poems and speeches. For   **71**
the orator must be mindful of what is fitting, not only in his arguments,
but also in his words. For not every social condition, not every office,
not every level of authority, not every age, location or time or every audience can be approached by using the same kind of words or arguments.
One must always consider what is fitting in every part of a speech, as
one does in life: this depends on the matter under consideration, as well
as on the personality of the speakers and the audience ... **22** Now in   **73**
all things one must be mindful of limits. And although everything has
its proper measure, nevertheless too much offends more than too little. For this reason Apelles also criticized those painters who had no
sense of what was enough ... for 'one ought to' refers to fulfilling one's   **74**
duty, which one must follow always and in all things, but 'it is fitting'
means to be, as it were, appropriate and suitable for time and person.
This principle most often concerns both what we do and what we say,
and furthermore our facial expressions, gestures and gait, the opposite
of which is 'unbecoming'. Now if the poet – who already offends even
when he puts the honourable words of a wise man into the mouth of a
villain or a fool – avoids this as the greatest flaw; if, furthermore, that

---

[2] Cf. Cicero, *On Duties* 1.27.93–9 (pp. 136–7), which supplies additional information on *decorum* in
speech.

painter[3] saw that in the scene of sacrificing Iphigenia, where Calchas was sad, Ulysses sadder yet and Menelaus lamenting, Agamemnon's head had to be wrapped up because the painter's brush was not capable of depicting that highest degree of grief; if, finally, the actor seeks what is fitting, what would we think the orator is supposed to do?

51.173

For the whole theatre cries out in disapproval if even one syllable in a verse is pronounced shorter or longer than it is supposed to be. Yet the crowd is not knowledgeable about poetic metres, nor can it count syllables, nor does it understand what the fault is, or why and how exactly it displeases them.[4] Nevertheless nature has endowed our ears with the ability to make judgements regarding long and short sounds in syllables, just as it gave us the ability to discern high and low pitches of musical tones.

53.177–8[5]

177 Once we have established who the pioneers and inventors of well-composed speech are, whom I just mentioned, and we have found the origin of it, let us look for its cause. Now its cause is so evident that I am surprised that the ancients missed it, especially since, as it happens, often they would say something aptly and well by chance. Surely when such a phrase stirred the ears and minds of the audience so as to make it clear that that chance remark had a pleasing effect, one would expect them to notice the general tendency and keep reproducing it. Indeed, the ears, or rather the mind through the ears, possesses in itself some natural

178 capacity for measuring all sounds. Accordingly, it can judge what is long or short and always expects something complete and well proportioned.

---

3 Timanthes of Sicyon, a Greek painter of the fourth century BC, a contemporary of Parrhasius and Zeuxis. None of his works survive. However there is a first-century AD Roman copy of 'The Sacrifice of Iphigenia', discovered at Pompeii and now in the Museum at Naples.

4 'or why ... displeases them': I translate according to the reading *aut cur aut in quo offendat intelligit* contained in 9 MSS. An alternative reading from one MS *aut curat ut in quo offendit intelligat*, translated as 'nor does it care to understand what exactly the fault is', assumes a less favourable view of the 'crowd'.

5 Cicero here speaks of using metres in prose speeches. Cicero's account of how the art of metres came to be is closely paralleled by Augustine's account of the invention of artistic principles in *On True Religion* 30.54 (pp. 220–1).

Thus it senses that some sounds and speech patterns are too short and, as it were, mutilated, and it takes offence, as if it were deprived of something due to it. At the same time, others are too long and, as it were, unbounded, which our ears detest even more. (Indeed, in speech, just as in most other areas, what is excessive offends more than that which is deficient.) Therefore, just as poetry and verse[6] arise from the judgement of the ears observed by perceptive people, in the same way in speech it was noticed (much later, to be sure, but on the same natural grounds) that there are certain fixed sequences and concluding cadences of words.[7]

55.183–4

The fact that a certain rhythmic principle, or metre, is present in speech 183
is easily noticed. For it is our sensory faculty itself that makes this judgement, which forces us to acknowledge the actual experience even if we cannot find the reason why this happens. For even verse itself was not at first recognized by reason, but by our sensory faculty acting naturally, while reason later explained what happened through measurements. Thus taking good notice of natural tendencies gave birth to art. However, metres are more pronounced in verse, although even there, if we deprive certain poetic metres of their musical accompaniment, they would appear to be mere speech. This is most evident among the best of those poets that are called 'lyric' by the Greeks: if the musical element is removed, their verses almost become plain speech. There are some similar examples 184
even among our own authors, e.g., this line in *Thyestes*:[8]

> What thus should I call you? Who, old and decrepit …

and what follows. These lines, unless accompanied by a flautist, sound almost exactly like plain speech. Also, the senarii[9] of the comic poets are often so down-to-earth on account of their likeness to common speech that at times it is hard to detect rhythm and verse in them. This is why it is all the more difficult to identify rhythm in prose than in verse.

---

[6] MSS give several textual variants here which do not affect the general meaning.
[7] I.e., metric *clausulae*.
[8] Cicero is quoting from Ennius' lost tragedy *Thyestes*. The metre here is bacchius ($\cup$ − −), difficult to identify and, due to the nature of Latin quantitative verse, difficult to illustrate in English.
[9] The senarius is a form of trimeter that contains three metra of two iambic feet each.

On Moral Ends

2.14.45

Thus under excellent (*honestum*) we understand something that is such that, apart from all utility, it could rightfully be considered praiseworthy in itself, without any promise of rewards or gains.[1] And its nature can be understood not so much through the definition that I used – although it can be to some extent – as through the common judgement of all and the occupations and deeds of all really good people, who do very many things for that one reason alone that the deed is appropriate, that it is right and that it is honourable and noble, even though they expect no benefit to follow from it.

2.14.47

After mentioning these three kinds of excellence (*honesta*), there follows the fourth[2] that possesses the same beauty and arises fittingly from the above three, in which there is order and moderation, so that perceiving its likeness in the beauty and dignity of material forms, one passes over

---

[1] The theory of *honestum* (τὸ καλόν) introduced through Cicero's *On Moral Ends* and *On Duties* (pp. 135–9), and in particular the claim that all καλόν is good, was the cornerstone of Stoic ethics although the idea itself dates as far back as Plato (cf. *Timaeus* 87c). The usual translations of *honestum* as 'honourable' or 'morally right' miss the aesthetic overtones, so the current translation renders the term and its derivatives according to the context as 'excellent/excellence', 'noble/nobility', or 'fine', which all preserve some of the aesthetic sense.

[2] I.e., *decorum*.

to the nobility (*honestas*) of what is said and done. Indeed, thanks to those three praiseworthy qualities that I mentioned above, one both dreads rashness and is careful not to harm anyone by an insolent statement or action, at the same time being anxious not to do or say anything that would appear less manly.

On the Nature of the Gods[*]

2.5.15[1]

The fourth and, surely, the greatest proof is the uniformity of motion in the revolution of the heavens, as well as the distinctive character, variety,[2] beauty and order of the sun, the moon and all the stars. The very sight of these things, according to him [i.e., Cleanthes], sufficiently indicates that they are not fortuitous. Consider the case when someone happens to enter a house or a gymnasium or a market-place, and sees the rational arrangement, measure and design in all things. He will not decide that these happened to be like this without a cause, but will think that there is someone who is in charge of all this and to whom all this is subject. All the more so, observing such great movements and alternations, the ordered arrangement of so many bodies of such great magnitude, which have never erred over boundless and infinite periods of time, one would decide that such great natural motions must necessarily be governed by some mind.

---

[*] The cosmological proof of the existence of the gods from the order and beauty of the universe also appears in other texts, such as Cicero, *On the Ideal Orator* 3.178–9 (pp. 120–1); Plato, *Timaeus* (pp. 71–2); Seneca, *On the Award and Reception of Favours* (pp. 144–5); and Augustine, *On True Religion* 29.52 (p. 219).

[1] Cleanthes' fourth proof of the existence of gods.
[2] Reading *varietas* (instead of *utilitas*) with Manutius and some of the MSS.

2.6.17[3]

Now it will not even cross your mind, should you happen to see a great and beautiful house (even though you could not see its owner), that it was built for[4] mice and weasels, will it? Then if you were to consider a world so lavishly adorned, such great variety and beauty of heavenly things, such great power and size of the sea and lands to be your dwelling, and not that of the immortal gods, would you not clearly seem to be insane?

2.7.18–19

But surely of all things nothing is better than the world, nothing more **18** stable, nothing more beautiful:[5] moreover, not only is there nothing better but no such thing can even be thought of. And if nothing is better than reason and wisdom, these are of necessity present in the world, which we concede to be the best. What now? Considering such a harmonious, con- **19** tinuous intimate connection and accord among things, who would not be forced to agree with what I say? Otherwise could the earth blossom at one time and then at regular intervals look rough and horrid? Or, given all the changes in things, could one know the exact position of the sun through summer and winter solstices? Or could ocean tides and narrow-ness of channels be governed by the rising and setting of the moon? Or could the diverse courses of the stars be preserved by the unified motion of the whole sky? All this clearly could not happen, with all parts of the world in harmony with each other, were it not governed by one continu-ous divine spirit.

2.34.87

So let someone demonstrate that the world could have been better; but no one will ever be able to do so, and should anyone wish to correct

[3] An opinion of Chrysippus.
[4] Another possibility is 'by mice'; however a dative of indirect object expresses the meaning better, and the latter part of the paragraph, which indicates that the world is the home *for* the gods, not for humans, supports the dative.
[5] Cf. *On the Nature of the Gods* 2.22.58: '... that the world is most fit for continuous existence; also, that it lacks nothing; however, mostly that it possesses extraordinary beauty and every sort of ornament'; 2.22.60 mentions the 'most beautiful form' of the world.

something, he will either make it worse or desire something impossible. But if all parts of the world have been put together in such a way that they could neither be more useful nor more beautiful in appearance, let us see if they happened to be like this by chance or whether their state is such that they could in no way cohere, were it not for some governing intelligence and divine providence. Now if those things that are accomplished by nature are superior to those produced by art, and if art does not make anything without applying reason, nature too should not be considered devoid of reason. For how does this make sense, to recognize the presence of art when one sees a statue or a painted picture, or to have no doubt, after seeing a ship sail from afar, that it moves by reason and skill, or to understand, upon seeing a sun-dial or a clepsydra, that it indicates the hours through art and not by chance, yet at the same time to consider the world, which embraces those very works of art, and their artificers, and all in its entirety, to be devoid of purpose and reason?

2.57.145–58.146[6]

145 **57** In addition, all human senses are far superior to those of animals. First of all, the eyes perceive many things more subtly in the arts that are judged by eyesight: painted, sculpted and engraved forms, as well as the movement and postures of bodies. Moreover, the eyes judge the beauty, order and, so to say, appropriateness of colours and shapes; but they judge other more important things as well, for they perceive both virtues and vices, recognizing angry, gracious, joyful, sorrowful, brave, **146** cowardly, daring and timid expressions. **58** Next, there is an admirable and artful judgement of the ears that judges the variety of tones, intervals and differences of pitch in the sound of the voice or of wind and string instruments, as well as the numerous kinds of voice qualities – sonorous or hoarse, smooth or rough, low or high, modulated or sustained – which can be judged only by human ears.

---

[6] As opposed to the usual opinion that animals have better, i.e., keener senses (cf. Augustine, *On True Religion* 29.53; p. 220), Cicero stresses that human sensation is more attuned to modulations and patterns in aesthetic forms.

Tusculan Disputations

4.13.28–31

For just as there are diseases, infirmities and flaws in the body, the same **28** is observed in the soul. Disease is the corruption of the whole body, infirmity is disease with weakness, flaw is when the parts of the body do not fit properly with each other, whence follows crookedness, distortion and deformity of the limbs. And in this way these two, disease **29** and infirmity, result from disturbance in the health of the body as a whole, while a flaw stands out as something on its own, even if health as a whole is intact. But as regards the soul we can distinguish disease from infirmity only in our mind, while fault or vice is a wayward disposition that affects and disturbs one's whole life. So it happens that one type of corruption of mental powers leads to disease and infirmity, and another to disturbance and dissent ... And just as the nature of the **30** soul is analogous to the body when conditions are unfavourable, so it is when things turn for the better. For just as there are such qualities as beauty, strength, health, firmness and swiftness in the body, so there are such qualities in the soul. Just as the balanced composition of the body, when those elements of which we consist agree with each other, is called bodily health, so, when judgements and opinions in the soul are in agreement, this is called its health, which is the same thing as virtue, which some pronounce to be precisely this balanced composition ... And just as there exists some fitting shape of bodily members with some **31**

sweetness of colour, which is called beauty, so the uniformity and consistency of opinions and judgements in the soul – which, together with
some firmness and steadfastness, results from virtue or even contains
the very essence of virtue – is called beauty.

On Duties

1.4.14–15[1]

Nor is this an insignificant arrangement of nature and reason, that this **14** living being alone [i.e., man] perceives what order is, or what the appropriate thing is, or what proper limits exist in deeds or words. In the same way, no other living being senses the beauty, charm and harmonious arrangement of parts in those things that are perceived by sight. Now our natural capacity and reason, drawing an analogy between the visual domain and the soul, judge that beauty, regularity and order must be even more carefully observed in decision-making and actions, and try to avoid doing anything in an unbecoming or effeminate way ... These things taken together produce that excellence (*honestum*) which we seek: which ... as we say, is praiseworthy by nature, even if it is not praised by anyone. Here you see, my son Marcus, the very form and, as it were, face of excel- **15** lence, 'which, if it were to be perceived by our eyes', as Plato says, 'would arouse wondrous desire' for wisdom.[2] But the excellent can be reduced to four kinds: it consists in the ability to perceive truth and in intelligence, or in preserving human society by rendering to each what is his due and being faithful in keeping agreements, or in the firmness and greatness of an elevated and unconquered spirit, or in the order and proper limits

[1] Cicero's (originally Stoic) idea that our aesthetic experience of the beauty of things leads to preserving the beauty of speech and morals has direct parallels in Plato's *Republic* 3. 400d–e (p. 49) and 401c–d (p. 50) as well as much later in Kant.
[2] *Phaedrus* 250d (p. 70).

of all that is done or said, in which there is moderation and due balance. And although these four are tightly linked and connected to each other, nevertheless taken separately they yield particular kinds of obligations.

I.27.93–9

93 It remains to discuss one last variety of excellence (*honestas*) where one sees modesty and, as it were, some adornment of life, as well as temperance, moderation, complete calming of the soul's passions and due limits in things. Here is contained that which can be called *decorum* (the fitting) in Latin, but is called *prepon* in Greek: whose nature is such that it can-

94 not be separated from the excellent or fine (*honestum*). For both what is fitting is fine and that which is fine is fitting: it is easier to understand the difference between fine and fitting than to explain it. For whatever is fitting shows itself only when excellence is already present. In this way that which is fitting appears not only in this subdivision of excellence of which we are speaking now, but also in the aforementioned three. For it is fitting to use reason and speech prudently and do what you do considerately, as well as discern and preserve the truth in all matters. On the contrary it is as unfitting and indecorous to be mistaken, err, fail and be deceived as to be mad or delirious. In the same vein, all just things are fitting, and the unjust, on the contrary, are ugly and therefore unfitting. The nature of courage fits the same pattern. For whatever is done in a manly way with a greatness of spirit is worthy of a man and appears fitting, and that

95 which is done to the contrary is ugly and therefore unfitting. Therefore that which I call fitting, first of all, pertains to all excellence and, moreover, pertains in such a way that it is immediately evident, and not perceived by some obscure reasoning. For there is, indeed, something – and it is perceived in every virtue – that is fitting: which can be more easily distinguished from virtue conceptually than in reality. Just as the charm and beauty of the body cannot be distinguished from health, so this fitting, about which we speak, is totally blended with virtue, though at the same time distinguishable from it conceptually by the mind.

96 There are two subdivisions of the fitting. For we can think of a universal type of appropriateness which is found in all excellence, but also of a specific type subject to the first one, which pertains to particular varieties of excellence. And the former type is usually defined in this sort of way: the fitting is that which is in accord with human excellence

as regards those areas where human nature differs from that of other animals. As for the latter type, subordinate to this universal genus, it is habitually defined in the following way: the fitting is that which is so in accord with nature that in it moderation and inner harmony become manifest with a noble appearance. That it is understood this way we can **97** deduce from that ideal of the fitting that the poets follow (of which kind much is written elsewhere).[3] But we say that the poets preserve what is fitting precisely when a certain character does or says what is appropriate for the represented person. For example, if Aeacus or Minos[4] were to say 'let them hate, as long as they fear'[5] or 'behold, the father is himself the grave for his sons' it would seem unfitting, for we believe them to have been just. At the same time when Atreus[6] says that, it generates applause: for the speech is appropriate for the person. Now poets will determine what is fitting for whom on the basis of a particular character. In our case, however, it is great nature itself that gave us the ideal of character that surpasses in excellence that of all other living things.

Therefore poets, among the great variety of characters, will perceive **98** what is appropriate and fitting even for flawed individuals. As for us, to whom nature has assigned the role of steadfastness, moderation, temperance and modesty – moreover since the very nature instructs us to pay attention to the way we behave regarding other people – it happens that we are able to perceive clearly both the broadly dispersed type of the fitting that pertains to excellence or fineness as a whole, and the fitting that is observed in any particular kind of virtue. For just as the beauty of the body moves the eye by a fitting arrangement of its members and delights by the very fact that all parts harmonize with each other with a certain gracefulness, in the same way what is fitting, which shines forth in life, brings about the approval of those with whom we live through order, steadiness and moderation in all words and deeds. Therefore one must show certain respect towards people, not only **99** those of the best kind, but also others. For to disregard someone's personal feelings is not only arrogance but a mark of complete carelessness. For there is some conceptual difference between the human notions of

---

[3] I.e., in treatises on poetics and rhetoric, cf. *Orator* 21.71 (p. 125).
[4] Sons of Zeus, supposed to have been so just and good during their lives that after death they were made judges of the dead.
[5] Words of Atreus from Accius' *Atreus* (also quoted in Seneca, *On Anger* 1.20.4).
[6] Atreus killed the children of his brother Thyestes and fed the flesh to their father.

justice and modesty. Justice demands that one not harm people, modesty that one not offend them. It is in this latter that the nature of the fitting shines through most powerfully. This having been said, I think that we made it sufficiently clear what it is that we call 'to be fitting'.

1.35.126–36.130

126   **35** This fitting shows in all that is said and done, and in addition in the motion and posture of the body, and consists of three things: shapeliness, order and adornment appropriate for the action (these things are difficult to articulate but it will be sufficient to understand what they are). Our concern to be approved by the people with whom or among whom we live relates to these three, so let us say a few words about them. First of all, nature itself seems to have created a great design for our body by placing in plain view our external shape and the rest of the forms that exhibit noble appearance, but at the same time concealing and hiding away the bodily parts that, although necessary for natural operations, end

127   up being misshapen and ugly to look at. It is this careful craftsmanship of nature that the human sense of modesty imitates. For whatever nature has concealed, all sane people also hide from view and engage in certain necessary activities in the most secretive ways possible. Also, neither the bodily parts that perform such functions, nor the functions themselves, are called by their proper names. Thus that which is not shameful to perform, so long as it is done in a concealed way, is nevertheless obscene to name. So it is impudent either to engage in such activities openly or to use obscene speech to describe them.

128   Nor should one listen to the Cynics, or, for that matter, to those Stoics who were close to the Cynics, who condemn and ridicule the fact that we consider it shameful to name those things that are in fact not disgusting, while we call by their proper names the things that are really shameful. Thus robbery, fraud, adultery are actually disgraceful but the terms for them are not indecent. At the same time, to produce children is a noble activity, but the name for it is obscene. And they say many similar things when arguing against modesty. As for us, let us follow nature and avoid anything that is abhorrent to the judgement of our eyes and ears. Let our posture, walk, sitting and lying down positions, facial and eye expressions, as well as hand movements, observe the principle of the fitting.

Among those things there are two that one should avoid the most: any- **129**
thing effeminate or unmanly on the one hand, or boorish and rustic on
the other. Nor should one allow actors and orators – as if it were appropriate for them – what is dissolute to us ... **36** There are two kinds of **130**
beauty: one of them contains charm, and the other dignity. We should
consider charm a feminine quality, and dignity a masculine one. For this
reason one should both remove all ornament unsuitable for a male from
one's external appearance and avoid a similar flaw in posture and motion.
For wrestling motions are often unappealing, and some gestures of actors
are full of silliness, and in both cases we praise what is simple and to
the point. The dignity of form should be supplemented by good colour,
which is maintained through the exercise of the body. In addition, one
must preserve a certain neatness: not too pronounced so as to become
offensive, but only to the point of avoiding rustic and uncivilized carelessness. The same principle should be observed regarding one's clothing, in which, just as in other things, avoiding extremes is best.

1.40.145–41.146

40 However that which is seriously incompatible with civilized behaviour, **145**
such as singing in a public place or some other serious misbehaviour, is
immediately evident and does not require a great deal of admonishing
or instruction. However, it is those seemingly lesser breaches, not easily
detected by many, that we must more carefully avoid. As is the case with
the string and wind instruments, where an expert usually detects even the
slightest dissonance, in the same way in our life we must be careful lest
something perchance sound out of tune: nay, rather a lot more careful,
given that the consonance of actions is more important than, and superior to, that of sounds. **41** So, just as musicians' ears sense even the slight- **146**
est changes in the sound of string instruments, in the same way all of us,
should we decide to turn our attention towards a keener perception of
vices, will often detect something greater by looking at something small.
Indeed, from the expression of the eyes, frowning or relaxing of eyebrows,
from the sad or joyful expression, laughter, verbosity or reticence, from
the raised or lowered voice and other similar signs, we can easily discern
which of these happen in an appropriate manner, and which deviate from
nature and from what is appropriate. In this situation it is quite advan-
tageous to form an opinion about these sorts of signs by observing other

people, so that we could ourselves avoid what we find unbecoming in them. For it happens somehow that we have a better chance of detecting what is aberrant in others, rather than in ourselves. That is why students easily improve if their teachers imitate their mistakes for the purpose of correcting them.

SENECA

Letters to Lucilius

Letter 65.2–10

As you know, our own Stoics proclaim that there are two principles in   **2**
nature that are responsible for the existence of everything: cause and
matter. Matter is something inert in the state of rest, ready to become
anything, which would remain idle if nothing moved it. At the same time,
cause, or reason,[1] shapes matter and moulds it into whatever it wishes,
producing various things out of it. Therefore there must be the material out of which something is produced, and then the agent of production: the former is the matter, the latter is the cause. All art consists in   **3**
imitation of nature; therefore apply what I said about the world in general
to human products. Thus in the case of a statue, there is both matter that
is subject to the activity of the artist, and the artist who gives external
shape to matter. In a statue bronze is the matter and the sculptor is the
cause. All things share the same condition: they consist of that which
becomes and of that which produces.

The Stoics believe there is one kind of cause: that which produces.   **4**
Aristotle[2] thinks that 'cause' is predicated in three different ways: 'the
first cause', he says, 'is the matter itself, without which nothing can be
produced; the second is the producer; the third is the form, which is
impressed on every product, as on a statue'. That last one Aristotle calls

---

[1] Seneca's *ratio* here translates the Stoic term λόγος: a universal principle that permeates and
sustains all of the universe.
[2] Cf. Aristotle, *Physics* 2.3.194b16–195a3; 7.198a14–b10; *Metaphysics* 1 (A).3.983a24–b3.

eidos (form, shape). 'And the fourth cause,' he says, 'added to these three,
5 is the projected purpose of the product as a whole.' I will clarify what this
all means. The bronze is the first cause of the statue, for it would never
have been produced had there been nothing to cast and make it from. The
second cause is the artist: for that bronze could not have been moulded
into the shape of a statue without any help from skilled hands. The third
cause is the form. Indeed, that statue would not have been called 'The
Man with the Spear' or 'The Man tying up his Headband' if this or that
particular shape had not been given it. The fourth cause is the projected
purpose of production: for if it did not exist, the product would never
6 have been made. What is this purpose? That which attracted the artist,
that which he aimed at when he made the statue. And this is either the
money, if he made it for sale, or glory, if he worked to make a name for
himself, or piety, if he was preparing a gift for a temple. Therefore this
is also a cause: 'that for the sake of which' something is produced. For
surely you must admit that something, without which a product would
never have been produced, must be counted among its causes?
7   To these four, Plato adds a fifth: the exemplar or model which he himself calls *idea*. For it is this that the artist contemplated as he carried out
what he had planned. And it does not really matter for the present discussion whether the artist had an external exemplar, which he could look
at, or an internal one, conceived and set up by the artist himself. God has
such exemplars of all things within himself, and his mind encompasses
the number and measure of all that needs to happen. He is filled with
these shapes that Plato calls *ideai*: immortal, immutable, indefatigable.
So, although individual humans die, nevertheless humanity itself – in
accordance with which a human is shaped – remains forever, and suffers
8 nothing, even though humans struggle and perish. Accordingly, there are
five causes, as Plato says: that from which, that by which, that in which,
that in reference to which, and that for the sake of which. Finally, we
have that which results from them all. For example, as regards the statue
(for we initially started with the statue) 'that from which' is the bronze,
'that by which' is the artist, 'that in which' is the form that is given to it,
'that in reference to which' is the exemplar that the maker imitates, 'that
for the sake of which' is the goal of the maker, and 'that which results
9 from them all' is the statue itself. All these five also apply to the world,
as Plato says: the maker, that is, god; 'that from which', or matter; the
form, which is the condition and orderly arrangement of the world as we

see it; the exemplar, contemplating which god created a work so beautiful and of such a magnitude; the goal, 'for the sake of which' he created it. You may ask what god's goal is? Goodness. This at any rate is what Plato says:[3] 'what reason did god have for creating the world? He is good. And someone who is good can grudge no good at all. Therefore he created this world as good as he was able'.

10

---

[3] Cf. *Timaeus* 29d7–e3.

On the Award and Reception of Favours

4.22.2

Clearly, in the case of fulfilling your moral obligations, a great reward is in the deed itself. Indeed, the power of the noble to attract human minds is immense: its beauty inundates souls and, charmed, they are seized with admiration for its light and splendour.

4.23.1–24.1

1 **23** Is there any doubt that the course and circumstances of human life are governed by the circular motions of the sun and the moon? That the heat of the former nourishes bodies, soothes the lands, eliminates excess moisture and breaks the harshness of winter that arrests everything, while the penetrating and powerful warmth of the latter controls the ripening of crops? That human fertility is affected by its movement? Or that the former's circular course measures out the observable year, while the 2 latter's smaller circles create months? However, to put aside those useful aspects, would not the sun by itself provide a suitable spectacle for the eyes that is worthy of reverence, even if all it were doing was to go by? And would not the moon be worthy of esteem, even if it were only passing by, an idle star? How many times through the night does the cosmos itself pour down its lights and glimmer with such a great multitude of innumerable stars, keeping everyone fixed on the show? And who thinks 3 of any profit while admiring these things? Look at these great multitudes

gently sliding along their course above our heads: how they conceal their speed behind the facade of a motionless structure at rest! How much happens during this night that you simply regard as the divider that sep-arates days! What a great number of events unfolds under the cover of silence! What a thread of destinies is spun with such precision! Each of 4 those things that you think are scattered about for decoration only, has a function of its own ...

24 What? You would not be taken by the sight of such a great magni- 1 tude, even if it did not protect, guard, cherish, generate and nourish you by its spirit? For just as these things are extremely useful, necessary and vital, but nevertheless it is their majestic appearance that fills the whole mind at once, in the same way virtue of any kind, and especially that of a grateful soul, is certainly of great benefit, but this is not what it is cher-ished for! Indeed, even if the reason why virtue is classified as useful is not always understood adequately, still it possesses something more than its benefit (and it is this 'more' that makes it attractive).

LONGINUS

On Sublimity

1–2

1 My dear Postumius Terentianus,

You will recall that when we were reading together Caecilius'
monograph *On Sublimity*,[1] we felt that it was inadequate to its high subject, and failed to touch the essential points. Nor indeed did it appear to
offer the reader much practical help, though this ought to be a writer's
principal object. Two things are required of any textbook: first, that it
should explain what its subject is; second, and more important, that it
should explain how and by what methods we can achieve it. Caecilius tries
at immense length to explain to us what sort of thing 'the sublime' is, as
though we did not know; but he has somehow passed over as unnecessary
the question how we can develop our nature to some degree of greatness.
However, we ought perhaps not so much to blame our author for what he
has left out as to commend him for his originality and enthusiasm.

You have urged me to set down a few notes on sublimity for your own
use. Let us then consider whether there is anything in my observations
which may be thought useful to public men. You must help me, my friend,
by giving your honest opinion in detail, as both your natural candour and
your friendship with me require. It was well said that what man has in
common with the gods is 'doing good and telling the truth'.

---

[1] Caecilius of Caleacte was an influential critic, active in the first century BC. Most of our knowledge of his views about sublimity has to be inferred from Longinus' refutation.

3   Your education dispenses me from any long preliminary definition. Sublimity is a kind of eminence or excellence of discourse. It is the source of the distinction of the very greatest poets and prose writers and the means by which they have given eternal life to their own fame.

4   For grandeur produces ecstasy rather than persuasion in the hearer; and the combination of wonder and astonishment always proves superior to the merely persuasive and pleasant. This is because persuasion is on the whole something we can control, whereas amazement and wonder exert invincible power and force and get the better of every hearer. Experience in invention and ability to order and arrange material cannot be detected in single passages; we begin to appreciate them only when we see the whole context. Sublimity, on the other hand, produced at the right moment, tears everything up like a whirlwind, and exhibits the orator's whole power at a single blow.

1   2 Your own experience will lead you to these and similar considerations. The question from which I must begin is whether there is in fact an art of sublimity or profundity. Some people think it is a complete mistake to reduce things like this to technical rules. Greatness, the argument runs, is a natural product, and does not come by teaching. The only art is to be born like that. They believe moreover that natural products are very much weakened by being reduced to the bare bones of a textbook.

2   In my view, these arguments can be refuted by considering three points:

(i)   Though nature is on the whole a law unto herself in matters of emotion and elevation, she is not a random force and does not work altogether without method.

(ii)   She is herself in every instance a first and primary element of creation, but it is method that is competent to provide and contribute quantities and appropriate occasions for everything, as well as perfect correctness in training and application.

(iii) Grandeur is particularly dangerous when left on its own, unaccompanied by knowledge, unsteadied, unballasted, abandoned to mere impulse and ignorant temerity. It often needs the curb as well as the spur.

3   What Demosthenes[2] said of life in general is true also of literature: good fortune is the greatest of blessings, but good counsel comes next, and the lack of it destroys the other also. In literature, nature occupies the place

---

[2] See Demosthenes, *Against Aristocrates* (23).113.

148

of good fortune, and art that of good counsel. Most important of all, the very fact that some things in literature depend on nature alone can itself be learned only from art.

If the critic of students of this subject will bear these points in mind, he will, I believe, come to realize that the examination of the question before us is by no means useless or superfluous ...

6–10

6 At this stage, the question we must put to ourselves for discussion is how to avoid the faults which are so much tied up with sublimity. The answer, my friend, is: by first of all achieving a genuine understanding and appreciation of true sublimity. This is difficult; literary judgement comes only as the final product of long experience. However, for the purposes of instruction, I think we can say that an understanding of all this can be acquired. I approach the problem in this way.

7 In ordinary life, nothing is truly great which it is great to despise; wealth, honour, reputation, absolute power – anything in short which has a lot of external trappings – can never seem supremely good to the wise man because it is no small good to despise them. People who could have these advantages if they chose but disdain them out of magnanimity are admired much more than those who actually possess them. It is much the same with elevation in poetry and literature generally. We have to ask ourselves whether any particular example does not give a show of grandeur which, for all its accidental trappings, will, when dissected, prove vain and hollow, the kind of thing which it does a man more honour to despise than to admire. It is our nature to be elevated and exalted by true sublimity. Filled with joy and pride, we come to believe we have created what we have only heard. When a man of sense and literary experience hears something many times over, and it fails to dispose his mind to greatness or to leave him with more to reflect upon than was contained in the mere words, but comes instead to seem valueless on repeated inspection, this is not true sublimity; it endures only for the moment of hearing. Real sublimity contains much food for reflection, is difficult or rather impossible to resist, and makes a strong and ineffaceable impression on the memory. In a word, reckon those things which please everybody all the time as genuinely and finely sublime. When people of different trainings, ways of life, tastes, ages and manners all agree about something, the judgement

and assent of so many distinct voices lends strength and irrefutability to the conviction that their admiration is rightly directed.

1   8 There are, one may say, five most productive sources of sublimity. (Competence in speaking is assumed as a common foundation for all five; nothing is possible without it.)

- (i) The first and most important is the power to conceive great thoughts; I defined this in my work on Xenophon.[3]
- (ii) The second is strong and inspired emotion. (These two sources are for the most part natural; the remaining three involve art.)
- (iii) Certain kinds of figures. (These may be divided into figures of thought and figures of speech.)
- (iv) Noble diction. This has as subdivisions choice of words and the use of metaphorical and artificial language.
- (v) Finally, to round off the whole list, dignified and elevated word-arrangement.[4]

2   Let us now examine the points which come under each of these heads. I must first observe, however, that Caecilius has omitted some of the five – emotion, for example. Now if he thought that sublimity and emotion were one and the same thing and always existed and developed together, he was wrong. Some emotions, such as pity, grief and fear, are found divorced from sublimity and with a low effect. Conversely, sublimity often occurs apart from emotion. Of the innumerable examples of this I select Homer's bold account of the Aloadae:

> Ossa upon Olympus they sought to heap; and on Ossa
> Pelion with its shaking forest, to make a path to heaven
> and the even more impressive sequel
> and they would have finished their work ...[5]

3   In orators, encomia[6] and ceremonial or exhibition pieces always involve grandeur and sublimity, though they are generally devoid of emotion. Hence those orators who are best at conveying emotion are least good

---

3 This work no longer survives.

4 Longinus proceeds to discuss the first, third, fourth and fifth sources of sublimity in turn but, surprisingly, does not discuss emotion as a separate topic, despite the importance which he clearly attaches to it. The selection from his work presented here omits much of the rather technical discussion of figures, diction and word-arrangement.

5 Homer, *Odyssey* 11.315–17.   6 Encomia were formal speeches of praise.

at encomia, and conversely the experts at encomia are not conveyers of emotions. On the other hand, if Caecilius thought that emotion had no contribution to make to sublimity and therefore thought it not worth mentioning, he was again completely wrong. I should myself have no hesitation in saying that there is nothing so productive of grandeur as noble emotion in the right place. It inspires and possesses our words with a kind of madness and divine spirit.   4

9 The first source, natural greatness, is the most important. Even if   1
it is a matter of endowment rather than acquisition, we must, so far as is possible, develop our minds in the direction of greatness and make them   2
always pregnant with noble thoughts. You ask how this can be done. I wrote elsewhere something like this: 'Sublimity is the echo of a noble mind.' This is why a mere idea, without verbal expression, is sometimes admired for its nobility just as Ajax's silence in the Vision of the Dead[7] is grand and indeed more sublime than any words could have been. First   3
then we must state where sublimity comes from: the orator must not have low or ignoble thoughts. Those whose thoughts and habits are trivial and servile all their lives cannot possibly produce anything admirable or worthy of eternity. Words will be great if thoughts are weighty. This is   4
why splendid remarks come naturally to the proud; the man who, when Parmenio[8] said, 'I should have been content'[9]... the interval between earth and heaven. One might say that this is the measure not so much of Strife as of Homer.[10]

Contrast the line about Darkness in Hesiod – if the *Shield* is by Hesiod: 5

> Mucus dripped from her nostrils.[11]

This gives a repulsive picture, not one to excite awe. But how does Homer magnify the divine power?

> As far as a man can peer through the mist,
> sitting on watch, looking over the wine-dark sea,
> so long is the stride of the gods' thundering horses.[12]

[7] In *Odyssey* 11.563 Ajax turns away from Odysseus in the Underworld without speaking.
[8] Parmenio, one of Alexander the Great's generals, is reported to have said that if he were Alexander, he would stop fighting, to which Alexander retorted, 'So would I, if I were Parmenio.'
[9] About six pages of the manuscript of *On Sublimity* are missing here.
[10] Homer in *Iliad* 4.440ff. describes Strife as having her head in the sky and walking on earth. Longinus means that Homer too is a figure of cosmic dimensions.
[11] Line 267 in the *Shield of Heracles*, a poem attributed to Hesiod.
[12] *Iliad* 5.770–2.

He uses a cosmic distance to measure their speed. This enormously impressive image would make anybody say, and with reason, that, if the horses of the gods took two strides like that, they would find there was not enough room in the world.

6   The imaginative pictures in the Battle of the Gods are also very remarkable:

> And the great heavens and Olympus trumpeted around them.
> Aïdoneus, lord of the dead, was frightened in his depths;
> and in fright he leapt from his throne, and shouted,
> for fear the earth-shaker Poseidon might break through the ground,
> and gods and men might see
> the foul and terrible halls, which even the gods detest.[13]

Do you see how the earth is torn from its foundations, Tartarus laid bare, and the whole universe overthrown and broken up, so that all things – Heaven and Hell, things mortal and things immortal – share the warfare

7   and the perils of that ancient battle? But, terrifying as all this is, it is blasphemous and indecent unless it is interpreted allegorically; in relating the gods' wounds, quarrels, revenges, tears, imprisonments and manifold misfortunes, Homer, or so it seems to me, has done his best to make the men of the Trojan War gods, and the gods men. If men are unhappy, there is always death as a harbour in trouble; what he has done for his gods is to make them immortal indeed, but immortally miserable.

8   Much better than the Battle of the Gods are the passages which represent divinity as genuinely unsoiled and great and pure. The lines about Poseidon, much discussed by my predecessors, exemplify this:

> The high hills and the forest trembled,
> and the peaks and the city of Troy and Achaean ships
> under the immortal feet of Poseidon as he went his way.
> He drove over the waves, the sea-monsters gambolled around him,
> coming up everywhere out of the deep; they recognized their king.
> The sea parted in joy; and the horses flew onward.[14]

9   Similarly, the law-giver of the Jews, no ordinary man – for he understood and expressed God's power in accordance with its worth – writes at the beginning of his *Laws*: 'God said' – now what? – '"Let there be light", and there was light; "Let there be earth", and there was earth.'

---

[13]   Longinus here combines *Iliad* 21.388 and 20.61–5.
[14]   This passage conflates *Iliad* 13.18–19, 20.60 and 13.27–9.

Perhaps it will not be out of place, my friend, if I add a further Homeric   **10**
example – from the human sphere this time – so that we can see how the
poet is accustomed to enter into the greatness of his heroes. Darkness
falls suddenly. Thickest night blinds the Greek army. Ajax is bewildered.
'O Father Zeus!', he cries,

> 'Deliver the sons of the Achaeans out of the mist,
> make the sky clear, and let us see;
> in the light – kill us.'[15]

The feeling here is genuinely Ajax's. He does not pray for life – that would
be a request unworthy of a hero – but having no good use for his courage
in the disabling darkness, and so angered at his inactivity in the battle, he
prays for light, and quickly: he will at all costs find a shroud worthy of his
valour, though Zeus be arrayed against him.

In this passage, the gale of battle blows hard in Homer; he   **11**

> rages like Ares, spear-brandishing, or the deadly fire
> raging in the mountains, in the thickets of the deep wood.
> Foam shows at his mouth.[16]

In the *Odyssey*, on the other hand – and there are many reasons for add-
ing this to our enquiry – he demonstrates that when a great mind begins
to decline, a love of story-telling characterizes its old age. We can tell that   **12**
the *Odyssey* was his second work from various considerations, in particular from his insertion of the residue of the Trojan troubles in the poem
in the form of episodes, and from the way in which he pays tribute of
lamentation and pity to the heroes, treating them as persons long known.
The *Odyssey* is simply an epilogue to the *Iliad*:

> There lies warlike Ajax, there Achilles,
> there Patroclus, the gods' peer as a counsellor,
> and there my own dear son.[17]

For the same reason, I maintain, he made the whole body of the *Iliad*,   **13**
which was written at the height of his powers, dramatic and exciting,
whereas most of the *Odyssey* consists of narrative, which is a characteristic of old age. Homer in the *Odyssey* may be compared to the setting
sun: the size remains without the force. He no longer sustains the tension

---

[15] *Iliad* 17.645–7.   [16] *Iliad* 15.605–7.
[17] These words are spoken by the aged Nestor in *Odyssey* 3.109–11.

as it was in the tale of Troy, nor that consistent level of elevation which never admitted any falling off. The outpouring of passions crowding one on another has gone; so has the versatility, the realism, the abundance of imagery taken from the life. We see greatness on the ebb. It is as though the Ocean were withdrawing into itself and flowing quietly in its own bed. Homer is lost in the realm of the fabulous and incredible. In saying this, I have not forgotten the storms in the *Odyssey*, the story of Cyclops, and a few other episodes; I am speaking of old age – but it is the old age of a Homer. The point about all these stories is that the mythical element in them predominates over the realistic.

14

I digressed into this topic, as I said, to illustrate how easy it is for great genius to be perverted in decline into nonsense. I mean things like the story of the wineskin, the tale of the men kept as pigs in Circe's palace ('howling piglets', Zoilus[18] called them), the feeding of Zeus by the doves (as though he were a chick in the nest), the ten days on the raft without food, and the improbabilities of the murder of the suitors. What can we say of all this but that it really is 'the dreaming of a Zeus'?

15

There is also a second reason for discussing the *Odyssey*. I want you to understand that the decline of emotional power in great writers and poets turns to a capacity for depicting manners. The realistic description of Odysseus' household forms a kind of comedy of manners.

1

10 Now have we any other means of making our writing sublime? Every topic naturally includes certain elements which are inherent in its raw material. It follows that sublimity will be achieved if we consistently select the most important of these inherent features and learn to organize them as a unity by combining one with another. The first of these procedures attracts the reader by the selection of details, the second by the density of those selected.

Consider Sappho's treatment of the feelings involved in the madness of being in love. She uses the attendant circumstances and draws on real life at every point. And in what does she show her quality? In her skill in selecting the outstanding details and making a unity of them:

2

> To me he seems a peer of the gods, the man who sits
> facing you and hears your sweet voice
> and lovely laughter; it flutters my heart in my breast. When

---

[18] Zoilus, a philosopher and rhetorician of the fourth century BC, was notorious for his severe criticisms of Homer.

I see you only for a moment, I cannot speak;
>   my tongue is broken, a subtle fire runs under my skin; my
> eyes cannot see, my ears hum;
>   cold sweat pours off me; shivering grips me all over; I am
> paler than grass; I seem near to dying;
>   but all must be endured ...[19]

Do you not admire the way in which she brings everything together –   **3**
mind and body, hearing and tongue, eyes and skin? She seems to have
lost them all, and to be looking for them as though they were external to
her. She is cold and hot, mad and sane, frightened and near death, all by
turns. The result is that we see in her not a single emotion, but a complex
of emotions. Lovers experience all this; Sappho's excellence, as I have
said, lies in her adoption and combination of the most striking details.

A similar point can be made about the descriptions of storms in
Homer, who always picks out the most terrifying aspects. The author of   **4**
the *Arimaspea*[20] on the other hand expects these lines to excite terror:

> This too is a great wonder to us in our hearts:
> there are men living on water, far from land, on the deep sea:
> miserable they are, for hard is their lot;
> they give their eyes to the stars, their lives to the sea;
> often they raise their hands in prayer to the gods,
> as their bowels heave in pain.

Anyone can see that this is more polished than awe-inspiring. Now com-   **5**
pare it with Homer (I select one example out of many):

> He fell upon them as upon a swift ship falls a wave,
> huge, wind-reared by the clouds. The ship
> is curtained in foam, a hideous blast of wind
> roars in the sail. The sailors shudder in terror:
> they are carried away from under death, but only just.[21]

Aratus tried to transfer the same thought: **6**

> A little plank wards off Hades.[22]

---

[19] Sappho, fr. 31.
[20] The *Arimaspea* was a lost poem attributed to Aristeas of Proconnesus, a prophet of Apollo in
the seventh century BC. The Arimaspi are described by Herodotus (4.27) as a one-eyed people
perpetually attempting to steal a hoard of gold guarded by griffins.
[21] *Iliad* 15.624–8.   [22] Aratus, *Phaenomena* 299.

But this is smooth and unimpressive, not frightening. Moreover, by saying 'a plank wards off Hades', he has got rid of the danger. The plank *does* keep death away. Homer, on the other hand, does not banish the cause of fear at a stroke; he gives a vivid picture of men, one might almost say, facing death many times with every wave that comes. Notice also the forced combination of naturally uncompoundable prepositions: *hupek*, 'from under'. Homer has tortured the words to correspond with the emotion of the moment, and expressed the emotion magnificently by thus crushing words together. He has in effect stamped the special character of the danger on the diction: 'they are carried away from under death'.

7 Compare Archilochus on the shipwreck, and Demosthenes on the arrival of the news ('It was evening ...').[23] In short, one might say that these writers have taken only the very best pieces, polished them up and fitted them together. They have inserted nothing inflated, undignified or pedantic. Such things ruin the whole effect, because they produce, as it were, gaps or crevices, and so spoil the impressive thoughts which have been built into a structure whose cohesion depends upon their mutual relations ...

13–15

1 13 To return to Plato, and the way in which he combines the 'soundless flow' of his smooth style with grandeur. A passage of the *Republic* you have read makes the manner quite clear: 'Men without experience of wisdom and virtue but always occupied with feasting and that kind of thing naturally go downhill and wander through life on a low plane of existence. They never look upwards to the truth and never rise, they never taste certain or pure pleasure. Like cattle, they always look down, bowed earthwards and tablewards; they feed and they breed, and their greediness in these directions makes them kick and butt till they kill one another with iron horns and hooves, because they can never be satisfied.'[24]

2 Plato, if we will read him with attention, illustrates yet another road to sublimity, besides those we have discussed. This is the way of imitation

---

[23] Several extant fragments by the lyric poet Archilochus relate to storms and shipwreck, but we do not know just which passage Longinus is referring to here. The passage of Demosthenes is the famous description of the panic at Athens when news came one evening in 339 BC that Philip of Macedon had captured Elatea (*On the Crown* 169).
[24] Plato, *Republic* 9.586a–b (slightly adapted).

and emulation of great writers of the past. Here too, my friend, is an aim to which we must hold fast. Many are possessed by a spirit not their own. It is like what we are told of the Pythia at Delphi: she is in contact with the tripod near the cleft in the ground which (so they say) exhales a divine vapour, and she is thereupon made pregnant by the supernatural power and forthwith prophesies as one inspired.[25] Similarly, the genius of the ancients acts as a kind of oracular cavern, and effluences flow from it into the minds of their imitators. Even those previously not much inclined to prophesy become inspired and share the enthusiasm which comes from the greatness of others. Was Herodotus the only 'most Homeric' writer? **3** Surely Stesichorus and Archilochus earned the name before him. So, more than any, did Plato, who diverted to himself countless rills from the Homeric spring. (If Ammonius had not selected and written up detailed examples of this, I might have had to prove the point myself.)[26] In all this **4** process there is no plagiarism. It resembles rather the reproduction of good character in statues and works of art. Plato could not have put such a brilliant finish on his philosophical doctrines or so often risen to poetical subjects and poetical language, if he had not tried, and tried wholeheartedly, to compete for the prize against Homer, like a young aspirant challenging an admired master. To break a lance in this way may well have been a brash and contentious thing to do, but the competition proved anything but valueless. As Hesiod says, 'this strife is good for men'.[27] Truly it is a noble contest and prize of honour, and one well worth winning, in which to be defeated by one's elders is itself no disgrace.

14 We can apply this to ourselves. When we are working on something **1** which needs loftiness of expression and greatness of thought, it is good to imagine how Homer would have said the same thing, or how Plato or Demosthenes or (in history) Thucydides would have invested it with sublimity. These great figures, presented to us as objects of emulation and, as it were, shining before our gaze, will somehow elevate our minds to the greatness of which we form a mental image. They will be even more **2** effective if we ask ourselves 'How would Homer or Demosthenes have reacted to what I am saying, if he had been here? What would his feelings

---

[25] It was widely believed in antiquity that the Pythia, the priestess of Apollo at Delphi, inhaled a vapour which sent her into a prophetic trance.
[26] Ammonius was a second-century BC critic, a pupil of the famous Alexandrian scholar Aristarchus. He wrote a work on Plato's borrowings from Homer.
[27] Hesiod, *Works and Days* 24.

have been?' It makes it a great occasion if you imagine such a jury or audience for your own speech, and pretend that you are answering for
3   what you write before judges and witnesses of such heroic stature. Even more stimulating is the further thought: 'How will posterity take what I am writing?' If a man is afraid of saying anything which will outlast his own life and age, the conceptions of his mind are bound to be incomplete and abortive; they will miscarry and never be brought to birth whole and perfect for the day of posthumous fame.

1   **15** Another thing which is extremely productive of grandeur, magnificence and urgency, my young friend, is visualization (*phantasia*). I use this word for what some people call image-production. The term *phantasia* is used generally for anything which in any way suggests a thought productive of speech; but the word has also come into fashion for the situation in which enthusiasm and emotion make the speaker *see* what
2   he is saying and bring it *visually* before his audience. It will not escape you that rhetorical visualization has a different intention from that of the poets: in poetry the aim is astonishment, in oratory it is clarity. Both, however, seek emotion and excitement.

> Mother, I beg you, do not drive them at me,
> the women with the blood in their eyes and the snakes –
> they are here, they are here, jumping right up to me.

Or again:

> O! O! She'll kill me. Where shall I escape?

The poet himself saw the Erinyes, and has as good as made his audience see what he imagined.[28]

3   Now Euripides devotes most pains to producing a tragic effect with two emotions, madness and love. In these he is supremely successful. At the same time, he does not lack the courage to attempt other types of visualization. Though not formed by nature for grandeur, he often forces himself to be tragic. When the moment for greatness comes, he (in Homer's words)

> whips flank and buttocks with his tail
> and drives himself to fight.[29]

---

[28] The first quotation comes from Euripides, *Orestes* 255–7, the second from Euripides, *Iphigenia in Tauris* 291. Both are spoken by Orestes who sees the Furies (the Erinyes) pursuing him in vengeance for his killing of his mother, Clytemnestra.

[29] Homer, *Iliad* 20.170–1.

For example, here is Helios handing the reins to Phaethon: **4**

> 'Drive on, but do not enter Libyan air –
> it has no moisture in it, and will let
> your wheel fall through – '

and again:

> 'Steer towards the seven Pleiads.'
> The boy listened so far, then seized the reins,
> whipped up the winged team, and let them go.
> To heaven's expanse they flew.
> His father rode behind on Sirius,
> giving the boy advice: 'That's your way, there:
> turn here, turn here.'[30]

May one not say that the writer's soul has mounted the chariot, has taken wing with the horses and shares the danger? Had it not been up among those heavenly bodies and moved in their courses, he could never have visualized such things.

Compare, too, his Cassandra:

> Ye Trojans, lovers of horses ...[31]

Aeschylus, of course, ventures on the most heroic visualizations; he is   **5**
like his own Seven against Thebes

> Seven men of war, commanders of companies,
> killing a bull into a black-bound shield,
> dipping their hands in the bull's blood,
> took oath by Ares, by Enyo, by bloodthirsty Terror –[32]

in a joint pledge of death in which they showed themselves no mercy. At the same time, he does sometimes leave his thoughts unworked, tangled and hard. The ambitious Euripides does not shirk even these risks. For   **6**
example, there is in Aeschylus a remarkable description of the palace of Lycurgus in its divine seizure at the moment of Dionysus' epiphany:

> the palace was possessed, the house went bacchanal.

---

[30] These two passages come from Euripides' *Phaethon*, a play which told how Phaethon, on discovering that he was the son of Helios, the sun-god, asked to be allowed to drive the chariot of the sun across the sky, with disastrous consequences. Substantial fragments of the play survive.
[31] This line may come from Euripides' lost play, *Alexandros*.
[32] Aeschylus, *Seven against Thebes* 42–6.

Euripides expresses the same thought less harshly:

> the whole mountain went bacchanal with them.[33]

7 There is another magnificent visualization in Sophocles' account of Oedipus dying and giving himself burial to the accompaniment of a sign from heaven, and in the appearance of Achilles over his tomb at the departure of the Greek fleet.[34] Simonides has perhaps described this scene more vividly than anyone else; but it is impossible to quote everything.

8 The poetical examples, as I said, have a quality of exaggeration which belongs to fable and goes far beyond credibility. In an orator's visualizations, on the other hand, it is the element of fact and truth which makes for success; when the content of the passage is poetical and fabulous and does not shrink from any impossibility, the result is a shocking and outrageous abnormality. This is what happens with the shock orators of our own day; like tragic actors, these fine fellows see the Erinyes, and are incapable of understanding that when Orestes says

> Let me go; you are one of my Erinyes,
> you are hugging me tight, to throw me into Hell,[35]

he visualizes all this *because he is mad.*

9 What then is the effect of rhetorical visualization? There is much it can do to bring urgency and passion into our words; but it is when it is closely involved with factual arguments that it enslaves the hearer as well as persuading him. 'Suppose you heard a shout this very moment outside the court, and someone said that the prison had been broken open and the prisoners had escaped – no one, young or old, would be so casual as not to give what help he could. And if someone then came forward and said "This is the man who let them out," our friend would never get

10 a hearing; it would be the end of him.'[36] There is a similar instance in Hyperides' defence of himself when he was on trial for the proposal to liberate the slaves which he put forward after the defeat. 'It was not the proposer,' he said, 'who drew up this decree: it was the battle of Chaeronea.'[37]

---

[33] The first quotation comes from Aeschylus, *Lycurgus* fr. 58 Radt, the second from Euripides, *Bacchae* 726.

[34] The first part of the sentence refers to the final scene of Sophocles' *Oedipus at Colonus*, the second perhaps to the appearance of Achilles' ghost in Sophocles' lost play, *Polyxena*.

[35] Euripides, *Orestes* 264–5.   [36] Demosthenes *Against Timocrates* (24).208.

[37] Philip of Macedon defeated the southern Greek states, led by Athens and Thebes, at the battle of Chaeronea in 338 BC. The orator Hyperides played a leading role in Athenian opposition to Philip after the battle.

Here the orator uses a visualization actually in the moment of making his factual argument, with the result that his thought has taken him beyond the limits of mere persuasiveness. Now our natural instinct is, in all such **11** cases, to attend to the stronger influence, so that we are diverted from the demonstration to the astonishment caused by the visualization, which by its very brilliance conceals the factual aspect. This is a natural reaction: when two things are joined together, the stronger attracts to itself the force of the weaker.

This will suffice for an account of sublimity of thought produced by **12** greatness of mind, imitation, or visualization ...

33–36

33 Let us consider a really pure and correct writer. We have then to ask **1** ourselves in general terms whether grandeur attended by some faults of execution is to be preferred, in prose or poetry, to a modest success of impeccable soundness. We must also ask whether the greater *number* of good qualities or the greater good qualities ought properly to win the literary prizes. These questions are relevant to a discussion of sublimity, **2** and urgently require an answer.

I am certain in the first place that great geniuses are least 'pure'. Exactness in every detail involves a risk of meanness; with grandeur, as with great wealth, there ought to be something overlooked. It may also be inevitable that low or mediocre abilities should maintain themselves generally at a correct and safe level, simply because they take no risks and do not aim at the heights, whereas greatness, just because it is greatness, incurs danger.

I am aware also of a second point. All human affairs are, in the nature **3** of things, better known on their worse side; the memory of mistakes is ineffaceable, that of goodness is soon gone. I have myself cited not a few **4** mistakes in Homer and other great writers, not because I take pleasure in their slips, but because I consider them not so much voluntary mistakes as oversights let fall at random through inattention and with the negligence of genius. I do, however, think that the greater good qualities, even if not consistently maintained, are always more likely to win the prize – if for no other reason, because of the greatness of spirit they reveal. Apollonius makes no mistakes in the *Argonautica*; Theocritus is very felicitous in the *Pastorals*, apart from a few passages not connected with the theme;

5 but would you rather be Homer or Apollonius? Is the Eratosthenes of that flawless little poem *Erigone*[38] a greater poet than Archilochus, with his abundant, uncontrolled flood, that bursting forth of the divine spirit which is so hard to bring under the rule of law? Take lyric poetry: would you rather be Bacchylides or Pindar? Take tragedy: would you rather be Ion of Chios or Sophocles? Ion and Bacchylides are impeccable, uniformly beautiful writers in the polished manner; but it is Pindar and Sophocles who sometimes set the world on fire with their vehemence, for all that their flame often goes out without reason and they collapse dismally. Indeed, no one in his senses would reckon all Ion's works put together as the equivalent of the one play *Oedipus*.

1   **34** If good points were totted up, not judged by their real value, Hyperides would in every way surpass Demosthenes. He is more versatile, and has more good qualities. He is second-best at everything, like a pentathlon competitor; always beaten by the others for first place, he

2 remains the best of the non-specialists. In fact, he reproduces all the good features of Demosthenes, except his word-arrangement, and also has for good measure the excellences and graces of Lysias. He knows how to talk simply where appropriate; he does not deliver himself of everything in the same tone, like Demosthenes. His expression of character has sweetness and delicacy. Urbanity, sophisticated sarcasm, good breeding, skill in handling irony, humour neither rude nor tasteless but flavoured with true Attic salt, an ingenuity in attack with a strong comic element and a sharp sting to its apt fun – all this produces inimitable charm. He has moreover great talents for exciting pity, and a remarkable facility for narrating myths with copiousness and developing general topics with fluency. For example, while his account of Leto is in his

3 more poetic manner, his Funeral Speech is an unrivalled example of the epideictic style.[39] Demosthenes, by contrast, has no sense of character. He lacks fluency, smoothness, and capacity for the epideictic manner; in fact he is practically without all the qualities I have been describing. When he forces himself to be funny or witty, he makes people laugh at him rather than with him. When he wants to come near to being

---

38 Eratosthenes, like Apollonius and Theocritus, was an Alexandrian poet of the third century BC. His lost poem, *Erigone*, told the story of the death of Icarius and the suicide of his daughter, Erigone.

39 Hyperides' account of Leto occurred in a lost speech, the *Deliacus*. His Funeral Speech, on those who fell in the Lamian War, largely survives.

charming, he is furthest removed from it. If he had tried to write the little speech on Phryne or that on Athenogenes,[40] he would have been an even better advertisement for Hyperides. Yet Hyperides' beauties, **4** though numerous, are without grandeur: 'inert in the heart of a sober man', they leave the hearer at peace. Nobody feels frightened reading Hyperides.

But when Demosthenes begins to speak, he concentrates in himself excellences finished to the highest perfection of his sublime genius – the intensity of lofty speech, living emotions, abundance, acuteness, speed where speed is vital, all his unapproachable vehemence and power. He concentrates it all in himself – they are divine gifts, it is almost blasphemous to call them human – and so outpoints all his rivals, compensating with the beauties he has even for those which he lacks. The crash of his thunder, the brilliance of his lightning, make all other orators of all ages insignificant. It would be easier to open your eyes to an approaching thunderbolt than to face up to his unremitting emotional blows.

35 To return to Plato and Lysias, there is, as I said, a further difference **1** between them. Lysias is much inferior not only in the importance of the good qualities concerned but in their number; and at the same time he exceeds Plato in the number of his failings even more than he falls short in his good qualities.

What then was the vision which inspired those divine writers who dis- **2** dained exactness of detail and aimed at the greatest prizes in literature? Above all else, it was the understanding that nature made man to be no humble or lowly creature, but brought him into life and into the universe as into a great festival, to be both a spectator and an enthusiastic contestant in its competitions. She implanted in our minds from the start an irresistible desire for anything which is great and, in relation to ourselves, supernatural.

The universe therefore is not wide enough for the range of human **3** speculation and intellect. Our thoughts often travel beyond the boundaries of our surroundings. If anyone wants to know what we were born for, let him look round at life and contemplate the splendour, grandeur and beauty in which it everywhere abounds. It is a natural inclination that **4**

---

[40] Hyperides' defence of Phryne, a courtesan, is lost. His speech *Against Athenogenes*, a large part of which survives, concerns a contract for the purchase of slaves.

leads us to admire not the little streams, however pellucid and however useful, but the Nile, the Danube, the Rhine and above all the Ocean. Nor do we feel so much awe before the little flame we kindle, because it keeps its light clear and pure, as before the fires of heaven, though they are often obscured. We do not think our flame more worthy of admiration than the craters of Etna, whose eruptions bring up rocks and whole hills out of the depths, and sometimes pour forth rivers of the earth-born,

5 spontaneous fire. A single comment fits all these examples: the useful and necessary are readily available to man, it is the unusual that always excites our wonder.

1   **36** So when we come to great geniuses in literature – where, by contrast, grandeur is not divorced from service and utility – we have to conclude that such men, for all their faults, tower far above mortal stature. Other literary qualities prove their users to be human; sublimity raises us towards the spiritual greatness of god. Freedom from error does indeed

2 save us from blame, but it is only greatness that wins admiration. Need I add that every one of those great men redeems all his mistakes many times over by a single sublime stroke? Finally, if you picked out and put together all the mistakes in Homer, Demosthenes, Plato, and all the other really great men, the total would be found to be a minute fraction of the successes which those heroic figures have to their credit. Posterity and human experience – judges whose sanity envy cannot question – place the crown of victory on their heads. They keep their prize irrevocably, and will do so

> so long as waters flow and tall trees flourish.[41]

3   It has been remarked that 'the failed Colossus is no better than the Doryphorus of Polyclitus'.[42] There are many ways of answering this. We may say that accuracy is admired in art and grandeur in nature, and it is by nature that man is endowed with the power of speech; or again that statues are expected to represent the human form, whereas, as I said, something higher than human is sought in literature.

4   At this point I have a suggestion to make which takes us back to the beginning of the book. Impeccability is generally a product of art; erratic

---

[41] A line from the 'epigram on the tomb of Midas' ascribed to Homer.
[42] It is disputed whether this refers specifically to the very large 'Colossus of Rhodes' or just to any colossal statue. The Doryphorus of Polyclitus was famous for its beautiful proportions.

excellence comes from natural greatness; therefore, art must always come to the aid of nature, and the combination of the two may well be perfection.

It seemed necessary to settle this point for the sake of our enquiry; but everyone is at liberty to enjoy what he takes pleasure in.

PHILOSTRATUS

Life of Apollonius of Tyana

2.22

Apollonius spent a long time in the temple, until the king had been told that the strangers had arrived. During this time the following conversation took place.

'Damis,' said Apollonius, 'is there such a thing as painting?'

'Yes indeed,' he replied, 'if there is also such a thing as truth.'

'What does this art do?'

'It mixes all the different colours together,' said Damis, 'blue with green, white with black and red with yellow.'

'For what purpose does it mix them?' Apollonius asked. 'For it is not just to obtain a bright colour, like dyed wax.'

'The purpose is imitation,' said Damis, 'to make likenesses of dogs and horses and people and ships and everything under the sun. And what is more, it makes a likeness of the sun himself, sometimes in a four-horse chariot, as he is said to appear in this world, and sometimes actually carrying a torch across the sky, when the painting depicts the upper air and the home of the gods.'

'So is painting imitation, Damis?'

'What else could it be?' said Damis. 'If it did not do this, we would think it ridiculous, foolishly concocting colours.'

'What will you say about the shapes we see in the sky when the clouds are torn apart from each other, the centaurs and goat–stags and, by Zeus, the wolves and the horses? Are they not products of imitation?'

'So it seems,' he said.

'Then is God a painter, Damis, who leaves the winged chariot on which he travels, ordering both divine and human affairs, and sits down at these times and plays and paints these things, like children drawing in the sand?'

Damis blushed when the argument seemed to descend into such absurdity. Apollonius did not look down on him, since he was not harsh when he refuted people, but said, 'Do you not rather mean something like this, Damis: shapes wander through the sky without meaning and by chance, as far as God is concerned, but we fashion and arrange them because we have a natural tendency to imitation?'

'Yes, let us believe that instead, Apollonius, since it is more convincing and a much better idea.'

'In that case, Damis, there are two kinds of imitation. We should hold that there is one kind which imitates with both hand and mind – this is painting – and another kind which makes likenesses with the mind alone.'

'We ought not to think that there are two kinds,' said Damis. 'The more perfect kind of imitation is painting, which can make likenesses both with the mind and with the hand; the other kind is just a part of that, since its possessor understands and imitates in his mind, even without being a painter, and would not be able to use his hand for painting.'

'Do you mean, Damis,' he said, 'someone whose hand has been maimed by a blow or an illness?'

'No,' said Damis. 'I mean someone who cannot paint because he has never touched a paintbrush or any of the painter's tools or colours, and has never learned how to paint.'

'In that case, Damis,' he said, 'we both agree that imitation comes naturally to human beings, but painting is acquired by art. This would seem to apply to sculpture as well. As for painting itself, you do not seem to me to be thinking only about painting in colours – for indeed one colour sufficed for the painters of old and, as painting developed, it then employed four or more colours. It is appropriate to call an outline drawn without any colour but composed of light and shade "painting". There too we can see likeness and form and intelligence, modesty and boldness, even though such pictures lack colour. This kind of picture does not show blood or the colour of a person's hair or beard; nevertheless compositions in monochrome are likenesses of both brown-skinned and white-skinned people.

Even if we draw one of these Indians with a white outline he will look like a black man, I suppose, since the flat nose, the stiff, curly hair, the protruding jaw and the expression of shock around the eyes makes what we see look black and suggests an Indian to intelligent observers. Therefore I would say that even those who look at works of painting need a capacity for imitation. For no one would praise a picture of a horse or a bull without thinking about the animal which it resembles; no one would marvel at the *Ajax* of Timomachus, in which Ajax is depicted as mad, without in some way conceiving in their mind an image of Ajax and how he would probably be sitting after the slaughter of the flocks at Troy, exhausted and planning to kill himself as well.'[1]

6.19

'What about sculptors like Phidias and Praxiteles? Surely they did not go up to heaven, model the forms of the gods and then reproduce them by their art? Was there something else which presided over their moulding?'

'There was something else,' said Apollonius, 'something full of wisdom.'

'What sort of thing was that?' asked Thespesion. 'You cannot mean anything other than imitation.'

'It was imagination, a wiser craftsman than imitation, which made those things,' he replied. 'Imitation will fashion what it has seen, whereas imagination can also fashion what it has not seen, since it will conceive of that with reference to what actually exists. Moreover imitation is often disrupted by shock; nothing disrupts imagination which proceeds unperturbed in pursuit of what it has conceived.'

---

[1] The Greek hero Ajax went mad when the arms of Achilles were awarded to Odysseus and not to him, after Achilles' death. In his madness he killed flocks of sheep and cattle, thinking they were the other leaders of the Greek army at Troy. When he realized what he had done he killed himself.

Pictures

Preface

Anyone who does not care for painting offends against truth and also offends against all the wisdom relating to the poets, since both painting and poetry alike deal with the deeds and appearance of heroes; such a person also does not appreciate symmetry, by which art actually attains reason. Now to anyone who wants to be clever, we can say that painting is a divine invention because of the patterns with which the Seasons paint the fields on earth and the phenomena to be seen in the heavens, but to anyone who investigates the origin of the art, we can say that imitation is a very ancient invention, very closely related to nature; wise men discovered it, calling one part of it painting and another part sculpture.

There are many kinds of sculpture: modelling, imitation in bronze, carving white or Parian marble, work in ivory and, by Zeus, gem-cutting. Painting, on the other hand, works with colours; not only does it do this but it can also cleverly do more with this one medium than another art with many; it depicts light and shade and recognizes the look in the eye of the madman, the man in pain and the happy man – all different from each other. Moreover, the sculptor is quite unable to reproduce the light in his subject's eyes as it really is, whereas painting knows how to depict grey, blue and black eyes as well as auburn, red and golden hair, the colour of clothing and armour, bedrooms and houses, groves, mountains and springs, and the sky above them.

PHILOSTRATUS THE YOUNGER

Pictures

Preface 3–7

The practice of painting is most noble and concerned with matters of **3**
no small significance. One who is going to master the art correctly must
have thoroughly studied human nature. He should be able to discern the
signs of people's characters even when they are silent, understanding
what appears in the state of the cheeks, the expression of the eyes, the
character of the eyebrows and, in short, everything which shows what
they are thinking. Once he has sufficient grasp of these he will put everything together and his hand will successfully interpret the story appropriate to each subject, whether a madman, perhaps, or someone in a rage,
or thoughtful, or happy, or impulsive, or in love and, in a word, he will
paint what is fitting for each one. There is a pleasant deception involved, **4**
with no blame attached; surely encountering things which are not real as
if they were real and being led by them to think that they are real, in a
way which causes no harm, is enough to provide attractive and blameless
entertainment?

I think that wise men of old wrote a great deal about symmetry in **5**
painting, laying down rules, as it were, for the proportion of each of the
limbs, as if it were not possible to convey mental agitation really well
unless the arrangement of the limbs conformed to the natural measurements; according to them an abnormal figure, which exceeds these measurements, cannot convey agitation of a normal nature. If one considers the **6**
matter, one finds that the art of painting has a kind of kinship with poetry

and that an element of imagination is common to both of them. For the poets introduce the gods as present on the stage along with everything impressive, solemn and attractive. Painting does the same thing, showing

7   in the picture things which the poets are able to describe in words. What need is there to say what has been admirably said by many others? By saying more I might give the impression of embarking on an encomium of painting.[1] Even these words, few as they are, are enough to show that our effort will not have been wasted: when I have encountered paintings by a clever hand, in which past deeds are artistically presented, I have not thought it right to pass over them.

[1] An encomium was a formal speech of praise.

ARISTIDES QUINTILIANUS

On Music

Book 1, chapter 1

I am constantly astonished, my most admirable friends Eusebius and
Florentius, at the enthusiasm with which the ancient philosophers
devoted themselves to every branch of learning, and at the way in which,
after discovering some things for themselves and inheriting some which
other people had found out, they carried them on to their proper com-
pletion, and ungrudgingly explained and bequeathed to their successors
the benefits which flow from them. But I marvel at their greatness of
mind most especially on the occasions when we discuss music with one
another, as we often do. This pursuit was not for them among those that
are of merely casual interest, as many who are ignorant about the matter
have supposed, especially nowadays: rather, it was held in honour for its
own sake, and was also exceedingly admired for its value in relation to the
other sciences, to which it offers an account both of a first principle and,
one might almost say, of a final objective.

Another merit peculiar to the art, and one which seems to me especially significant, is this. Unlike the others, its usefulness is not thought
to be restricted to one subject matter or to a short period of time: every
stage of life, life as a whole and every action can be perfectly ordered only
through music. Painting and all similar arts, in their pursuit of visual
beauty, yield only a tiny fragment of benefit, and since they are easy for
everyone to grasp, they display no increase, as time goes on, in the intri-
cacy of the understanding. Medicine and gymnastics benefit the body,

but cannot begin in childhood to confer on those who pursue them the rewards which flow from learning. Dialectic and its counterpart advance the soul towards wisdom, so long as the soul they lay hold on is purified by music, but without music they not only fail to advance it: they sometimes even bring it to ruin. The art we have mentioned is the only one that extends through virtually every subject matter, and lasts through the whole of time, putting the soul in order with the beauties of *harmonia*[1] and setting up the body with decorous rhythms. It provides children with the benefits that melody brings, and to those who are getting older it gives the beauties of metrical diction, and indeed of discourse in general: when they are older still, it explains to them the nature of numbers and the intricacies of proportions, and reveals the *harmoniai* that arise from them in all bodies. Most important and most perfect of all is its capacity to yield the ratios of that which men find hardest to understand, the soul, and not only the individual soul, but the soul of the universe as well. The inspired utterance of Panaceus the Pythagorean bears witness to what I say: he asserts that the task of music is not merely to relate to one another the parts of musical sound, but to bring together in a harmonious relation all natural things.[2] These points will be demonstrated later, as the argument progresses.

Chapter 2

What has principally stimulated me to attempt this treatise is the low opinion which most people have of the subject, and I am determined to show how excellent a branch of learning it is that they unjustifiably despise. Other sciences are neglected either, like medicine, because they are difficult, or, like geometry, because most people get no pleasure from them. Music is not to be rejected for either of these reasons. It presents no great difficulty, and through its presence it cannot fail to give well-proportioned pleasure to those who pursue it: it can quickly give benefits to those who are prepared to work, and yield honourable and outstanding pleasure as its fruits. Besides, anyone who labours in the other arts needs some different activity by way of diversion, whereas those who study music find their recreation in the work itself, which brings no less joy to

[1] The word *harmonia* (plural *harmoniai*), left untranslated here, refers to music's melodic aspect.
[2] Nothing substantial is known about Panaceus.

the spirit than profit to the mind. Most people give this fact no weight, preferring the pleasure which comes from idleness and ignorance to that which accompanies reason and brings benefit.

It is also, however, because there are those who have brought to the art no little love, but who, because they have not attended to every part of it, passed on nothing of significance to their associates, and earned from them no praise on account of music. Again, it is also because virtually none of the ancient writers put together their accounts of music as a complete whole in a single study: instead, they discussed particular topics piecemeal in disconnected writings. They said nothing about most of its principles and natural causes, and more or less confined their attention to technical matters and to the subject of the use of melodies. But that is enough of preliminaries.

Chapter 3

Now we must set out upon our course, after calling in due form on the god who leads the Muses. For the poets, even though what they are working on is not music – of which they use only a small fraction in their descriptions of deeds of old – nevertheless call upon the Muses, and Apollo their leader. But we shall not be narrating ancient myths with the help of a part of music. We are attempting to present music itself, in its entirety, and to describe its nature and character. We are seeking to reveal all the forms which it takes in sound and all its instantiations in bodies; to reveal whether certain relations to numbers are also ratios of resemblance between it and our most valuable element, the soul; and to explain everything about this whole universe which a man who advances higher may reveal without violating the principles of music. Upon whom should we first call to aid us in so great an undertaking? Should it not be him who has fitted together harmoniously the whole of this visible world with invisible devices, and devised every soul most perfectly with the ratios of *harmonia*? – whether it is right to call him Craftsman, giving him a title suitably derived from the things he has made, or reverent to call him Form, thus indicating his powers to men through that which he imparts to his subordinates, or proper to call him Ratio or Unit, or, as men of divine wisdom have done, Unitary Ratio, revealing by the first title how he harmonizes and orders everything, and by the second how he has arrested the multiplicity and diversity of things, and holds them together in one with unbreakable bonds.[3] Upon him let us call, and pray him to supply us with every secure perception, and to grant us complete leisure to speak adequately of the subject we have undertaken. Let that be a sufficient supplication; and let us at once begin to present our account of the whole of music, as we have promised.

Book 2, chapter 1

After this we ought to investigate whether it is possible to educate by means of music or not; whether such education is useful or not; whether it can be given to all or only to some; and whether it can be given through just one kind of composition or through several. We must also enquire whether the kinds thought unsuitable for education have no use at all, or whether even these can sometimes be found beneficial. The educational side of our subject includes all these questions. But first we must give some account of the soul. Just as none of the other arts can be understood until we have grasped the nature of the object at which its energies are directed, so too we cannot understand musical education until we have a clear grasp of the soul, to which it directs all its concern. What the soul is, and from what it is composed, we shall explain in due course. For the present let us give a brief account, sufficient for our immediate purposes.

Chapter 2

Inspired men of ancient times, it seems, strongly maintained the following thesis, among many others: that the soul is not one of the simple entities, nor one of those whose nature and capacities are unitary. Things in this world, they argued, if they were to be equipped with rhythm and order, needed the leadership of soul.[4] But the soul cannot be present and actively engaged among the things on earth without being confined in the fetters of the body, which, borne downwards as it is towards the heaviness

---

[3] 'Craftsman' is the title given to the maker of the universe in Plato's *Timaeus* 28a (p. 71). The references to 'Form', 'subordinates', 'Ratio', 'Unit' and 'Unitary Ratio' all go back to passages such as *Timaeus* 29e–32c, 41a and 47e–52c. The explanation of these titles was probably developed in the Platonist/Pythagorean tradition of the early centuries AD.

[4] Aristides here seems to be thinking primarily of Plato. See, for example, Plato *Phaedrus* 245c and *Timaeus* 34b–c. The rest of the chapter is also full of Platonic allusions.

whose nature it shares, drags down the soul and prevents it from flying away. Nor can the soul accomplish its designs for things in this world rightly and in concord with the whole, if it does not also have an understanding and perception of the beauties of the other. Thus it needed a double nature, equipped with wisdom, and yet also, because of its affinity with the body, not disposed wholly to reject the things of this world. For he who orders the universe, so they say, when he constructed the soul to take charge of bodies, gave it, out of what is proper to the divine, an instantiation of reason, by which it was to order things on earth; and out of what belongs to the irrational he attached to it desire, through which it would seek after things in this world. And to ensure that its long stay here would not make it forget completely the beauties of the other world, and that it would not be shackled by its sympathy for things less worthy than itself, he providently instilled in it memory, as an antidote against irrationality, and sent the sciences, in their indescribable beauty, to be its companion in its downward journey. To this beauty it could direct the love that its nature gave it, so living its life here in holiness, adorned with virtuous impulses and deeds, and making as happy an end as is possible. These, then, are its two aspects, the rational, through which it accomplishes the works of wisdom, and the irrational, through which it engages in the business of the body. The activities of the irrational aspect gave it, in turn, a two-fold nature: that which is addicted to much slackness they called 'appetitive', and that which is displayed in excessive tension they named 'spirited'.

Chapter 3

There have also come to be two different kinds of branches of learning. Some maintain the rational part in its natural freedom, making it sober and keeping it pure by gifts of wisdom; while others take the irrational part, as though it were some savage beast that is moved without order, and heal and tame it, allowing it neither to pursue excesses nor to be wholly subdued. Of the first kind philosophy is the leader and high priest. The ruler of the others is music, which from earliest childhood moulds the character with its *harmoniai*, and makes the body more melodious with its rhythms. The very young could not be educated through unadorned words, which contain instruction but no pleasure, nor could they be wholly neglected. For them there remained an education which did not

stir up the rational part before its time, this being left in peace because
of their youth, and which gave benefit along with pleasure to the other
part, training it by habituation. Nature itself taught the means through
which education should be applied: for it is not through things of which
we know nothing, but through those with which reason and experience
have made us familiar, that some of us are led to be convinced and others
work to produce conviction. Song always comes readily to all children, as
we can see, and so do patterns of joyful movement: nor would anyone in
his senses forbid them the pleasure they get from such things. It may be
that the delightfulness of the activity enchants their minds; or perhaps
the soul, released from the torpor which enfolded it in infancy because
of the softness of its coverings, springs with enthusiasm into its natural
movements as soon as it senses that its body is becoming firm.[5]

Chapter 4

Since all this is so, we have a reply to those who doubt whether everyone
is moved by melody. To begin with, they have failed to realize that learning is for children, all of whom, as we can see, are naturally overcome by
this kind of delight. Secondly, they have not noticed that even if it does
not at once capture those whose way of life makes them less amenable
to it, nevertheless it enslaves them before long. Just as one and the same
drug applied to the same kind of complaint in several bodies does not
always work in the same way, depending on the slightness or severity of
the condition, but cures some more quickly, others more slowly, so music
too arouses those more open to its influence immediately, but takes longer
to capture the less susceptible.

The reasons why music is effective are clear. Our earliest learning
comes from similarities, which we assess by bringing them to the attention of our senses. Though painting and the plastic arts teach through
sight alone, they nevertheless arouse and startle the soul: how then could
music fail to capture it, given that it creates its imitation through several of the senses and not just through one? Poetry, with the medium
of words alone, uses only the sense of hearing: but without melody it
does not always arouse the emotions, and without rhythms it cannot
bring the emotions into conformity with its subject matter. Here is some

---

[5] Cf. Plato, *Laws* 2.653d–e, 664e, *Timaeus* 44a–c.

evidence: if we are to arouse an emotion in the course of a performance, this cannot be done without inclining the voice in some way towards melody. Only music teaches both by words and by images of actions, and through agents that are not static or fixed in a single pattern, but are alive, and alter their form and their movement to fit every detail of what the words express. This is clear both from the dances of the choruses of ancient times, whose teacher was the science of rhythm, and also from what has been written by most authors about performing. The other arts, which work with their own specialized materials, cannot bring us quickly to a conception of the action they represent, for some things are based upon colours, others on solids, others on words, all of which are alien to the reality. Music, however, persuades most directly and effectively, since the means by which it makes its imitation are of just the same kind as those by which the actions themselves are accomplished in reality. For instance, in actual trains of events deliberation comes first and speech follows, and after them comes the performance of the action: music imitates the characters and emotions of the soul through its conceptions, speech through *harmoniai* and the moulding of the voice, action through rhythm and bodily movement. Hence education of this sort should attend most especially upon children, so that through the imitations and likenesses they encounter when they are young they may come, through familiarity and practice, to recognize and to desire the things which are accomplished in earnest in adult life.

Why then are we surprised to find that it was mostly through music that people in ancient times produced moral correction? – for they saw how powerful a thing it is, and how effective its nature makes it. Just as they applied their intelligence to such other human attributes as health and bodily well-being, seeking to preserve one thing, working to increase another, limiting to what is beneficial anything that tended towards excess, so also with the songs and dances to which all children are naturally attracted. It was impossible to prohibit them without destroying the children's own nature: instead, by cultivating them, little by little and imperceptibly, they devised an activity both decorous and delightful, and out of something useless made something useful.

No human activity is complete without music. Music beautifies hymns to the gods, and their worship; it brings good cheer to private celebrations and public festivities; it gives vigour and support to those at war or on journeys; it takes away the hardship from sailing and rowing, and from the hardest kinds of manual labour, easing their toil; and among some foreign peoples it is used even in mourning, where it blunts with melody the sharpness of grief. It has also been observed that there is no one single cause that makes us turn to making melody. For those who are happy it is pleasure, for those in sorrow it is grief, and for those possessed by the impulse of a divine breath it is inspiration: and in certain conjunctions of circumstances these causes are mixed, when children, because of their age, or their elders, because of some weakness in their nature, are subjected to such emotions.

Chapter 5

Even though not everybody is stirred up by these emotions, as the wise, for instance, are not,[6] and though not all emotions make us sing, as untempered ones do not, nevertheless it was found expedient to use this treatment on the emotions which do so arouse us, and the people whom these emotions affect, thus making citizens who were useful when the time for serious activity arrived. No cure could be found in reason alone for those who were burdened by these emotions; for pleasure is a very powerful temptation, captivating even the animals that lack reason (as is shown by the shepherd's *syrinx* and the goatherd's *pēktis*),[7] and grief which remains unsolaced casts many people into incurable illnesses; while inspired ecstasies, if not kept in moderation, do not advance to the right end, but bring on superstition and irrational fears.

These emotions were understood on the basis of their derivation from the different parts of the soul. People saw that pleasure is rife in its appetitive part, grief and its offspring anger in the spirited part, and inspired ecstasy in the rational. But for each of these there was a fitting style of treatment through music, which brought the sufferer gradually, and without his knowledge, into a proper condition. A person who is under the moderate influence of any of these emotions makes music of his own accord, while one who has succumbed to untempered emotion may be taught through his hearing. For a soul subject to excesses of disorder cannot be benefited except through the means by which it acts itself when it

---

[6] The imperturbability of the wise man is a Stoic theme, though one with Platonic roots.

[7] The *syrinx* was any kind of pipe played without a reed mouthpiece. The *pēktis* was usually the name of a kind of harp but sometimes, as here, indicates an instrument similar to the *syrinx*.

is affected only moderately. The susceptibility of souls to different types
of melody varies also with their sex and age: the souls of children are
led to sing by pleasure, those of women, for the most part, by grief, and
those of old men by divine possession, by breaths of inspiration during
festivals, for example.

Chapter 6

In view of all this, they required everyone to cultivate music from
childhood throughout their lives, and made use of properly authorized
melodies, rhythms and dances.[8] They prescribed certain melodies, which
they called *nomoi*, for customary usage both in private revelries and in
public religious festivals, employing their role in religion as a device to
ensure their stability – even the name they gave them was a promise
that they would remain unchanged.[9] Again, they tried to bring calm,
in one way or another, to the movements which the soul at times performs within itself when seized by untempered desires, and to transport
it into that sweetness of mood which comes through ear and eye – just as
if they were diverting a stream, which was rushing through impassable
crags or dispersing itself in marshy places, into an easily trodden and
fertile plain.

Their anxieties about musical matters were two-sided. They saw that
those who neglected music, melody and unaccompanied poetry alike,
were utterly crude and foolish; while those who had involved themselves
in it in the wrong way fell into serious errors, and through their passion for worthless melodies and poetry stamped upon themselves ugly
idiosyncrasies of character. Accordingly, they employed for the most part
those melodies which are suitable for education, and only very occasionally those that are more relaxed, either to discover men's characters, in
the same way that drunkenness was often used as a test (and just as the
great Plato tests the young people in the *Republic* by means of pleasures),[10]
or else to divert towards education anything that was over-excited by
desires, in the way I have already described. All education influences

---

[8] By 'they' here Aristides means the 'people in ancient times' mentioned in Chapter 4. In fact
however he is drawing not so much on historical sources as on Plato's *Republic* and *Laws*.
[9] See, for example, Plato, *Laws* 2.656b–657b, 660b, 3.700a ff., 7.799e–800b. Outside musical contexts, the word *nomos* means 'law', 'custom' or 'convention'.
[10] For the test of drunkenness, see *Laws* 1.637a ff., 649d; the reference to the *Republic* is to 3.413d–e.

people either by imposing something on them, as the laws do, or by pressure of persuasion, such as that of the company we keep. Music has both kinds of power, both enslaving the hearer by words and melodies, and inveigling him, by subtle variations of sound and posture, into conformity with what the words express. They assigned educational music to as many as a hundred days, the relaxing kind to no more than thirty.[11] Through the serious songs and dances they educated persons of the better sort – audiences and performers alike – while through the pleasurable kind they gave recreation to the common people. Where all the guardians of the state were men of serious worth, as in the wise Plato's *Republic*, use was made only of melodies conducive to education. But where there was diversity among those who welded together the whole complex of the state, as in all other cities, amusements suited to each one of them were also necessary ...

It can be shown both that music is the most powerful agent of education, rivalled by no other, and that our characters commonly deteriorate if they are left undisciplined, lapsing into base or brutal passions. My argument will not deal with facts about the individual, which are hard to discern, but with facts about cities and entire races, since research is always easier when its objects are on a large scale. So far as education is concerned, there are two undesirable conditions, lack of culture and corruption of culture. The first comes from absence of education, the second from poor teaching. Now the soul is found to contain two generic varieties of emotion, spirit and appetite. Hence of the races that have never tasted the beauties of music at all, those that truckle to their appetites are insensitive and bovine, as are the peoples of Opicia and Leucania, while those that encourage their spirited side are savage, like wild beasts, as are the peoples of Garamantis and Iberia.[12] Of those among whom music has been perverted against its nature into depravity and cultural corruption, the peoples that cultivate the appetites have souls that are too slack, and improper bodily affectations, like those who live in Phoenicia and their descendants in Africa;[13] while those that are ruled by the spirited part lack

[11] The reference is to the institution of festivals, to each of which appropriate music was assigned. Cf. Plato, *Laws* 2.653c ff., 7.799a–b, 803c ff. The mention of thirty days for specifically non-educational music is somewhat puzzling; it does not correspond to anything either in Plato or in the extant works of Aristotle.
[12] Opicia and Leucania are in southern Italy, Garamantis in northern Africa. Iberia is northern Spain.
[13] That is, the Carthaginians.

all mental discipline – they are drunkards, addicted to weapon-dances no matter whether the occasion is right, excessive in anger and manic in war, like the Thracian peoples and the entire Celtic race. But the races that have embraced the learning of music and dexterity in its use, by which I mean the Greeks and any there may be who have emulated them, are blessed with virtue and knowledge of every kind, and their humanity is outstanding. If music can delight and mould whole cities and races, can it be incapable of educating individuals? I think not.

Again, no other activity has so great a capacity both for establishing a community and for sustaining it once it is established. When a constitution has already begun to incline in one direction or the other, the other activities follow in its wake: but music directs all such changes. Of all branches of learning it is first in order and in power, and with its melodies it moulds the will of each man in suitable ways from his earliest youth.

Let me also give you an indication of the way it serves to detect character. Whatever the qualities of the melodies and rhythms in which each group of people takes pleasure, publicly and privately, the qualities of character which they find agreeable will turn out to be the same. From lack of concern about the fact that bad things are promoted by song, there arises conformity of habit, and from habit springs character, the source of impulses towards action. Pleasure joins them, to confirm and intensify the evil, treating postures, styles and even words quite indiscriminately, till in the end it turns upside down the whole of private and public life.[14] The reverse is also true: from fine song arise good words, characters and habits, noble impulses and most excellent deeds.

Thus it was that in the earliest times, when political institutions were nowhere firmly established, the cultivation of music in association with virtue corrected civil discord and put an end to hostilities with neighbouring cities and races. It specified set times for communal assemblies, and through the celebrations and revels customary at such occasions it restrained their aggressiveness towards one another, replacing it with kindliness – just as skilful farmers first clear their fields of weeds and barren scrub, making a safe place to sow seeds of the highest value.

If in these days every city and virtually every race has come to love good order and human friendship, music has not therefore become useless. Medicine is not something to be called upon when we are ill and to

---

[14] Cf. Plato, *Republic* 4.424b–425e. The last clause quotes *Republic* 424e almost word for word.

be treated with ingratitude when we are healthy: we should acknowledge that we owe to it our good health, and make it our guide through the rest of our lives, so that we do not fall back through idleness and self-indulgence into our original condition. It is the prerogative of one and the same art both to instil an excellence when it is missing, and to preserve and augment that same excellence when it is already present. That is how we should speak of music too. We should acknowledge our debt to it for bringing each of us into friendship with himself and with one another in the community; and we should practise it always, looking for a safeguard of our mutual fellow-feeling. The task should be pursued privately as well as communally. Just as there is a kind of health that belongs to the community and one that belongs to the individual, so there is a concord that holds between a whole city and itself, and one that holds between a single soul and its own parts.

No one, I believe, could now deny that we should educate the young through music, and that we should ourselves cultivate it throughout our lives wherever it is possible.

PLOTINUS

Enneads

1.6

The beautiful is mostly found in sight but also in things that we hear, in   I
arrangements of words and also in music, that is, in all kinds of music –
for indeed, tunes and rhythms are beautiful. For those who are advancing
upwards, away from the realm of perception, practices are also beautiful, as are actions, dispositions and types of knowledge; and there is also
beauty of the virtues. If there is any further beauty prior to these, this
discussion will make it plain.

So what is it that has made us imagine bodies to be beautiful and has
made hearing approve of sounds as beautiful? How are all the things
beautiful which depend, one after another, on the soul? Is everything
made beautiful by one and the same beauty or is bodily beauty different
from other kinds? What are these things, or this thing? Some things,
such as bodies, are beautiful not because of what they are in themselves
but by participation, while others, like the nature of virtue, are beautiful
in themselves. The same bodies appear sometimes beautiful, sometimes
not since being bodies and being beautiful are different things. So what is
this which is present in bodies? We should consider this first. What is it
that attracts the eyes of spectators, turns them towards itself, draws them
on and makes them enjoy the sight? For if we discover this we can perhaps 'use it as a ladder'[1] and have a view of the rest.

---

[1] Cf. Plato, *Symposium* 211c (p. 24).

More or less everyone says that symmetry of parts with one another and with the whole, with the addition of fine colour, produces visual beauty and that both for the objects of sight and, generally, for everything else being beautiful is a matter of being symmetrical and measured.[2] According to this view, it is necessarily the case that nothing simple will be beautiful, only what is composite. The whole will be beautiful, in their view, while the individual parts will not have the quality of being beautiful in themselves but will contribute to making the whole beautiful. But if the whole is beautiful, the parts must be beautiful too; it could not be composed of ugly parts – all the parts must have beauty. Moreover, on this view, beautiful colours and the light of the sun, for example, will not be classed as beautiful because they are simple and do not owe their beauty to symmetry. How then is gold beautiful? What makes lightning at night and stars beautiful to see? Simple sounds will similarly be discounted, although often each sound which is a part of a beautiful whole is also beautiful itself. Furthermore, when the same face appears beautiful at one time, not beautiful at another, although its symmetry remains the same, surely we have to say that the beautiful is something else, other than the symmetrical, and that something else makes the symmetrical beautiful?

If they move on to practices and beautiful expressions of thought and claim that here too the symmetrical is responsible for beauty, what could be meant by symmetry in beautiful practices, or laws, or types of learning and knowledge? How could theories be symmetrical with one another? If the point is that they are in harmony, bad ideas can be consistent and in harmony with one another: the claims that 'self-control is folly' and that 'justice is noble silliness'[3] are harmonious and in tune and consistent with each other.

All virtue is beauty of soul, a truer beauty than the ones mentioned earlier. How is virtue symmetrical? It is not symmetrical in the same way as magnitudes or numbers. Since there are several parts of the soul, what is the formula for the combination or mixture of the parts or the theories? What would be the beauty of intellect on its own?

2   So let us start again and say what the origin of beauty in bodies is. It is something which becomes perceptible at the first glance; the soul speaks

---

[2] This was a standard Stoic view.
[3] See *Republic* 1.348c and 8.560d; cf. *Gorgias* 491e.

of it as if it understood it, recognizes and welcomes it and, as it were, adapts to it. By contrast, when it encounters the ugly, it shrinks back, rejects it and turns away from it, since it is not in harmony with it and finds it alien.[4] Our explanation of this is that the soul, with the nature it has, related to superior reality in the realm of being, rejoices when it sees something akin to it or a trace of what is akin to it; it is thrilled, returns to itself and remembers itself and the things which belong to it. What likeness is there between things in this world and the beauties in the higher world? If there is a likeness, we assume the things are alike. How are both the things in that world and the things in this world beautiful? We say the things in this world are beautiful because they participate in form. For everything which is shapeless, although naturally able to receive shape and form, is ugly and outside divine rational principle as long as it has no share in rational principle and form; this is the utterly ugly. Also ugly is that which is not measured by shape and rational principle because its matter has not allowed itself to be completely shaped in accordance with form. Form approaches and arranges what is going to be one ordered whole composed of many parts; it brings it into a completed unity and makes it one by agreement of its parts, since form itself is one and what is shaped by it must be one in so far as that is possible for a thing composed of many parts. So beauty settles on it once it has been unified, giving itself to both parts and wholes. When beauty takes hold of something that is one and uniform in its parts, it gives the same gift to the whole. Similarly, sometimes art gives beauty to a whole house, with all its parts, and sometimes nature gives beauty to a single stone. That is how the beautiful body comes into being, by sharing in a rational principle which comes from the divine realm.

Beauty is recognized by the power in the soul appointed for this task; **3** there is nothing more authoritative in judging its own affairs, especially when the rest of the soul judges along with it. Perhaps the rest of the soul also makes a statement by matching up the beautiful body with the form inside itself and using this form for judgement like a ruler used to judge what is straight. How is something bodily in harmony with what is prior to body? How does the architect match up the house before him with the form of a house within him and declare it to be beautiful? He can do this because, if one abstracts from the stones, the house before him is that

---

4 Cf. *Symposium* 206d (p. 23).

inner form divided into parts by the external mass of matter; the form has no parts, yet appears divided into many parts. So when sense-perception sees the form in bodies binding together and mastering the contrary nature which is shapeless, and sees some shape conspicuously over and above other shapes, it gathers together into one what is dispersed, takes it up and refers it, now without parts, to the soul's interior and presents it to that which is within as something harmonious, matching and dear to it. Similarly a good man delights in seeing a trace of virtue in a young man, in harmony with his own inner truth.

The simple beauty of colour derives from shape, from mastery of the darkness in matter thanks to the presence of incorporeal light which is rational principle and form. That is why fire itself is beautiful compared to the other bodies, because it holds the rank of form in relation to the other elements, placed at the top and more subtle than the other bodies, since it is near the incorporeal.[5] It alone does not admit the others, while the others do admit it. For it warms them but does not itself become cold and it is coloured primarily while the others take the form of colour from it. It shines and gleams as if it were form. The weaker colour which fades in a fire's light is no longer beautiful since it does not participate in the whole form of the colour.

The imperceptible harmonies in sounds which bring about the perceptible ones make the soul conscious of their beauty in the same way, showing the same thing as regards another of the senses. It follows that perceptible harmonies are measured by numbers, not according to any and every formula but according to one which serves to produce form in order to master matter. So much for perceptible beauties, images and shadows, which, as it were, sally forth and arrive in matter, adorning it and exciting us when they appear.

4   We must leave sense-perception to stay down below; we must go on up and consider the beauties beyond, which it is no longer the role of sense-perception to see but which the soul sees and describes without sense-organs. Perceptible beauties cannot be discussed by people who have neither seen them nor grasped them as beautiful, such as those who have been blind from birth. In the same way the beauty of practices cannot be discussed by those who have not accepted the beauty of practices,

---

[5] This appears to be a Platonist adaptation of the Stoic view that pure fire is the formative element in the universe.

types of knowledge and other things of that kind, and the 'light' of virtue cannot be discussed by those who have not even imagined how beautiful is 'the countenance of justice' and self-control, 'more beautiful than the evening or the morning star'.[6] But there must be people who see this beauty by that with which the soul sees things of this kind; when they see it they feel pleasure and shock and are far more excited than when they saw the previous beauties because now they are grasping true beauties. These are the feelings people must experience in relation to beauty of any kind: awe, a pleasant sense of shock, longing, love and excitement accompanied by pleasure. It is possible to experience these feelings in response to invisible beauties, and more or less all souls do experience them but those souls which are more inclined to love invisible beauties experience them more strongly. So too where bodies are concerned: everyone sees but not everyone is stung by their beauty to the same extent; there are some who are stung particularly severely who are actually said to be in love.

We must ask those who are in love with the imperceptible the following questions: 'What do you feel about practices which are called beautiful and beautiful ways of behaving and self-controlled types of character and, in general, virtuous activities and dispositions and the beauty of souls? What do you feel when you see your own inner beauty? How are you stirred up into a frenzy and long to spend time on your own, gathering yourselves together away from bodies?' These are the feelings experienced by those who are really in love. What is the object about which they have these feelings? It is not a shape, nor a colour, nor any size, but soul which itself has no colour and possesses self-control, something with no colour, and all the other 'light' of the virtues. You feel like this when you see, either in yourself or in someone else, greatness of soul, an upright character, pure self-control, courage with its fearsome face,[7] dignity, modesty moving swiftly in a peaceful, calm, unperturbed manner and godlike intellect shining down on them all. We love and admire these things but why do we call them beautiful? They are real and appear to us and one who has seen them can never say anything else except that they are really real. What does 'really real' mean? It means they are beautiful.

5

---

[6] See Plato, *Phaedrus* 250b (p. 69) and Aristotle, *Nicomachean Ethics* 5.3.1129b, quoting the lost *Melanippe* of Euripides.
[7] See Homer's description of Ajax going into battle at *Iliad* 7.212.

But the argument still requires us to show why real things have made the soul lovable. What is it that shines on all the virtues like a light?

Would you like to consider the opposite case, the ugly qualities which develop in the soul, and contrast them with these? Perhaps considering what the ugly is and why it appears like that will contribute to our finding what we are looking for. Suppose an ugly soul, dissolute and unjust, full of numerous desires and extensive disturbance, beset by fear because of cowardice and by envy because of pettiness, thinking only low, mortal thoughts insofar as it thinks at all, crooked all over, fond of impure pleasures, living a life of bodily sensations and taking pleasure in its ugliness. Shall we not say that this ugliness has become attached to it like a beauty brought in from outside? It has damaged it and made it impure and 'soiled with much evil'.[8] It no longer possesses either a pure life or pure perception but experiences life feebly, diluted with a great deal of death, because evil is mixed into it. It no longer sees what a soul should see and is no longer left in peace with itself because it keeps on being dragged out, and down, towards the dark. In my opinion it is impure and pulled in all directions towards the objects of sense-perception, with a great deal of bodily stuff stirred into it. Consorting with much that is material and accepting that into itself, it has exchanged its form for another, with a mixture which makes it worse. It is as if someone sank into mire or mud: he would no longer show the beauty he had before but we would see what he had wiped off on himself from the mire or mud. Ugliness has come upon him by the addition of something that does not belong to him and if he is to be beautiful again, it will be his business to wash himself clean and purify himself so that he is as he was before.

We would be right in saying that the soul becomes ugly by mixture and dilution and by inclining towards the body and matter. This is ugliness for the soul: not being pure and unmixed, like gold, but being filled up with earthiness. If someone takes the earth away, the gold is left behind and is beautiful, isolated from everything else, alone by itself. In the same way the soul too, isolated from the desires which it has because of the body, with which it has spent too much time, freed from the other emotions and purified from the results of its embodiment, when it remains alone, puts off all the ugliness due to the other nature.

---

[8] Cf. Plato, *Phaedo* 66b.

For, as the ancient teaching tells us, self-control, courage and all virtue, **6** including wisdom itself, are a form of purification. That is why the mysteries are right to present us with an allegory, saying that one who has not been purified will lie in mud even when he goes to Hades because the impure is fond of mud on account of its badness.[9] Similarly pigs too, which are unclean in body, enjoy that kind of thing. What else would true self-control be other than not consorting with bodily pleasures, but avoiding them as impure and not belonging to the pure? Courage is not being afraid of death. And death is the separation of the soul from the body. A person does not fear this if he likes being by himself. Greatness of soul is despising the things in this world. Wisdom is the process of thought which turns away from the things below and leads the soul upwards. So the purified soul becomes form and rational principle, entirely incorporeal and intellectual, belonging completely to the divine whence comes the source of beauty and everything of that kind related to it. When soul is raised to the level of intellect it becomes still more beautiful. Intellect and the things which come from intellect are the soul's beauty, its own beauty, not foreign to it, since only then is it really soul. That is why it is right to say that the soul's becoming something good and beautiful is becoming like God, because the beautiful comes from God, and so does everything else which falls to the lot of real beings. Or rather, Beauty personified is reality and the other nature is the ugly, and the same thing is primary evil, so that for God good and beautiful, or the Good and Beauty, are the same. So we must follow the same line of enquiry to discover beauty and goodness, ugliness and evil. First we should posit the personified Beauty which is also the Good; intellect, which is the beautiful, derives immediately from that; soul is beautiful because of intellect; and everything else is beautiful as soon as it is shaped by soul, including the beauties in actions and practices. Moreover bodies that are said to be beautiful are beautiful as soon as soul makes them so; because soul is something divine and, as it were, a portion of the beautiful, it makes everything it grasps and masters beautiful insofar as it is possible for them to participate in beauty.

We must go back up to the Good which every soul desires. Anyone **7** who has seen it knows what I mean when I say it is beautiful. For it is desired as good and the desire for it is directed to good; it can be attained

[9] Cf. Plato, *Phaedo* 69c.

by those who proceed upwards and turn around and take off the garments in which we were clothed when we descended. Similarly those who go up to sacred rites must be purified and take off their previous clothes and go up naked. The ascent continues until, going past everything alien to God, one sees with oneself alone that which is in itself alone, unmixed, simple and pure, on which everything depends; everything looks towards it and exists, lives and thinks in relation to it, for it is responsible for life, intellect and being. If someone were to see this, what love and longing would he feel, wanting to be united with it? How would he not feel a shock of pleasure?[10] It is possible for one who has not yet seen it to desire it as good, but one who has seen it admires it as beautiful and is filled with pleasurable awe, shocked without being hurt; he feels true love and sharp pangs of longing, laughs at all other loves and despises what he previously thought beautiful. It is similar to what happens to people who have encountered appearances of gods and spirits and no longer appreciate the beauty of other bodies in the same way.

'Then what do we think it would be like if it were possible for someone to see beauty itself in a pure state, not tainted by flesh and the body, not on earth, not in the heavens, so that it may remain pure?'[11] For all these things are added on and mixed and not primary but derived from it. If one could see that which orchestrates everything, which remains by itself, giving to all but receiving nothing into itself, if one were continually looking at a sight like that and enjoying becoming like it, what other beauty would one need? For that itself is the supreme and primary beauty and it makes those who love it beautiful and lovable. Here indeed the greatest, the ultimate contest confronts our souls;[12] all our efforts are directed towards it, efforts not to be left without a share in the noblest vision. He who attains this is blessed, gazing at a blessed sight, but he who fails to attain it is a complete failure. For a failure is not someone who fails to win beautiful colours or bodies, or who fails to win power or office or kingship, but someone who fails to win this and only this. To attain this one should renounce gaining kingship and sovereignty over all the earth, the sea and the heavens if only by abandoning and spurning these things one can turn to the Good and see it.

---

[10] In inserting a negative here I follow the *addenda ad textum* of Henry and Schwyzer's OCT.
[11] Cf. Plato, *Symposium* 211a (p. 24) and 211d–e (p. 25).
[12] Cf. Plato, *Phaedrus* 247b.

What then is the way? What is the means? How could one see 'incon-   **8**
ceivable beauty'[13] as it remains in the holy sanctuary and does not come
out where even the uninitiated may see it? Let the one who can, follow
and go inside; he should leave the sight of his eyes outside and not turn
back to the bodily splendours he saw before. For when he sees bodily
beauties he must no longer run after them; recognizing that they are
images, traces and shadows he must hurry away towards that of which
they are images. If someone runs after bodily beauty, wanting to grasp
it as if it were real, like a beautiful reflection playing on water – there is
a story somewhere, I think, which presents an allegory about a man who
wanted to grasp a reflection and sank down into the stream and disappeared; in the same way someone who clings to beautiful bodies and does
not let go will sink not with his body but with his soul into dark depths
in which the intellect takes no pleasure where he will remain, blind in
Hades, and will spend his time with shadows both here and there. 'Let us
flee to our own dear country',[14] as someone might more truly advise us.
What is the way of escape and how are we to find it? We shall put out to
sea, as Odysseus did, escaping from the witch, Circe, or from Calypso,
as Homer says – I think in an allegory – not content to stay, despite having visual pleasures and spending his time with abundant sensual beauty.
Our country, where we came from, and our father are there. What is our
course and what is the way of escape? We cannot get there on foot; for
our feet carry us everywhere on earth, from one place to another. Nor do
you need to prepare a chariot with horses or a boat. You must let all these
things go and not look. Close your eyes, change your point of view and
awaken another kind of sight which everyone has but few use.

What does this inner sight look at? When it is just waking up, it is   **9**
quite unable to look at the bright objects presented to it. The soul itself
must be trained, first to look at beautiful practices, then beautiful works,
not works of art but the works of men who are regarded as good; then
look at the soul of those who produce beautiful works.

How can you see the sort of beauty that a good soul has? Go back
into yourself and look. If you do not yet see yourself as beautiful, be like
a sculptor making a statue which has to be beautiful: he takes away one
part, polishes off another, makes one part smooth and another clean until
he has revealed a beautiful face on the statue. In the same way you must

---

[13] Cf. Plato, *Republic* 6.509a, *Symposium* 218e.   [14] Homer, *Iliad* 2.140.

take away what is superfluous, straighten what is crooked, clean up what is dark and make it shine, and do not stop 'working on your statue' until the godlike splendour of your virtue shines out, until you see 'self-control enthroned on its holy seat'.[15] If you have become this and have seen it and are at home with yourself, clean and pure, with no impediment to becoming one in this way, no inner mixture of anything else, completely yourself, nothing but true light, not measured by any dimensions, neither circumscribed and reduced by shape nor increased and expanded by the absence of limit, but unmeasured in all directions because greater than any measurement and superior to any quantity – if you see yourself become this, at that moment you have become sight itself. Take courage: at that point you have already ascended and no longer need a guide; gaze without blinking and see, for this eye alone sees the great beauty.

However, if anyone comes to the sight, bleary with vices and not purified, or weak, unable through cowardice to look at very bright objects, he sees nothing, even if someone else shows him what is there to be seen. For looking at anything requires a power of sight akin to what is seen and like its object. No eye ever saw the sun without becoming sun-like and no soul can see the beautiful without becoming beautiful. Let everyone first become godlike and beautiful, if he intends to look at God and beauty. As he ascends he will come first to intellect and there he will know the Forms to be beautiful and will say that beauty is this, the Ideas.[16] Everything is beautiful because of these, the products of intellect and being. We say that what is beyond this, the nature of the Good, holds beauty as a screen in front of it. So in a general way of speaking it is the primary beauty; but if one distinguishes the intelligibles from the Good, one will say that the place of Forms is intelligible beauty and that the Good is that which lies beyond, the source and origin of beauty. Otherwise one will place the Good and primary beauty on the same level; in any case, beauty is in the intelligible world.

5.8.1–2

1 We maintain that one who has reached the vision of the intelligible world and has grasped the beauty of true intellect will also be able to

---

[15] Cf. Plato, *Phaedrus* 252d and 254b.
[16] Plotinus here is referring to the Platonic Forms or Ideas in the intelligible world. In Plotinus' metaphysics, as in Plato, *Republic* 6, the Good is superior to the Forms.

come to understand its father, which is beyond intellect. Since that is the case, let us try to see and explain to ourselves, in so far as it is possible to explain such things, how anyone can contemplate the beauty of intellect and of that world. Let us suppose, if you like, two lumps of stone lying side by side, one shapeless and untouched by art, the other already mastered by art and turned into a statue of a god or a human being – if a god, a Grace or one of the Muses, if a human being, not any particular human being but one produced by art from every sort of human beauty. The one in which the beauty of form has been realized by art will appear beautiful, not because it is a stone – for in that case the other lump of stone would be just as beautiful – but because of the form which art has put into it. This form was not in the material but in the person who had it in his mind even before it entered the stone. It was in the craftsman, not in so far as he had eyes or hands but because he had a share in art. So this beauty was in the art, and far better there; for what enters the stone is not the beauty in the art – that beauty remains unchanged and it is another, inferior beauty, derived from it, that enters. Even this beauty does not remain pure in the stone, as the craftsman intended, but only in so far as the stone has submitted to the art.

If art makes its product like what it is and has – and it makes it beautiful according to the rational principle of what it is making – it is beautiful to a greater degree, and more truly, since it has the beauty of art which is greater and more beautiful than the beauty in anything external. For the more a thing expands as it enters into matter, the weaker it becomes compared to that which abides in unity. Everything that is extended loses its own nature: strength becomes less strong, heat becomes less hot, power in general becomes less powerful and beauty becomes less beautiful. Every original cause must in itself be more powerful than the effect which it produces; it is not lack of music but music that makes a person musical, and music in the perceptible world is caused by music prior to this world. If anyone despises the arts, on the grounds that they make their products by imitating nature, we should reply, first, that natural things are also imitations and secondly, he should know that the arts do not simply imitate what we can see but go back to the rational principles from which nature derives. Furthermore, the arts do a great deal by themselves and since they possess beauty, they make additions where nature is defective. So Phidias too made his statue of Zeus, not from any perceptible model, but by grasping what Zeus would look like if he chose to appear before our eyes.[17]

2　　Let us leave the arts aside and consider the things whose works they are said to imitate, i.e., beauties which come about naturally and are said to be such: all rational and irrational animals, especially all the most successful examples where the craftsman who modelled them has mastered the matter and bestowed on them the form he wanted. What is the beauty in these things? It is certainly not the blood and the menstrual fluid. The colour of these is different and their shape is no shape, or it is a shapeless shape or like that which circumscribes something simple [such as matter].[18] From what source did the beauty of Helen, over whom men fought, shine forth? What about all the other women who were like Aphrodite in beauty? Where did the beauty of Aphrodite herself come from, or of any totally beautiful human being, or of any god who has appeared for us to see or who has not appeared but has a beauty which could in principle be seen? Surely in all cases this is form, coming from the maker into what has been generated, just as, in the case of the arts, it was said to come from the arts into their products? Well then: is it the case that things which are made and the rational principle in matter are beautiful but the principle which is not in matter but in the maker which is first and immaterial [and certainly unifying] is not beauty?

If the mass was beautiful, in so far as it was mass, it would follow that the rational principle which made it was not beautiful because it was not mass; on the other hand, if the same form, whether in something small or in something large, moves and influences the soul of the observer in the same way by its own power, we should not attribute beauty to the size of the mass. The following point is further evidence: we do not yet see a thing while it is outside us, but when it comes inside it influences us. However it enters through our eyes as form only. How else could it get through something small? The size is drawn in along with it, since it has become not large in mass but large in form.

Moreover the maker must be either ugly or neutral or beautiful. If it were ugly, it would not produce the opposite, and if it were neutral, why would

[17] Cf., for example, Cicero, *Orator* 2.8–9 (p. 124), Philostratus, *Life of Apollonius of Tyana* 6.19 (p. 169), Proclus, *Commentary on the Timaeus* 1.265.18–26 (p. 235).
[18] Both the text and the interpretation of this sentence are uncertain. I follow the interpretation of A. H. Armstrong in the Loeb translation. The words 'such as matter' do not belong here, since for Plotinus, as Armstrong says, 'matter cannot have an outline, even the simplest'.

it produce something beautiful rather than something ugly? Indeed nature which shapes such beautiful things is far more beautiful but we, unaccustomed to see the things within and ignorant of them, pursue the external, not knowing that it is what lies within that moves us. We are like someone who sees his own reflection or pursues it, not knowing where it came from.

That what we pursue is something else and that beauty is not a matter of size is clearly shown by the beauty in types of knowledge and in practices and generally in souls. It is precisely here that a greater beauty can be found, when you see and admire wisdom in someone, not looking at their face – for that might be ugly – but putting aside all shape and pursuing their inner beauty. If it does not yet move you so that you can call someone like this beautiful, you will not be pleased with yourself as beautiful when you look within. While you are in this state, it would be futile for you to seek beauty, for you will be seeking with something ugly and impure. That is why discussions about things like this are not for everyone; but if you have seen your own inner beauty, remember!

6.7.22.24–36

In this world too we should say that beauty is what illuminates symmetry rather than symmetry itself, and this is what is lovable. Why is the light of beauty more noticeable on a living face, and only a trace evident on a dead one, even if the face, with its flesh and its symmetry, has not yet wasted away? Why are the more lifelike statues more beautiful even if the others are better proportioned? Why is a rather ugly living person more beautiful than a beautiful statue? It is because the living is more desirable. This is because it has soul; and soul is more like the good, since it is coloured in some way by the light of the Good and, being so coloured, it wakes and rises up and lifts up what belongs to it and makes it good, as far as it can, and awakens it.

6.7.31–33

Since the beauty and light in everything comes from that which is prior to them, Intellect[19] obtained from there the light of intellectual activity with 31

---

[19] Here and elsewhere in this extract I use capital letters for 'Intellect' and 'Soul' when Plotinus is referring not to an individual intellect or soul but to Intellect and Soul as hypostases, or levels, within his metaphysical system.

which it illuminated nature and Soul obtained power towards life since a fuller life entered into it. Intellect was raised up there and remained there, content in the presence of the Good; and the soul that could do so returned to it and, when it knew and saw, rejoiced in the sight and was shocked and amazed in so far as it could see. It saw as if in a state of shock and, since it had something of the Good in itself, it became aware of it and was moved to longing for it, just as the image of their beloved arouses in lovers a desire to see the actual object of love. In this world lovers shape themselves to become like their beloved, making their bodies better looking and their souls more alike since, as far as possible, they do not want to fall short of the beloved in self-control or any other virtue – otherwise they would be rejected by those they love who have these qualities – and these are the lovers who are able to have intercourse. In the same way the soul too loves the Good, moved by it to love from the beginning. The soul which has its love ready to hand does not wait to be reminded by the beautiful things in this world. Since it has love, even if it does not realize that it has it, it is always seeking. Wanting to be carried towards the Good, it despises things in this world and when it sees the beauties in this universe here it is suspicious of them because it sees that they are in bodies of flesh, polluted by their present dwelling and fragmented by extension, not the things that are beautiful in themselves; for those beauties, being what they are, would not venture to enter the mud of bodies and soil and obscure themselves.

When the soul sees the things of this world flowing past, it already fully understands that the beauty diffused over them comes from elsewhere. Then it is carried off there, since it is skilled in finding out what it loves, and does not desist until it grasps hold of it, unless perhaps someone takes even its love away. There indeed it sees that everything is beautiful and true and it gains strength from being filled with the life of real being; having itself become really real and having really gained understanding, it perceives that it is near to what it had been seeking for a long time.

32 Where then is the one who made such great beauty and life and generated reality? You see the beauty which rests upon all the Forms themselves in their variety.[20] It is beautiful staying here; but when one is in the midst of

---

[20] By 'Forms' here Plotinus means the Platonic Forms, located at the level of Intellect in his metaphysical system.

beauty, one should consider what is the source of these things and of their beauty. This source cannot be any one of them, for being one of them, it will be a part. So it cannot be a shape of any kind, or a particular power, or the sum of powers and shapes which have come to be and exist there; it must be beyond all powers and beyond all shapes. The origin of all this is the formless, formless not in the sense of needing shape but as the source of all intellectual shape. That which came to be, if it came to be, necessarily became a particular thing and had a specific shape; how could something that no one has made have a particular shape? So it is none of these things, and all of them; it is none of them because real beings are posterior to it, but it is all of them because they derive from it.

What size could it have when it has the power to make everything? It would be infinite, but if it were infinite it would have no size. Size belongs to the last and lowest things. Even if it is going to make size, it cannot itself have it. The greatness of reality is not quantitative. Something else posterior to it would have size. Its greatness consists in the fact that nothing is more powerful than it nor can be compared with it: for how could anything be equal to any aspect of it when they have nothing in common? Eternity and universality give it neither measure, nor indeed measurelessness; for then how could it measure everything else? It does not have any form either. Indeed when you cannot grasp the form and shape of what is longed for, it would be most longed for and most desired, and the love of it would be measureless. Love is not limited in that case, because the beloved is not limited either, but the love of this would be infinite – which means that its beauty too would be of another kind, beauty beyond beauty. For if it is nothing, what beauty can it be? However if it is lovable, it would be the generator of beauty. So the power to produce everything is the flower of beauty, the beauty that makes beauty. It generates beauty and makes it more beautiful by the excess of beauty which comes from it, so that it is both the origin and the limit of beauty. Since it is the origin of beauty it makes beautiful that of which it is the origin and makes it beautiful not in shape; indeed the beauty itself which comes to be is without shape, and yet, in another way, it is shaped. For what is called this very thing, shape, is only shape in another, but shapeless in itself. So what participates in beauty has shape, but beauty does not.

So even when it is called beauty, you should avoid shape like this still more, and not put it before your eyes so that you do not fall from beauty to what is called beautiful by faint participation. Form without shape **33** is beautiful, as form; it is beautiful to the extent that you have stripped away all shape, for example, the 'shape' in reasoning by which we say one thing differs from another, as when we say that justice and self-control are different from each other and yet are both beautiful. When the intellect thinks of something particular, it is diminished, as it is also even if it grasps everything in the intelligible world all together. If it thinks of an individual thing, it has one intelligible shape; if it thinks of things all together, it has a kind of variegated shape, still asking how it should view what is beyond it, the wholly beautiful which is both variegated and not variegated, which the soul desires without saying why it longs for such a thing – but our reasoning says that this is the real thing since the nature of the best and most lovable is in the completely formless. So if you bring something into form and show it to the soul, the soul seeks something else beyond this which gave it shape. Reasoning tells us that what has shape, as well as shape and form itself, is all measured, and such things are not complete or self-sufficient or beautiful in themselves but are mixed. So these beautiful things must be measured but not the really beautiful or the 'super-beautiful'; and if this is the case it must not be shaped or be a form. So the primarily beautiful and first is without form and Beauty personified is that, the nature of the Good.

The experience of lovers bears witness to this: while one's attention is on the impression perceived by the senses, the lover is not yet in love; but when the lover himself generates from that an imperceptible impression in himself, in his partless soul, then love springs forth. He seeks to see the beloved, so that he may revive that fading impression. But if he could understand that he should move on to what is more shapeless, he would desire that. Indeed what he experienced from the beginning was the love of a great light, aroused by a faint gleam.

Indeed the trace of the shapeless is shape; for it is the shapeless that generates shape, not vice versa, and it generates it when matter comes to it. Matter is necessarily furthest away from it because it does not have any shape of itself, not even the last and lowest ones. So if what is lovable is not the matter but what is formed by the form, and the form upon the matter comes from soul, and soul is more form and more lovable, and intellect is more form than soul and still more lovable, then we should assume that the first nature of beauty is formless.

AUGUSTINE

On Order

2.11.32–19.51[1]

11   Thus[2] I see two cases in which the powers of our ruling faculty are   32
affected by the senses themselves: the visible products of human activity, and audible sounds and words. In either case our mind is in need of
an additional judgement[3] of the senses due to the fact that the body is
involved in both: in the former case, the judgement of the eyes, in the
latter of the ears. Accordingly, when we see something that is shaped
in such a way that its parts are in harmony with one another, it is not
inept for us to say that it 'appears to have order or regularity'. Also, when
we hear something that sounds harmonious, we do not hesitate to say
that the 'sound exhibits regularity or proportion'. At the same time,[4] no
one would escape ridicule if he said 'it smells with regularity', 'it tastes
proportionate', or 'it is orderly to the touch'...

---

[1] Although the nature of Augustine's statements used in this selection is clearly aesthetic, the general context of *On Order* is not: the work is mostly devoted to the discussion of providence and
the divine and human order.

[2] The key to an adequate rendering of the following passage into English is the meaning of the
Latin *ratio* and its derivatives *rationabilis* and *rationabiliter* as used by Augustine: see Note on
the texts and the translations.

[3] I.e., in addition to its own rational judgement. *Nuntius* (more appropriately 'witness') is freely
rendered as 'judgement'.

[4] Augustine here presents a division of the senses into higher (aesthetic) and lower, according to
whether they can be 'encoded' with regularity. Vision and hearing are traditionally considered as
the higher senses, up to modern times. In antiquity similar ideas were expressed, e.g., by Plato,
Hippias Major 297e, 298a (pp. 20–1) or *Philebus* 51b ff. where vision and hearing – but not only
these two – are listed among the pleasures that are pure and unmixed with pain, and Plotinus,
Ennead 1.6.1 (p. 185).

33   We have then, so far as we were able to investigate, certain traces of regularity or proportion in our senses and, in so far as it pertains to sight and hearing, in the pleasurable response itself … So far as vision is concerned, whenever parts harmonize with each other with regularity, this is usually called beautiful. However, as regards hearing, when voices sound good together according to some regularity or musical ratios,[5] or a song is composed with some regular rhythm, the proper name for this is sweetness. At the same time, when we are enticed by colour in beautiful things, or when, in the sweet realm of sounds, a plucked string sounds, as it were, clearly and purely, in neither case do we usually call this 'regular' or 'proportionate'.[6] It remains, therefore, to admit that in the pleasurable response of those senses it is only that which possesses a certain measure and modulation that pertains to the rational nature of proportion.

34   And so, carefully inspecting the details of this particular building, we cannot help being displeased at the fact that we see one door placed to the side, and the other almost in the middle, but not quite there. Clearly, in manufactured things positioning parts unevenly without any compelling reason almost seems to offend our sight.[7] As for the fact that the three windows inside this building – one in the middle, and one on each side of it – pour down sunlight[8] at equal intervals, how it delights us, after intent observation, and how it ravishes our mind! This is something evident and does not need too long an explanation. Whence architects themselves in their own terminology call this regularity 'proportion' and say that incongruously placed parts are 'out of proportion'.[9] This is a widely known fact and applies to almost all the arts and human products. Indeed, in

[5] The mathematical ratios that correspond to musical intervals (a discovery ascribed to Pythagoras), such as 1 : 1 1/2 (fifth), 1 : 1 1/3 (fourth), etc.
[6] Cf. Plotinus' observations in *Ennead* 1.6 (p. 186) regarding the beauty of pure sounds or colours. Despite the obvious influence of Plotinus on Augustine, their views on what constitutes the main principle of beauty or aesthetics seem to disagree at least in spirit. Plotinus reduces all to the principle of simplicity and oneness (*Ennead* 1.6). Although Augustine speaks of unity as the ultimate principle that governs all proportion in *On True Religion* 30.55 and 32.60 (p. 221, p. 224), in general he prefers to think of the aesthetic principle as inseparable from proportion and harmony, i.e., involvement of multiple parts. For an explanation one may look to the Christian doctrine of the Trinity (which is the ultimate source of beauty) as a coincidence of relations, i.e., not something altogether uniform like the Neoplatonic One.
[7] The expression 'without any compelling reason' can be taken both with the expression 'positioning parts' and 'seem to offend'. The translation reflects this ambiguity, although the second possibility is the more interesting one.
[8] The *PL* reading *solis* is chosen over the *CCSL solio*.
[9] I.e., beyond the rational principle.

On Order

poetry, where we say there is also regularity and proportion that pertains to the pleasure of the ears, who does not feel that it is a sort of measuring that is responsible for all this delight? How about a dancing actor? If one watches closely, all those gestures signify certain things. Accordingly, we say that there is some rationality in this dance, because it signifies and demonstrates something well, in addition to arousing sensible pleasure. At the same time, some measured rhythmic motion of the limbs delights our eyes by that very regularity.[10] Indeed, if an actor portrayed a winged and feathered Venus or a cloaked Cupid, no matter how admirable his postures or the movement of his limbs were, it is the mind, which detects these signs of things, that would be offended by way of the eyes, not the eyes themselves. The eyes, on the other hand, would be offended if he did not move beautifully. For it is this aspect, i.e., visible movement, that pertains to bodily sense. And it is through sense that the mind, by the very fact that it is mixed with the body in the act of sensation, perceives a pleasurable response. Therefore the 'sense' is one thing, and 'by way of the sense' is quite another. For the sense of sight is appeased by a beautiful movement, but the mind by way of the sense is appeased only by the beautiful way this movement signifies something. This phenomenon is even easier to detect in hearing. For whatever sounds agreeable is pleasing and enticing to the sense of hearing itself. However, that which is signified well by the same sound, although it is delivered by way of the ears, nevertheless pertains solely to the mind. Accordingly, when we hear the following verses:

why the sun hastens so much to plunge into the ocean in the winter,
or what cause prevents long nights in the summer ...[11]

it would be one thing to praise the metres and another to praise the sense, nor do we take it in the same way when we say 'it exhibits regularity in the way it sounds' and 'what is said makes good sense'.[12]

. . .

14 From this point on, our reason wished to be ravished to the most **39** blessed contemplation of the divine things themselves. But lest it might

---

[10] Augustine is trying to distinguish between rational signification or symbolism and our immediate 'quasi-rational' response to patterns, both of which can be rendered in Latin through the same term *ratio* ('reason' in one sense and 'regularity' in the other).
[11] Virgil, *Aeneid* 1.745–6; *Georgics* 2.481–2.
[12] I.e., exhibits rational patterns. In both cases Augustine uses the same term *rationabiliter*.

fall from the heights, it sought supporting steps[13] and attempted to make its own way using its own achievements and orderly nature. For it desired that sort of beauty which it could contemplate alone in its pure state, without these eyes. However, it was impeded by the senses. Therefore, for a little while it turned its gaze towards the senses which, proclaiming that they possessed the truth, with their discordant clamour called back reason that hastened to proceed to other things.

. . .

41 Thus at this fourth step reason perceived that it is numbers that reign and perfect everything in either rhythms or melodies. It carefully pondered of what kind they were. It found them to be divine and eternal, especially because it had constructed all the previous steps with their help. Now it could hardly bear the fact that their splendour and clarity was stained with the corporeal matter of sounds. In fact, it is precisely for the reason that what the mind sees is always present and is acknowledged to be immortal (and numbers appeared to be of this kind),[14] but the sound, because it belongs to the sensible realm, flows by into the past and is impressed in the memory, that the poets, in a lie that is not far from truth, made the Muses into daughters of Zeus and Memory.[15] Whence this discipline that shares in both the senses and the intellect is called music.

42   15 Hence reason proceeded to the domain of the eyes and, inspecting the earth and the heavens, felt that it was pleased by nothing else except beauty, and in beauty by shapes, in shapes by proportions, in proportions by numbers. Then it asked itself, whether visible lines or circles or any other forms or shapes matched in quality those contained by the intellect. It found visible shapes to be much inferior: what the eyes saw could not possibly compare in any way to what the mind contemplated. Accordingly, it isolated these proportions into a separate area of science and arranged them into an academic discipline called geometry. Reason was also greatly moved by the motion of the heavens, which invited a

---

[13] This is Augustine's famous 'ladder' of beauty that leads to the divine. The metaphor is common in the Platonic tradition: cf. Plato, *Symposium* 211c (p. 24) and Plotinus, *Ennead* 1.6.1 (p. 185).

[14] Augustine makes a distinction between 'eternal truths' that can always be accessed and verified by the intellect and the truths derived from sense data that are stored by the memory and can be forgotten, distorted, etc.

[15] The Muses are presented as daughters of Zeus and Mnemosyne in Homer, *Iliad* 2.491, 598 and Hesiod, *Theogony* 54f.

more thorough investigation. And it understood – from the most uniform changes of the seasons, from the calculated and precise movements of the stars, and from the regular succession of periods of time – that even in the heavens nothing else reigned but measure and numbers. In a like manner, then, it separated these regularities and arranged them in a certain order into the science of astrology, which provides a strong argument for religion and a constant torment for the inquisitive.

. . .

19 Gradually[16] the soul also comes to the idea of proper conduct and the   **50**
best way of life: this time not by faith alone, but with the help of sure reasoning. Indeed, it will seem most disgraceful and deplorable to it, whose gaze is fixed on the nature and power of numbers, that verses should run smoothly, and the cithara should sound harmoniously as a result of its own artistic skill, and that at the same time its own life and itself, i.e., the soul, should go astray, dominated by wantonness, and sound discordantly with the most disturbing clamour of vices.

But when the soul has arranged and organized itself, and made itself   **51**
harmonious and beautiful, it will then dare to look at God: the very source, whence all true things emanate and the father of truth himself.

---

[16] Augustine here expands the idea that detecting a parallel between the arrangement of musical sounds and the arrangement of psychic powers brings us to a conclusion that harmony must be preserved in both. For similar aesthetic-ethical parallels see Plato, *Republic* 3.401a–402a (pp. 50–1) and Cicero, *On Duties* 1.40.145–41.146 (p. 139).

On Music

6, 2.3 – 13.38

3 2 TEACHER: Therefore whatever it is that allows us, not by reason but naturally, to discern whether the sound we hear is agreeable or disagreeable, I call the number principle of the sense of hearing. However, this power of approval or disapproval is not dependent on the actual perception of sound by our hearing. (Clearly, our ears are equally open to both good and bad sound combinations.) So make sure you do not confuse the two in the least. For let us say now we recite a verse slowly, and now we do it faster. Clearly, the length of time each version occupies is different, but the metric pattern remains the same. What, then, is responsible for soothing our ears by the metric pattern itself? It is that power, by which we approve harmonious and reject discordant sounds. Let us take the case when a verse recited faster is perceived within a shorter time period than the one recited more slowly. Is there any other difference, apart from the length of time during which our ears are affected by the sound? Clearly, the condition of the ears when they are affected by the sound is in no way identical to the one when they are not affected. And just as hearing is different from not hearing, so is hearing this particular sound different from hearing some other sound. Therefore, this condition neither extends farther than, nor stops short of, the limits of that sound that produced it. And this affection of the mind is different in the case of an iambic verse as opposed to a tribrach,[1]

---

[1] A poetic foot consisting of three short syllables.

206

and lasts longer in a verse recited more slowly, and for a shorter time in one recited more quickly. There is none in the case of silence. And if it occurs when the sound has a certain numerical pattern, it must also have this pattern, and it cannot exist, except when the sound that effects it is present. It is similar to an impression in water, which is neither formed before an object is dipped in it, nor persists when the object is removed. At the same time, that natural power of judgement that our hearing possesses does not cease at the moment of silence. Nor is it generated in us by the actual sound, but it is rather the sound that is received by it, for either approval or disapproval. For this reason, these two[2] must be distinguished, unless I am mistaken, and we must admit that the numbers that exist in the affection of the ears itself at the time when something is heard are generated by the sound and silenced by its absence. This suggests that the numbers that exist in the sound itself can exist without those that are produced during the process of hearing, while the latter cannot exist without the former.

3   STUDENT: I agree.   **4**

T.: Now let us look at the third kind of numbers that exists in the very effort and activity of the one who is doing the enunciation. Can these numbers exist without those that are in the memory? For we can go through some rhythms,[3] even silently in our own mind, at the same pace as we would use when reproducing them out loud. It is clear that these involve some activity of the mind. And since this activity does not produce any sound and does not result in any affection of the ears, it proves that this kind can exist separately from the previous two, of which one is in the sound itself, and the other in the recipient of the sound when he hears it. But we ask if it could exist without the help of memory. Although, if it is the soul that drives those numbers that we detect in the rhythmic pulsation of the veins, the question is solved. For they clearly involve some activity, but at the same time do not require the assistance of memory. But if it is not clear regarding these latter whether they are a result of some activity of the soul, regarding those that are produced by the rhythm of breathing there is clearly no doubt, first, that they are numbers (judging by the intervals of time), and, second, that they are

---

[2] I.e., the power of judgement and sensory images of sounds.
[3] Here Augustine does not mean 'verses' as in previous examples, but 'number patterns' in general, such as musical rhythms, etc.

generated by the soul in such a way that they can even be manipulated in many ways at will, but at the same time the process requires no memory whatsoever.

s.: It seems to me that this type can exist without the others.[4] I do not doubt that the pulse and breathing rate vary depending on the constitution of the body. But who would dare to deny that these occur due to some activity of the soul? Sure enough, even the movement of a body is either slower or faster, depending on its shape and size. But there is surely none at all if the soul is not present and generating it.

т.: Now consider the fourth kind, namely those numbers that are stored in memory. For if we produce them in the act of recollection and then store them away again, as it were, in their secret hideaways, when we move on to other thoughts, I think it is clear enough that they can exist apart from the other kinds.

s.: I do not doubt that they can exist apart from the other kinds. At the same time, they could not have been memorized, had they not been heard or thought of before that. For this reason, although they do remain when the other ones cease, one must still keep in mind that they are impressed by those other kinds, which preceded them.

5   4   т.: I have no objection to that. I was also about to ask you which of these four kinds of numbers, in your opinion, is the most eminent, except that I believe that during our discussion we somehow came up with a fifth kind: the one that is contained in our innate sensory judgement itself, when we are delighted by the regularity of numbers and discomforted by their irregularity. For I do not despise your observation that we would have no power of sensory judgement whatsoever without some numbers lurking in our senses. Or do you think that this great power belongs to one of the aforesaid four kinds?

s.: No, as for me, I think that this last kind should be distinguished from all others. Indeed, sound is one thing, which is a bodily quality; hearing is something else, which is the way the soul that is in the body reacts to sounds; yet another is a faster or slower generation of numbers; add to this the memory of these things; finally, there is, as it were, some natural ability of judging all this by feeling affinity or discomfort.

---

[4] Augustine actually writes 'without the other three'; however, since he only speaks of the third kind at this point, this is clearly an error.

т.: Come, now, tell me which one of these five is the most eminent.　6
s.: I think this fifth one.
т.: You are right. For it would not have been able to pass judgement about the other ones, if it did not surpass them in eminence.

...

5　т.: To make it brief, it seems to me that when the soul in the body　10 senses something, it is not affected by it in any way, but simply becomes attuned to its own various reactions. As a result, it becomes aware of those bodily affections, either agreeable, as in the case of conformity,[5] or uncomfortable due to a misfit. And all this is precisely what is called sensation ...

т.: These are its own movements that the soul adds to the preceding　12 affections of the body, which delight it when it harmonizes with them and offend it when they become uncomfortable. However, when it is affected in some way by its own movements of this sort, the impact clearly comes from the soul itself, when it adjusts itself to the body, and not from the body. As a result, the soul switches some of the focus away from itself,[6] for the body always holds a lower position compared to the soul.

...

6　т.: I see five kinds of numbers that we distinguished and ordered　16 hierarchically in some way according to their status. Now we should find appropriate names for them: in this way later on we will have exactly as many terms as we have referents. Do you agree?
s.: I do.
т.: So let us call the first kind 'judging', the second kind 'progressing',[7] the third kind 'occurring'[8] the fourth kind 'mnemonic', and the fifth kind 'sounding'.
s.: I understand and will use these terms gladly.

...

7　т.: Now think again and tell me which of those seem immortal to you?　17 Or do you think that all of them fade and pass away when their time comes?

---

[5] I.e., between the body and the type of affection or motion.
[6] I.e., the soul loses some of its superior status.
[7] I.e., the ones that control the procession of rhythms and metres as the brain generates them. The Latin terms for these classes of numbers are: *iudiciales, progressores, occursores, recordabiles, sonantes* (unfortunately any conceivable English equivalents will sound awkward). On the functions of the five kinds of numbers see 6.2.3–4.6.
[8] I.e., the impressions that correspond to actually sounding numbers, see 6.2.3–4.6.

s.: I think that only the 'judging' ones are immortal. The rest, from my observation, are either in a constant flux as they exist, or are obliterated from memory through forgetfulness.

T.: Are you as certain about their immortality as you are about the demise of the other ones, or should we enquire more carefully whether they are really immortal?

s.: Yes, let us enquire.

T.: So tell me, when I recite a verse somewhat faster or more slowly, as long as I comply with the metric rule, by which in each foot one long syllable accompanies one short one, does this sound wrong to you or offend the judgement of your senses?

s.: Not at all.

T.: What now? Can the sound that is produced by reciting those shorter and, as it were, swifter syllables take up more time than the time it sounds for?

s.: How could it?

T.: Now suppose that those 'judging' numbers were constrained to the same length of time, which is allotted to these sounding numbers. In this case, could they have any hope of judging those same sounding numbers, arranged according to the same iambic metre, except if the latter were recited a bit slower?

s.: Not a chance.

T.: Then it is clear that those numbers that are in charge of judging are not constrained by any interval of time.

s.: Completely clear ...

19 T.: But how about judging single and double periods on the scale of hours, days, or even months and years? Can those individuals become so advanced in judging extended intervals, that they could grasp those, too, by that 'judging' sense of theirs, and approve of them, even despite interruptions created by sleep, as they approve of those iambic verses, by some synchronized motion in this sense faculty?[9]

s.: They cannot.

T.: And why not? Is it not because any living being whatsoever in its own kind is endowed with a sense for space and time that is commensurate

---

9 I take *motionis nutibus* in Latin together, which contains the idea of 'approbation', already expressed, and probably refers to 'moving to the rhythm', or 'nodding in synch', which is a physical image but also, perhaps, an attempt to describe the reaction of the senses to sounding rhythms and metres.

with its position in the universe? As a result, just as its body is of a certain size compared to the world's body, of which it is a part, and its lifetime is of a certain duration compared to the whole of time, of which it is a part, in the same way its sense is commensurate with its activities, which stand in a certain relation to the motion of the whole universe, of which they are a part. In this way, containing all things, this world (often called 'heaven and earth' in the Scriptures) is great. And even if all its parts shrink or increase in their dimensions proportionately, it will still maintain its level of greatness.[10] Indeed, there is nothing great in the intervals of space and time when they are considered on their own, but only in relation to something shorter or smaller. Again, nothing in those intervals is simply short, but only in comparison to something greater. Now, in order to enable the functions of its bodily life, human nature is endowed with sense of such a kind that it cannot judge temporal intervals greater than those that are commensurate with the periodic activities belonging to this kind of life. For this reason, since such human nature is mortal, I also think that this sort of sense is mortal ...

8   But whatever the status is of those 'judging' numbers, one thing about   20
them is surely superior, namely that whether they are mortal is in doubt and is difficult to prove. At the same time, there is not even a question about the other four kinds.

···

9   T.: Things being this way, let us try, if possible, to go beyond those   23
'judging' numbers and see if there are any that surpass them. For although we can hardly discern temporal intervals in the 'judging' kind, still they are applied only to judge the things that happen over a period of time; moreover, they are applied only to those of them that can be retrieved from memory. Or do you perhaps have any objections to this?

S.: I am greatly impressed by the power and nature of those 'judging' numbers. It seems to me that they are precisely what all the senses serve. Therefore I do not know if we can find anything superior to them among numbers.

T.: We lose nothing by enquiring more persistently. For we will either find a higher kind in the human soul, or confirm their supreme status in

[10]   Although Augustine frequently expresses the idea that the qualities imparted by proportions are eternal and unchangeable, he provides a corrective to this observation, e.g., in his commentary *On the Letter of John to the Parthians* 4.9 (Migne *PL*35, 2010) by stating that the thing is not the same if its size is different, even though its proportions remain the same.

it, if it becomes clear that no other numbers in it are more excellent ... Now it is true that when we recite that verse that we suggested, 'O God who does create all things', we perceive it by 'occurring' numbers, recognize it by 'mnemonic', enunciate it with the help of 'progressing' and delight in it by those 'judging' numbers. But I also think that, in addition to that, we assess it by means of some other mysterious numbers, and, with their help, pass another, more definitive judgement about that delight, which is itself, as it were, a judgement of 'judging' numbers. Or does it seem to you that the delight of the senses and assessment by reason is the same thing?

s.: No, I think these are different. But first of all I am concerned about terminology. Why not apply the term 'judging' to those numbers that have to do with reason, rather than those that deal with delight? But then I also wonder if that rational assessment is not simply some keener judgement that these numbers make of themselves. This way the numbers that deal with delight will be the same numbers as the ones that deal with reason. It is just that at one time they will pass judgement about those numbers that function in the body (when, as was demonstrated above, memory puts them forth), and at another time about themselves in a way more remote from, and less mixed with, the body.

24 T.: It is one thing to react with approbation or disapproval to those motions in the body, either when they are actually generated, or when they are recalled from memory: which is what happens when we delight in the harmony of such motions or affections, or are offended by their discord. It is quite another thing to assess whether these motions delight us appropriately or not, which is the domain of reason. Thus we must admit that these are two different kinds ... Further, consider this observation of ours: if our sensory capacity for delight itself were not endowed with some numbers, it could in no way express approval for regular intervals and displeasure with irregular ones. Now if this observation is correct, then the following is also: there is no way that reason, which is positioned above this sense of delight, could pass judgement about the numbers that are below it without the help of some more permanent numbers. And if this is all true, it seems that we found five kinds of numbers in the soul. And if you add to them those corporeal numbers that we called 'sounding', you will realize that there are six distinct kinds of numbers. But now, if you wish, let those numbers, to which we first inadvertently accorded

primacy, be called 'sensory'. The more noble name of 'judging', then, will go to those numbers that we found to be more excellent, although I would also change the name for the 'sounding' numbers. Indeed, if we call them 'corporeal' they can be more appropriately applied also to those numbers that are present in dance and other visible motions. That is, if you approve of what has been said.

s.: I surely approve, for all this seems to me both true and obvious. I even accept freely the adjustment of the terminology.

10 T.: Now go ahead and consider the nature and power of reason, to the extent that its activities can show us. First of all – to mention particularly that which is relevant to this investigation – it considered what good modulation is in itself, and it perceived that it consisted in some free motion for the sake of its own beauty. Then it detected two types of variation in the movement of bodies: one linked to the greater or lesser duration (i.e., how much time a motion takes), the other to how fast or slow the locomotion (motion from place to place) is. After making this division, it perceived that that, which related to duration, was capable of producing various numbers in patterns that were clear and moderately spaced, in the format that is suitable for the human sense. It further traced the evolution of the varieties and order of these numbers all the way to lines of verse. Finally it determined the role of the soul (of which it is the chief power) in adjusting, producing, perceiving and memorizing these numbers, and separated all those numbers that pertained to the soul from those pertaining to the body. And it realized that it could not itself perceive, distinguish, nor even precisely number all these things without some numbers of its own, and determined by some kind of judicial assessment that it preferred the latter to the other, lower ranking ones. At this point, it addressed its own sense of delight (which is its favourable reaction to the intervals of time, as well as a sign of approbation for modifying such numbers) in this way: what is it that we like in the numbered nature of sensory data? Is it anything else apart from some equality and evenly measured intervals? ... What beauty is in an iamb, a trochee or a tribrach, except that its longer section can be evenly divided into two of its shorter sections?[11]

25

26

...

---

[11] I.e., its longer section is exactly twice as long as its shorter section.

29   11   Therefore, let us not be envious of the things that are ranked lower than us, but let us position ourselves, with God our Lord's help, between those things that are below us and those things that are above us, in such a way that we are not troubled by the lower-ranking things and take delight only in those that are the highest. For delight is, as it were, the weight of our soul, and therefore it gives the soul its due position. 'For where your treasure is, there your heart will be also' (Matt. 6:21), where 'treasure' stands for delight, and 'heart' for the sense of happiness or misery. And what else can we call 'higher', apart from those things that are the seat of the loftiest, unmoved, unchangeable, eternal equality: where there is no time, for there is no change, and where time originates as it is formed, ordered and shaped in the image of eternity, as the revolution of the sky brings the celestial bodies back to their starting point, obeying the laws of equality, unity and order by means of the regular intervals of days, months, years, decades, and other periodic rotations of the stars? In this way earthly things, in their obedience to the heavenly, as it were, weave their numerous and repeated periodic revolutions into the song of the

30   universe. Now many things among these seem to us disorderly and confused, because we have been stitched into this order only according to our own capacity, and we do not know what sort of beautiful arrangement divine providence has for us. It is the same, for example, with a statue placed in some corner of a vast and most beautiful building: it will not be able to appreciate the beauty of the structure, of which it itself is a part! Nor can a soldier perceive the order of the whole army from his place in a rank. The same goes for verses. Surely, if individual syllables in a poem were allowed to live and perceive only for the time that they sounded, they could in no way appreciate that numeric texture and beauty of the work, because they could not perceive and approve it as a whole: despite the fact that it is made out of these very syllables that pass away and perish one by one ...[12]

31   But let us return to our main point, which originated the whole discussion. All this means that these numbers contained by reason surpass other kinds in beauty. Indeed, if we were completely cut off from them in our dealings with the body, 'progressing' numbers would not modify

---

[12] Cf. Augustine, *On the Nature of the Good* 8. Augustine frequently expresses the idea that beauty is only perceived in the whole, cf. *On True Religion* 40.76 (pp. 225–6), as do earlier authors, e.g., Seneca, *Letter* 33.

sensory numbers [and this would upset the whole process, because][13] the latter, in their turn, generate the sensible beauty of temporal intervals through bodily movements, which also results in the creation of 'occurring' numbers as a reaction to the 'sounding'[14] ones; ultimately, the same soul receives all of its impulses, amplifies them, as it were, and makes them suitable for memorization (this power of the soul is called memory, which is of great help in the most fundamental activities of this life of ours) ...

12   T.: Now regarding this equality, which we did not find to be certain and permanent in the numbers of the sensible world, but instead obscured and passing: surely, our intellect would not seek it anywhere, unless it were known from somewhere? However, that 'somewhere' is not in the intervals of space or time, for the former change shape and the latter pass away. So where is it? See if you can find an answer to this. For you cannot think it is in the shapes of bodies, which you would never dare to call equal on close examination. Nor is it in the intervals of time, for we are similarly unaware if something is a little longer or shorter than it is supposed to be, if it escapes our senses. I am asking you about a different kind of equality: the one we have before our mental gaze when we desire certain bodies or bodily motions to be even, and upon considering these bodies more carefully dare not trust them. Where do you think this sort of equality is?

34

S.: I think that it is in that which is more excellent than bodies, but whether this is in the soul itself or above it, I do not know.

T.: Then let us enquire in this way: do you think that the art of rhythm and metre that is used by those who compose verses contains some numbers that are used to produce verse?

35

S.: How can it be otherwise?

T.: Whatever these numbers are, do they seem to you to pass away with the verses or remain?

S.: To remain, for sure.

T.: Then you must agree that some passing numbers are produced by some permanent ones?

S.: Reason presses me to agree.

---

[13] This editorial addition is needed to preserve the flow of meaning.
[14] Augustine had already decided to rename them as 'corporeal', so this is how it should be understood here.

T.: What about that art: is it anything except some affection in the mind of the artist?

S.: I believe so.

T.: Do you also believe that this affection is present in someone who is ignorant of this art?

S.: Not at all.

T.: What about someone who has forgotten the art?

S.: Not in this one either, for such a person is also ignorant, even though once he was an expert.

T.: But what if someone reminds such a person of this art by way of questioning? Do you think that these numbers pass back into the forgetful one from the person who is doing the questioning? Or is there some inner motion in his mind towards something that will restore what he has lost?

S.: I think it happens inside this person himself …[15]

T.: However, as for forcing one and two not to amount to three, or two not to be twice one, that was not possible to anyone in the past, is not possible to anyone in the present, and will not be possible to anyone in the future.

S.: Nothing could be more obvious.

T.: What about the following scenario? Suppose we ask questions about all other things that pertain to those numbers, in the same way that we asked about one and two, which was such a clear process. Further, suppose that we ask a person who is ignorant not through forgetfulness, but because he has never learned these things. Do you not think that such a person can likewise learn this art, apart from the length of syllables?

S.: Who would ever doubt that?

T.: Now, in this case, what is the moving force that imprints in the mind of such a person[16] those numbers that bring about the affection that is called art? Would they not be given by the one who questions, at least in this case?

S.: No, I think such a person also undergoes some inner process, in the same way, so that he realizes the truth of the things that are the subject of enquiry,[17] and forms a response.

---

[15] In the short omitted passage the interlocutors find out that the memory of some chance things, such as details of one's life or length of syllables, cannot be restored.

[16] I.e., the one who has never learned.

[17] Reading *interrogantur* instead of *interrogatur*.

T.: Now go ahead and tell me whether it seems to you that those numbers 36
under discussion are subject to change.

S.: Absolutely not.

T.: Then you would not deny that they are eternal?

S.: Even more so, I must admit this.

T.: Are you sure? And there will not be any lurking suspicion of inequality in them that could let us down?[18]

S.: I cannot see anything more reliable than the equality they have.

T.: Where else, then, can the soul acquire something eternal and immutable, if not from the one eternal and immutable God?

S.: I do not see how we can believe anything else.

T.: So, finally, is it not evident that he who inwardly moves towards God
in order to understand the immutable truth when another person questions him, cannot be set on this path towards contemplating truth by any
external admonition,[19] unless this motion is retained by his memory?

S.: This is indeed clear …

13   T.: Tell me now, can we love anything but beautiful things? For even 38
if there are some people who seem to like ugly things – the Greeks commonly call them *saprophiloi* (lovers of rotten things) – the only difference
is in the degree of beauty: how much less beautiful those things are that
they like compared to those that are pleasing to most people. For clearly
no one loves those things that offend his senses with their hideousness.

S.: It is just as you say.

T.: Now in their turn these beautiful things please us by their numeric
nature, in which, as we have shown already, what we seek is equality.
And the latter is found not only in that beauty that pertains to hearing
or the movement of bodies, but also in visible forms themselves, where
it is more commonly called beauty. Do you think anything else apart
from the equality of number is at work when doubled elements always
come as equal counterparts, while unique elements are centred, in such
a way that the ones on each side are equidistant from the ones in the
middle?

S.: How can it be otherwise?

---

[18] Here syntax requires the reading *quid, metus ille non suberit* (and probably also *subierit* for
suberit) instead of *quid, metus ille nunc suberit*.

[19] 'External admonition' here must be interpreted broadly, so as to include such 'reminders' as
natural beauty of objects, aesthetic judgement, etc. The idea, then, is that the visible leads to the
invisible by way of triggering the process of 'internal recollection'.

T.: And what about the visible light itself, which is the origin of all colours? (We do enjoy colour in corporeal forms, do we not?) Do you think we seek anything else in light and colours, apart from that which is agreeable to the eye? For we turn away from extreme glare, and at the same time lose interest in things which are too dark and unclear: just as we shrink from sounds that are too loud and find no pleasure in something too quiet, at the level of whisper. The latter quality is not in temporal intervals, but in the sound itself, whose function in respect to these sounding numbers is similar to that of light in relation to visible patterns. The contrary of this quality is silence, just as darkness is the contrary of colours. In all these things, when we seek something agreeable to our own nature and reject what is disagreeable (at the same time understanding that it could be agreeable to other creatures), is it not, again, some law of equality that makes us rejoice in these, when we realize that equal elements are paired up with each other in some mysterious ways? We can also perceive this in the sense of smell, taste and touch, which is too long to discuss properly, but is the easiest thing to explore by trial. To conclude, there is no other thing except equality or similitude that would please us in those sensory experiences. And where there is equality or similitude, there are numeric principles. And clearly nothing is as equal or as similar as one and one, unless you have something to say here.

S.: I agree completely.

On True Religion

29.52–41.77

29   Let us see how far reason can proceed in its ascent[1] from the visible   **52**
to the invisible and from the temporal to the eternal. For one should not
vainly behold the beauty of the sky, the orderly arrangement of the stars,
the brightness of light, the alternations of night and day, the monthly
courses of the moon, the division of the year into the four seasons that
corresponds to the four-fold division of the elements, the great power of
the seeds that produce both the species and the scores of individuals, as
well as all other things that preserve their nature and the proper mode
of being of their kind. Considering these things must not feed vain and
short-lived curiosity, but become a step towards something immortal and
everlasting.

The nearest task at hand, however, is to investigate what this vital
power is that perceives all this. Clearly, since it gives life to the body it is
necessarily more eminent than the latter. For no matter how massive an
object is or how brightly it shines with this visible light, it is not worth
very much if it lacks life. Indeed, any living thing is naturally superior to
any non-living thing.

Further, since no one doubts that irrational life-forms also live and have   **53**
sensation, the most eminent power in the human soul must be not that
by which it senses sensible things, but that by which it makes judgements

---

[1] The idea of the ascent is presented at length in Plato, *Symposium* 210–12 (pp. 23–5) and Plotinus, *Ennead* 1.6 (pp. 185–94).

about them. For most beasts are superior to humans in detecting material objects: they have sharper eyesight and the rest of their organs of perception are more sensitive.[2] At the same time, it takes a rational, and not just a sentient, capacity to make judgements about bodies: something that animals lack but in which we humans excel. For it is the easiest thing to see that the one who judges is superior to that which is judged. Indeed, the rational faculty makes judgements not only about objects of sense, but also about the senses themselves ... This is why it is clear that just as sentient life-forms are superior to bodies, so rational life-forms are superior to both of the above.

54   **30**   Accordingly, if our rational faculty itself makes judgements about itself, there is no natural power superior to it. However, because it is clear that it is subject to change, for at various times it may either lack or possess a certain skill, and its ability to judge corresponds to its level of skill, and its level of skill depends on imparting some art or discipline or science to it, one must enquire into the nature of art itself. At this point I do not mean that art which originates from experience, but the one that is derived by a rational process. Indeed, what is so remarkable about knowing that the mixture of lime and sand holds masonry better than clay? The same goes for the practice of building with great elegance, when repeating architectural elements always have equal counterparts, while unique elements are centred,[3] although this sense-knowledge is already closer to reason and rationality. But this is what we need to investigate for sure: why does it displease us when, out of two windows positioned side by side, but not one above the other, one is larger or smaller than the other, as opposed to both being of equal size? At the same time, if they were of uneven size but positioned one above the other and centred, their inequality would not offend us in the same way. Further, if they are uneven, why do we not pay much attention to their respective sizes if they are only two? However, if they are three, sense itself seems to demand either that they all be of the same size, or that the window that is positioned between the smallest and the largest be of such a size that the size of the middle one would relate to the size of the smallest in the same way as the size of the largest would relate to the size of the middle

---

[2] Cf. Cicero, *On the Nature of the Gods* 2.57.145–58.146 (p. 132), where the human senses are presented as superior to those of the animals.

[3] This passage is almost identical to that in *On Music* 6.13.38 (p. 217); cf. a similar idea in *On Order* 2.11.34 (p. 202).

one.[4] Thus, nature itself is first consulted, as it were, to determine what it would approve. In connection to this, it is particularly interesting how something that does not displease us that much when considered on its own is rejected in comparison with something better.

We can thus conclude that 'art' as commonly understood[5] is nothing other than the memory[6] of experiences that we found pleasing, combined with some motor skills of the body. Now even if you lack the latter and are not able to manufacture artefacts, you can still make judgements about works of art, which is a far superior ability.

The source of pleasure in any art is harmony, which alone is respon- **55** sible for the beauty and wholesomeness of all things. At the same time, harmony aspires to equality and unity, either through the similarity of even parts or through a regular progression of uneven. But who could find the highest degree of equality or similarity in bodies? Or who would dare say, upon careful consideration, that any body has unity in a true and pure sense, when all things shift their shapes and change places, and consist of parts that are locally positioned and partition things according to spatial intervals? Furthermore, true equality and similarity, as well as true unity itself in its original form, cannot be perceived by the eye of the flesh, nor by any bodily sense, but can be contemplated by the mind alone. For where would one get the idea to search for any equality in bodies, or a firm conviction that such equality is a long way from perfect equality, were it not for the mind's ability to see the perfect kind? (That is, if 'perfect' is the right word for something that has not been 'perfected' by anyone.)[7]

Indeed, all sensual beauty – either natural or enhanced by the arts – **56** is beautiful in a spatial and temporal sense, as, for example, the body and its movements. At the same time, that sort of equality and unity that is grasped by the mind alone, and according to which one makes

---

[4] I.e., the respective sizes of the three windows would follow the proportion a:b = b:c, e.g., 4, 2, 1 and so forth.

[5] *Ars vulgaris*, i.e., craft, as opposed to higher forms of art (that are known to us as *liberales*), is something practical and mechanical as opposed to something purely intellectual and contemplative. Cf. the ancient and medieval understanding of the respectable discipline of music as the mathematical theory of music, as opposed to the lowly craft of musicians.

[6] Cf. a similar idea about the origin of art in Cicero, *Orator* 53.177–8 (p. 126) and in *On the Ideal Orator* 3.51.197 (p. 122).

[7] The last phrase is a pun in Latin based on the linguistic kinship between '*per-fectus*' and '*factus*': the former is perceived by a native Latin speaker as a result of the latter, while 'perfect equality' is eternal and therefore certainly not 'made'.

judgements about corporeal beauty through the mediation of the senses, neither changes shape spatially nor fluctuates in time. For it is not right to say that this perfect standard is used to determine that a wheel is round, but cannot be applied to a vase; or that it is used to determine that a vase is round but does not apply to a coin. The same holds true regarding time and the movements of bodies. Indeed, it is ridiculous to say that perfect equality is used to determine that years are equal, but does not apply to months; or that it is used to determine that months are equal, but is not applicable to days. In fact, whether something moves with regularity over these greater periods of time, or on an hourly basis, or every few seconds, one judges it by one and the same immutable law of equality.

But if one judges both greater and lesser intervals in spatial forms and temporal movements alike according to one and the same law of equality, similitude and correspondence, the law itself is greater than all of these – however, only in power. Yet, it is neither greater nor less in a spatial or temporal sense. Indeed, if it were greater in scale or duration, it could not be used in its entirety[8] to judge lesser things, and if it were smaller in scale, one could not use it to judge greater things.[9] In fact, however, the law of squareness in its entirety is used to judge both the square forum and the square stone, as well as square tablets or gems. Again, the law of equality in its entirety is used equally to judge the synchronized leg movement of a running ant and of a treading elephant. Who, then, would doubt that this law is neither greater nor less in a spatial or temporal sense, while surpassing all by its power? Now this law that governs all the arts is absolutely immutable. At the same time, the human mind, which enjoys the benefit of perceiving this law, can err and undergo change. It is sufficiently clear, then, that that law, which is called truth, is above our mind.

57   31   Nor should there be any doubt that that immutable nature, which is positioned above the rational soul, is God, and that this highest wisdom is also the highest life and being. For this is precisely that immutable truth that is rightly called the law of all the arts, as well as the art of the almighty artist. Accordingly, whenever the soul feels that it is not self-sufficient even in making judgements about the shape and movement

[8] Assuming the reading *totam* or *eam totam*, rather than *eam* as in *CCSL*.
[9] I.e., although it is greater in power, since it can judge any scale or object no matter how great, it is not itself 'greater' in scale or size, which would prevent it from judging something on a smaller scale.

of bodies, it necessarily realizes both that its own nature is superior to
that nature about which it judges, and that, at the same time, that nature
according to which it judges and about which it absolutely cannot judge
is superior to itself. Indeed, I can say why any particular body ought to
be proportioned by way of placing similar parts symmetrically on each
side: because I am delighted by the highest degree of equality, which I
perceive not by the eyes but by the mind. For this reason, the more the
things that I see with my eyes correspond in their nature to those that I
intuit by my intellect, the better I judge them to be. However, why those
intelligible things are the way they are, no one can say, nor would anyone
in his right mind presume to say that they ought to be like that, as if they
could be otherwise.

Thus pure minds are capable of knowing the eternal law, but they
cannot judge or evaluate it. The difference is as follows. Knowledge is
sufficiently constituted by perceiving whether something is or is not so.
Judging, in addition to that, involves something else, namely, an indication that the things could be otherwise, as when we say 'it ought to be like
this', or 'it ought to have been this way', or 'it will have to be that way', as
artists do when speaking of their own works.

32   To many, of course, the human response of delight is the end. They
have no wish to turn their gaze upward to find out why these visible things
are pleasing. Accordingly, if I ask an artist, after he constructs one arch,
why he intends to build another one just like it on the opposite side of the
building, he is likely to respond 'in order that equal parts of the building
might balance each other out'. Further, if I persist with my questioning,
asking why he prefers that very arrangement, he will say that 'it is fitting',
or that 'it is beautiful', or that 'it delights the beholder'. He will not find
anything more to say: with downcast eyes and his head bowed, he will be
at a loss about the cause of his perplexity.

However, if I happen upon a beholder of inward things who sees the
unseen, I will persist in pressing him to answer why these things are
pleasing, in order that he may dare to pass judgement about the human
response of delight itself. Indeed, when one judges that very delight, but
not according to its laws, he is above it and not confined by it. And first
I will ask whether things are beautiful because they please, or please
because they are beautiful. Without any doubt, I will get an answer that
they please because they are beautiful. I will further ask what it is that
makes them beautiful. If he hesitates I will add a hint: is it because they

58

59

have equal parts that come together in such a way that they form one harmonious arrangement?

60   Once this becomes clear to him, I will ask: do these things attain this unity in its highest form (for, as we found out, they are striving for it), or are they still far inferior to it and only somehow pretend to have it? Indeed, who would not see, after some pressure to think about it, that, on the one hand, there is no shape or body whatsoever that does not have some trace of unity, but that, on the other hand, no matter how beautiful a body is, it cannot attain that unity it strives for, because its parts are necessarily spread out in space over different locations? But if this is so, then I will ask him to tell me this: where or how does he see that unity? For if he does not see it, how would he know both what bodily shapes imitate and that they cannot attain this ideal? Listen how he tells material objects presently: 'If you were not bound by some unity, you would be nothing! But, again, if you were unity itself, you would not be bodies.' But we can rightly ask: 'How do you know this unity, according to which you judge bodies? For if you do not see it, you could not judge that bodies do not attain it. But if you do see it with these bodily eyes, you cannot be making a right statement when you say (on the premise that we see only corporeal things with these eyes) that "although there is a trace of unity in bodies, nevertheless they are a long way from reaching it".' Therefore we see this unity with our minds. But where do we see it? If it were in the same place as our body, someone in the East judging about bodies in this way would not see it. Therefore it is not contained in a place and, since it is present to the one who judges wherever he may be, it is not spatially in any particular place, but everywhere as far as its influence is concerned.

. . .

72   39   What obstacle, then, remains for the soul on its way to recalling the primal beauty, which it has abandoned, when it can do so even from its own vices? For thus the wisdom of God extends mightily to all boundaries. Through it, that supreme artist[10] constructed and ordered his works with one end in mind: beauty. Accordingly, in his goodness, he bears no grudge against any beauty (which owes its very existence to him), from the highest to the lowest, to make sure that no one is excluded from partaking

---

[10] For the metaphor of the artist cf. Plato's account in *Timaeus* 29 a, e (pp. 71–2).

in truth itself, just as no one is deprived of some sensible image and likeness of truth. Enquire what attracts you in the pleasurable experience
derived from bodies: you will not find anything else except harmony. For
just as discordant or incompatible things result in a painful sensation, so
harmonious things give pleasure. Examine, then, what the highest degree
of harmony would be. There is no need to go out: return within yourself,
for truth abides inside you. And if you find your own nature to be subject to change, transcend even yourself. But remember, as you transcend
yourself, that it is the rational soul that you are transcending. Therefore,
aim in that direction where the light of reason itself is kindled. For what
else does any diligent thinker attain, except truth? However, since truth
itself certainly does not attain itself by way of reasoning, but is the goal
for those who reason, you must perceive that harmony there, greater than
which none can exist, and strike an accord with it. Admit that you are
not as it is, for it does not seek itself. At the same time, you sought it and
came to it not through the reaches of space, but through an affection of
the mind, in order to reach an accord between your inner self and the
indwelling truth through a pleasure that is not low and carnal, but lofty
and spiritual.

. . .

40   Accordingly, all functions and ends of all things are designed to ensure   **76**
universal beauty, and that which horrifies us on its own, in fact, pleases
us very greatly when considered as part of the whole. Indeed, we should
not only consider one corner in judging a building, nor only hair in a
handsome man, nor only the movement of hands in a good orator, nor the
shape of the moon for only three days out of the whole cycle. For certain
things acquire a lower status precisely because they possess perfection
only as a whole, while their parts taken separately are imperfect. Now
such things, whether their beauty is revealed in motion or at rest, must be
considered as a whole if one wants to pass a fair judgement. For the truth
of our judgement does not depend on whether it is about the whole or a
part. However,[11] our judgement is beautiful only in so far as it covers the
whole world, and we do not focus on a particular part of it while trying to

---

[11]   The *CCSL* text at this point must be repunctuated in order to make sense: a semicolon or even a
full stop is needed before *pulchrum est*, instead of a comma. Augustine here makes a distinction
between 'truth' judgements (the 'truth of correspondence', according to contemporary classi-
fications) and 'beauty' judgements that are somehow also 'true' (the 'truth of coherence' that
takes into consideration the whole picture).

determine the truth. Indeed, even the error of focusing on a part of the world is in itself hideous. However, just as the black colour in a painting becomes beautiful as part of the whole, in the same way the immutable providence of God arranges this public spectacle of life as a whole most fittingly. For it assigns different roles to the vanquished, the contenders, the victorious, the spectators, and the tranquil whose sole function is contemplating God. Yet in all these cases there is nothing evil, except sin and punishment for sin, that is, a voluntary fall from the highest being and an involuntary suffering among the lowest: in other words, freedom from justice and slavery under sin.

77   41   For every orderly arrangement is beautiful. Just as the Apostle says: 'All order is from God.'¹² We must surely admit that a grieving human is still better than a rejoicing worm. Yet, I could praise even the worm profusely without any deceit. Indeed, consider the shiny colour, the rounded shape of its body, the segments in the front being equal to those in the middle, and those in the middle to the ones in the back, thus preserving unity inasmuch as its lowly nature permits! There is nothing on one side that would not have its equal counterpart on the other. As for the soul that animates its tiny body, see how rhythmically it moves it, how it seeks things suitable for it and overcomes or avoids obstacles as much as it can, and, guided on all occasions by the single sense of self-preservation, attains unity – that foundation of all natural things – in a much more prominent way than the body! I say this about a worm, or something alive, while many have poured praises on ashes and dung, and most convincingly!¹³ No wonder, then, if I say that the human soul – which, no matter where it is or what it is like, is better than any body – is beautifully ordered, and its punishment generates further beauty, when the soul in the state of misery occupies the place of the wretched, as is appropriate, instead of the place of the blessed.

¹² Cf. Rom. 13:1.
¹³ Cf. Cicero, *On Old Age* 15.54, about the utility of dung for agriculture. There was a long ancient tradition of writing encomia of trivial things.

On Free Choice of the Will

2.11.31–16.43

11 The fact is that divine wisdom posited numbers at the foundation of all things, even the most lowly ones, located on the farthest fringes of reality. Indeed, even all bodies, despite the fact that they occupy the lowest grade of reality, have their numbers. At the same time wisdom deprived bodies of understanding, and it did the same to some souls, except for the rational ones. It is as if it established its residence in rational souls, from which it could control even all those lowly things to which it had assigned numbers. Consequently, because we can easily judge about bodies, which are hierarchically lower than us, seeing that number is in their nature, we think that even numbers themselves are below us, and for this reason hold them in low regard. But when we start, as it were, our journey upwards, we find that they transcend even our minds and immutably abide in truth itself. At the same time, because only a few are wise, but even the stupid can count, people ordinarily admire wisdom and treat numbers with contempt.

. . .

12 Then what about that truth that we have been discussing for a long time now and which allows us to discern so much? Do you think that it surpasses our mind, or is at the same level as our mind, or even below it? Surely, if it were lower, we would judge about it, and not according to it, just as we judge about bodies because they are below us, and often not only acknowledge that they are or are not this way, but also insist that

227

they ought or ought not to be this way.[1] The same applies to our souls. Not only do we know that the disposition of the soul is such and such, but often also that it ought to be. An example of judging in this manner about bodies is when we say 'it is not as white as it ought to have been', or 'not as square', and many other like statements. An example about someone's character would be when we say 'it is not as accommodating as it ought to be', or 'not as meek', or 'not as forceful,' according to what our moral standards might be. Now we make these judgements according to those inner rules of truth that we all discern. However, in no way does one judge about these rules themselves. For while someone may say that 'eternal things are more powerful than temporal', or that 'seven and three equals ten', no one says that it ought to have been so. Indeed, learning no more than that it is so, one makes no attempt to correct as an examiner, and merely rejoices as a discoverer.

However if this truth were at the same level as our minds, it would have been equally changeable. For our minds see sometimes more and sometimes less of this truth, thus declaring that they are changeable. At the same time, truth, abiding in itself, neither increases when we see more of it, nor shrinks when we see less of it. In fact, it remains intact and incorruptible, blessing with its light those who turn to it, and punishing with blindness those who turn away from it. Do you not see that we even judge about our own minds according to it, while there is no way for us to judge about truth itself? For we say 'he understands less than he ought to', or 'he understands as much as he ought to'. But the degree of understanding for a given mind depends precisely on the degree of its proximity to immutable truth and its ability to cling to it. For this reason, if truth is neither lower than nor level with our minds, it must be higher and more excellent.

. . .

41   16   For wherever you turn, wisdom speaks to you through some vestiges with which it has stamped its creation, and when you slip towards external reality, it calls you back inside through the very forms of external things. For it enables you to see that whatever delights you in bodies and lures you through corporeal senses is proportioned, and to enquire where this quality comes from, and return into yourself. And then you understand that you could not approve or reject that which comes into

---

[1] Cf. a similar passage in *On True Religion* 31.57 (p. 223).

contact with your bodily senses, unless you had some laws of beauty within you, with which you could compare any beautiful things that you sense externally.

Look at the sky, the land and the sea and at whatever is there that shines   42
from above or crawls below or flies or swims. All these have form because they have number: take away their form and number and they will be nothing. Do they not have the same origin, then, as number? For indeed, they have being only to the extent that they have a numeric nature.[2] Look at artists skilled in the production of all corporeal forms: even their art consists of numbers, in accordance with which they fashion their works. For they move their hands and instruments in the process of production up to the point when the product that is being shaped externally is suf-ficiently adjusted to the standard set by that light of numbers which is inside: that is, until it releases them and pleases – through the mediation of the senses – the inward judge whose gaze is fixed on celestial numbers. Further, enquire who it is that moves the limbs of the artist himself. You will find that it is number, for they too move in accordance with number. And if you take away the actual product from his hands, and the inten-tion of making something from his mind, and let this movement of limbs itself serve the sole purpose of delight, it will be called dance. Now ask what delights in dance, and number will answer you: 'Behold, it's me.' Now examine the beauty of bodily form: you see numbers permeating space. And now look at the beauty of bodily movement: you see the pro-cession of numbers in time. Now look deeper, at the art from which these numbers proceed. Can you find time and place in it? Nowhere and never will you find them, but its life is number, and its region is not measured in feet, nor its age in days. And yet when those who aspire to become art-ists set to study the art, they conform their body to it by spatial and tem-poral movements, and their mind through temporal transformation, for they become more skilled with the passage of time. Therefore transcend also the mind of the artist, in order to see eternal number: and at this moment wisdom will flash out at you from its inner abode and from the very sanctuary of truth. And if at this point your weak sight is repelled by it, redirect the eye of your mind to the more pleasurable ways in which it used to show you things. But remember that you put aside this vision

---

[2] 'Numeric nature' renders Augustine's technical term *numerosus*: see Note on the texts and the translations.

simply out of caution and you can seek it again when you are stronger and bolder.

43   Woe to those who stray away from you, their guide, and wander about lost among your traces! Woe to those who love the signs that point to you, instead of loving you yourself, and to those who forget about you and your beckoning, O wisdom, the sweetest light of the purified mind! For you never cease to communicate to us through signs what and how great you are, and all the loveliness of creation is but these signals of yours! For even the artist somehow beckons the beholder of his work away from the very beauty of the work, lest they become totally fixed on it. Rather he wants them to glance over the beautiful appearance of the artist's creation in such a way that they may return with affection to him who has made it.

Confessions

3.2.2

I was ravished by theatrical shows that were full of images of my own miseries and fuelled my fires. Why is it that a man wants to grieve when he watches mournful and tragic things in the theatre, which, at the same time, he would not want to suffer himself? And nevertheless he wants to feel grief on their account as a spectator, and the very pain is his pleasure. Is this anything but extraordinary madness? Indeed, the worse such experiences make us feel, the more we are moved by them, although when we suffer ourselves it is usually called misery, and when we empathize with others, it is called pity. But, after all, what pity can there be in fictitious and theatrical situations? For the audience is not moved to help but only invited to suffer, and is more favourably disposed towards the actor who performs those scenes when its suffering is more intense. And if those human misfortunes, either because they are out of date or because they are too artificial, are enacted in such a way that the spectator does not suffer, he loathes the show and leaves in disapproval; but if he suffers, he remains riveted and rejoices through his tears.

7.17.23

I tried to find the source of my feeling of approval for the beauty of bodies, whether heavenly or earthly, and what that presence was that guided me in judging soundly about things that are mutable when I said: 'This ought to be so, and that not so.' And looking for the source of my judgements of this sort, I found the immutable and eternal truth residing above my mutable mind. In this way I ascended progressively from bodies to the part of the soul which perceives through the body, and thence to its inner power, to which bodily senses pass information about external things – the level still accessible to animals – and from there to the reasoning power, whose role is to judge the sensory data coming from the body. In its turn, the reasoning power, after discovering that in me it remained mutable, raised itself to its own level and purged the thought process of habit, detaching itself from the swarms of conflicting sensory images: all in order to find that light that pervaded it. For it declared without any doubt that the immutable was to be preferred to the mutable, whence it followed that it knew what that immutable was: for how else could it prefer with certainty what is immutable to what is mutable, if it did not somehow know the former? And so it attained that which is 'in the flash of a trembling glance'.[1] For at that moment I saw your 'invisible nature understood through the things that are made'.[2] But I could not maintain my focus, and in my weakness was driven back to my ordinary experiences. All I had left were dear memories that longed, as it were, for the things that I had smelled but was not yet able to eat.

[1] Cf. 1 Cor. 15:52.   [2] Rom. 1:20.

On the Trinity

9.6.11

Likewise, when I revolve in my mind, let us say, a beautifully and evenly curved arch that I have seen in Carthage, the mind becomes aware of a certain physical object through the eyes, which is then transferred to the memory and produces a picture in the imagination. But my mind also sees something else: namely, some criterion according to which this piece of work pleases me, and which would allow me to correct it if I did not like it. Therefore we judge about these material things according to that form of truth. Now this form of truth we perceive by the eye of our rational mind, but those material things we either detect by our bodily senses when they are present, or recall as images in the memory when they are absent; or, again, by analogy with those images we make up images of other things in our mind, such as we could actually produce if we wished and were able. Thus to picture the images of bodies in the mind and see bodies by bodily senses is one thing, but to capture by pure intelligence the principles of such images and the ineffably beautiful art that gives rise to them, which is all above the range of our mind, is quite another.

PROCLUS

Commentary on the Timaeus

I, 265.18–26

So too Phidias who made the statue of Zeus did not look at something that has come to be but arrived at a notion of the Homeric Zeus. If he had actually been able to reach the intellectual god himself, clearly his own work would have been a finer achievement. Beauty, or the lack of it, comes to the image from the model, likeness or unlikeness to the archetype comes from the sculptor. 'Image' is used of both, both the copy of the model and the work and product of the sculptor.

Commentary on the Republic

I, 177.7–179.32

Let us turn next to the discussion of poetry and consider what types of poetry there are according to Plato, what type he had in mind when he expounded his criticisms of poetry in the tenth book of the *Republic*, and finally how even here Homer is shown to be exempt from the criticisms which apply to most poets. To make this clear also, let us begin teaching about this with the following point: we say that, speaking generally, there are three kinds of life in the soul. The best and most perfect kind is that in which the soul is joined to the gods and lives the life that is most closely akin to them and united with them in extreme similarity: it belongs not to itself but to them, surpassing its own intellect, awakening in itself the ineffable symbol of the gods' unitary existence and joining like with like, its own light to the light of the gods and the most unitary aspect of its own being and life to the One which is beyond all being and life. The life second to this in dignity and power, holding an intermediate rank in the middle of the soul, is that in which the soul descends from the divinely inspired life and returns into itself. Placing intellect and knowledge as the principle of its activity, on the one hand it unravels multitudes of arguments and contemplates all kinds of changes of the forms and, on the other, it brings together the thinker and the object of thought and reflects intellectual being by comprehending the nature of the intelligibles in a single unity. The third kind of life is that which moves among the lesser powers and acts in concert with them, using

236

irrational images and perceptions and filling itself entirely with inferior things.

Since these are the three kinds of life seen in souls, let us consider the division of poetry in a similar order. Poetry also proceeds from above along with the many kinds of life of the soul and is diversified into first, middle and last types of activity. In poetry too there is one type which is the highest, full of divine goods. It sets the soul among the principles responsible for reality, joining the soul which is filled with that which fills it in a sort of ineffable union; it lays out the former for illumination immaterially and without touch and it summons the latter to share its light, 'accomplishing the works of imperishable fire as channels mingle', as the Oracle puts it.[1] It completes a single, divine binding together and a unifying mixture of participated and participant, setting the inferior wholly in the superior and bringing it about that the more divine of the two is active while the lesser is subordinate and conceals its own characteristics in the superior. In short, this is a madness better than sanity, defined by the divine measure itself. Just as other kinds of madness bring people to other gods, so too this one fills the inspired soul with a sense of measure. That is why it adorns its last activities with metre and rhythm. So, just as we say that prophetic madness exists in relation to truth and the madness of love exists in relation to beauty, so too we say that poetic madness is defined by reference to divine measure.

The next type of poetry, which is inferior to the first, inspired type and is seen to have a middle place in the soul, has its allotted existence by reference to the actual scientific and intellectual disposition of the soul. It understands the being of real things and loves to look upon fine and good words and deeds, bringing everything to expression in metre and rhythm. You can find many works by good poets that belong to this type of poetry, worthy of emulation by right-thinking people, full of admonition and excellent advice, brimming with intellectual good measure. They offer a share in wisdom and the other virtues to those who are so inclined by nature and enable them to recollect the cycles of the soul and the immortal principles and diverse powers within those cycles.

---

[1] Proclus here quotes from the *Chaldaean Oracles*, a Platonizing text probably composed in the second century AD and taken very seriously by the later Neoplatonists. The passage quoted is fragment 66 in the edition by E. Des Places (Paris: Les Belles Lettres, 1971).

There is a third type of poetry which is mixed with opinions and imaginings and composed by means of imitation. It is, and is said to be, simply imitative. Sometimes it provides only a copy but at other times it presents an apparent likeness which does not really exist, inflating the significance of small events and amazing the audience with words and expressions of this kind, altering the dispositions of their souls by changes of harmony and variety of rhythm and displaying the natures of things to the masses not as they are but as they may appear. It is a sort of shadow-painting[2] of reality, not accurate knowledge. Its aim is to enchant an audience and it looks especially to the element in the soul which is emotional and naturally inclined to joy and grief. As we said, one part of this type of poetry, the part which aims at correctness in imitation, is 'eikastic', concerned with copying, while the other part is, as we described, 'phantastic', concerned with appearance, and provides only apparent imitation.

2, 107.14–108.16

We should add to these points that souls are intellectual in their nature and full of incorporeal and intellectual principles; however, in our world of change they have assumed an imaginative intellect and cannot live without this here. For that reason some of the ancients say that imagination and intellect are the same and others, although they distinguish between the two, hold that there is no thinking without images.[3] Since, as we said, souls have become emotional instead of impassive and inclined to give things shape instead of having no concern with shape, it is reasonable to say that using this kind of story is an appropriate way of teaching them; these stories contain within them a great deal of the intellectual light of truth, but the fictional element forms a screen in front, concealing it with imitation, as imagination in us obscures our individual intellect. For stories which are entirely fictional are suitable only for those who live by the imagination alone and who in general have only passive intellect;[4] the bright light of knowledge and the self-revealing quality of intellectual

[2] 'Shadow-painting' was a technique for giving the impression of depth in two dimensions. Cf. Plato, *Republic* 10.602d (p. 60).
[3] Proclus is probably thinking here particularly of Aristotle, *On the Soul* 3.7.431a16 and 8.432a9 ff.
[4] On the later Neoplatonist notion of the 'passive intellect', often identified with the imagination, see H. J. Blumenthal, '*Nous pathētikos* in later Greek philosophy', in Blumenthal and H. Robinson (eds.), *Aristotle and the Later Tradition* (Oxford: Clarendon Press, 1991), 191–205.

cognition are suitable for those who concentrate all their own activity in pure thoughts. As for the kind of story which is fictional outside but intellectual inside, it remains for us to say, I suppose, that this corresponds to those who are a combination and have a double intellect – the one which we really are and the one which we have put on and use as a screen. That, I suppose, is the reason why we take pleasure in stories as natural to us; the double intellect in us enjoys them – the part of us which is nourished by the inner meaning has seen the truth, while the part which is impressed by the outer story has been put on the road to knowledge. Just as, if we are using our imaginations, we should employ images that are pure and not polluted by any base imaginings, so too, I suppose, mythical stories should have an outer dress appropriate to the intellectual figures within. That is why Plato rejected the telling of mythical stories in poetry, because they fill uninitiated souls with vulgar meanings.

Anonymous Prolegomena to the Philosophy of Plato

14.11–15.51

It is worth enquiring why Plato, who elsewhere criticizes variegated things – for example, he criticizes pipe-playing because it uses variegated instruments with many openings, playing the cithara because it uses a number of different strings, comedy because of the variety of its characters and tragedy for the same reason – why does Plato, who criticizes all these things for this reason, himself use the literary form of the dialogue which involves a variety of characters?[1] We should reply that the variety of characters in tragedy and comedy is not of the same kind as in Plato. In drama there are good and bad characters and they remain as they are, whereas in Plato, although we find good and bad characters there too, we can see the bad characters being changed by the good and instructed and purified; they always disengage themselves from their materialistic way of life. So the variety in drama is different from the variety in Plato; therefore Plato has not fallen into any contradiction here.

We must now give the reasons why Plato used this literary form. We say that he did this because the dialogue is, in a way, a universe. For just as in the dialogue there are different characters, each speaking in the way appropriate to him, so too in the universe as a whole there are different natural things uttering their different voices; each speaks according to

---

[1] Cf. Plato, *Republic* 3.394–9 (pp. 41–8).

241

its own nature. So he did this too in imitation of the works of the divine craftsman, I mean the universe.

He did it either for this reason or because the universe is a dialogue. For just as in the universe some natures are higher and some are lower, and the soul, during its stay in this world, sometimes combines with the higher natures and sometimes with the lower, so too in the dialogue there are some characters who refute and others who are refuted: our soul, being, as it were, a sort of judge, sometimes surrenders itself to those who refute and sometimes to those who are refuted.

Alternatively, since, as Plato himself says,[2] a speech is analogous to a living creature, so too the finest speech will be analogous to the finest living creature. The finest living creature is the universe; the dialogue is analogous to this, as we said above. Therefore the dialogue is the finest kind of speech.

A fourth reason is the following: since our soul enjoys imitation, and a dialogue is an imitation of different characters, Plato used the dialogue form in order, as it were, to bewitch our soul. That our soul enjoys imitation is shown by the fact that, as children, we love stories.

There is still another reason: Plato used this form of writing so as not to present us with facts in isolation and bare of characters. For example, when he discusses friendship, he does not want to tell us about friendship in isolation but about friendship as it appears in a particular person, and likewise when he discusses ambition not by itself but as it appears in a particular person. In that way our soul, seeing others refuted, for example, or praised is more effectively compelled to agree with the refutations or to emulate those who are praised. This is like what happens to the souls in the Underworld who see others punished for their sins and become better through fear of the punishments that are imposed on others.

Sixthly, Plato used the dialogue form in order to imitate dialectic. Just as dialectic proceeds by question and answer, so too the dialogue consists of characters asking questions and giving answers. Plato therefore used this form of writing in order to compel the reader to agree with what is being said, just as dialectic forces the soul to reveal the embryonic understanding

---

[2] See Plato, *Phaedrus* 264c (p. 70). Cf. also *Timaeus* 92c.

of things which it has within itself – for the soul, in Plato's view, is not like a blank tablet.

In the seventh place, Plato used dialogue so that the variety of speakers should make us pay attention to what is being said, so that we do not, so to speak, doze off because there is always the same one person teaching us.

Index

CAMBRIDGE TEXTS IN THE HISTORY OF PHILOSOPHY

Hume *An Enquiry Concerning Human Understanding* (edited by Stephen Buckle)
Kant *Anthropology from a Pragmatic Point of View* (edited by Robert B. Louden with an introduction by Manfred Kuehn)
Kant *Critique of Practical Reason* (edited by Mary Gregor with an introduction by Andrews Reath)
Kant *Groundwork of the Metaphysics of Morals* (edited by Mary Gregor with an introduction by Christine M. Korsgaard)
Kant *Metaphysical Foundations of Natural Science* (edited by Michael Friedman)
Kant *The Metaphysics of Morals* (edited by Mary Gregor with an introduction by Roger Sullivan)
Kant *Prolegomena to any Future Metaphysics* (edited by Gary Hatfield)
Kant *Religion within the Boundaries of Mere Reason and Other Writings* (edited by Allen Wood and George di Giovanni with an introduction by Robert Merrihew Adams)
Kierkegaard *Concluding Unscientific Postscript* (edited by Alastair Hannay)
Kierkegaard *Fear and Trembling* (edited by C. Stephen Evans and Sylvia Walsh)
La Mettrie *Machine Man and Other Writings* (edited by Ann Thomson)
Leibniz *New Essays on Human Understanding* (edited by Peter Remnant and Jonathan Bennett)
Lessing *Philosophical and Theological Writings* (edited by H. B. Nisbet)
Malebranche *Dialogues on Metaphysics and on Religion* (edited by Nicholas Jolley and David Scott)
Malebranche *The Search after Truth* (edited by Thomas M. Lennon and Paul J. Olscamp)
Medieval Islamic Philosophical Writings (edited by Muhammad Ali Khalidi)
Medieval Jewish Philosophical Writings (edited by Charles Manekin)
Melanchthon *Orations on Philosophy and Education* (edited by Sachiko Kusukawa, translated by Christine Salazar)
Mendelssohn *Philosophical Writings* (edited by Daniel O. Dahlstrom)
Newton *Philosophical Writings* (edited by Andrew Janiak)
Nietzsche *The Antichrist, Ecce Homo, Twilight of the Idols and Other Writings* (edited by Aaron Ridley and Judith Norman)
Nietzsche *Beyond Good and Evil* (edited by Rolf-Peter Horstmann and Judith Norman)
Nietzsche *The Birth of Tragedy and Other Writings* (edited by Raymond Geuss and Ronald Speirs)
Nietzsche *Daybreak* (edited by Maudemarie Clark and Brian Leiter, translated by R. J. Hollingdale)
Nietzsche *The Gay Science* (edited by Bernard Williams, translated by Josefine Nauckhoff)
Nietzsche *Human, All Too Human* (translated by R. J. Hollingdale with an introduction by Richard Schacht)
Nietzsche *Thus Spoke Zarathustra* (edited by Adrian Del Caro and Robert B. Pippin)
Nietzsche *Untimely Meditations* (edited by Daniel Breazeale, translated by R. J. Hollingdale)
Nietzsche *Writings from the Early Notebooks* (edited by Raymond Geuss and Alexander Nehamas, translated by Ladislaus Löb)

Nietzsche *Writings from the Late Notebooks* (edited by Rüdiger Bittner, translated by Kate Sturge)

Novalis *Fichte Studies* (edited by Jane Kneller)

Plato *The Symposium* (edited by M. C. Howatson and Frisbee C. C. Sheffield)

Reinhold *Letters on the Kantian Philosophy* (edited by Karl Ameriks, translated by James Hebbeler)

Schleiermacher *Hermeneutics and Criticism* (edited by Andrew Bowie)

Schleiermacher *Lectures on Philosophical Ethics* (edited by Robert Louden, translated by Louise Adey Huish)

Schleiermacher *On Religion: Speeches to its Cultured Despisers* (edited by Richard Crouter)

Schopenhauer *Prize Essay on the Freedom of the Will* (edited by Günter Zöller)

Sextus Empiricus *Against the Logicians* (edited by Richard Bett)

Sextus Empiricus *Outlines of Scepticism* (edited by Julia Annas and Jonathan Barnes)

Shaftesbury *Characteristics of Men, Manners, Opinions, Times* (edited by Lawrence Klein)

Adam Smith *The Theory of Moral Sentiments* (edited by Knud Haakonssen)

Spinoza *Theological-Political Treatise* (edited by Jonathan Israel, translated by Michael Silverthorne and Jonathan Israel)

Voltaire *Treatise on Tolerance and Other Writings* (edited by Simon Harvey)